DEMOCRACY
for the
NEW MILLENNIUM

DEMOCRACY

for the

NEW MILLENNIUM

Getting Money Out of Politics

Michael Karath

Thaddaeus Books

North Bay, California

Thaddaeus Books

North Bay, California

Copyright © 2020 by Michael Karath.

FIRST EDITION.

Printed in the United States of America

Library of Congress Cataloging-in-Publication Data is available.

For my father, George James Karath

ACKNOWLEDGMENTS

I wish to thank the following people and organizations for their inspiration, contributions, and assistance regarding this project: Marie Danziger for her positive energy, great input, and wonderful spirit; Mario Cuomo for his positive feedback on the original manuscript, Sue Williamson for her kindness and heart, Elaine Baur for her wonderful edits, K² for his sharp political insight and edits, Jeff Tangen for his book cover design, Steve Jarding for his political wisdom, David Gergen, Jeff Danziger for a perfect cartoon, Linda MacNeil of the Woodrow Wilson Presidential Library, Kathryn Harris of the Abraham Lincoln Presidential Library, Ryan Pettigrew of the Richard Nixon Presidential Library and Museum, The American Presidency Project at the University of California at Santa Barbara, Terri Gallego-O'Rourke of the Harvard Law Library, Federal Election Commission staff for the many questions they ably answered for me, Bureau of Labor Statistics staff, U.S. Census staff, Georgetown University, University of Chicago, University of California at Los Angeles, Center for Responsive Politics, Center for Public Integrity, Brennan Center for Justice; Joe Gaylord, Ben Ginsberg, Michael Deaver, Linda Bilmes, Elaine Karath, my wonderful Mom; Nancy, Scott, Diane, Danielle, Michael Caplan, Walter Merlington, Leonard, Kym, Francie, Richard Neiss, Cyril Penn, Rich Mainenti, Jeff McFarlane Johnson, JoAnn & Russ Melgar, Laurie Gage, Barb Bryson, Kenji Ruymaker, Tony Alvis, David Lovell, Nancy McDonnell, Suzanne Kaasa, Al Gold, Claudia Prevost, Rob Hampton, Demetrius Atsalis, Ellen Story, Matthew Patrick, George Levas, Lily Giambarba, Patrick & Lolita, Allen & DD McGarry, John Horgan, Stefanie Coxe, Tia & Daniel, Sheryl Plush, Allan Berman, Alison Tyman, Tim & Claudia, Michael & Lynnie, Aldo, Iris & Reggie, Rita, Hannah, Jay Goetting, Nina & Howard, Brad Wagenknecht, Mark Luce, Keith Caldwell, the Brancas, Robert Gold, Betty Rhodes, Amy Garcia—a true angel, Karen Taylor, Marc Flournoy, Linda Reynolds for putting up with all the manuscript copies you bound for me at Office Depot; and my wonderful wife, Leslie, who is simply the best—EVER!

TABLE OF CONTENTS

"If money is free speech, the big interests are sitting in front with megaphones, and the average citizens are sitting in the back." [1]

~ SENATOR JOHN McCAIN (R-AZ)

INTRODUCTION

C ampaign finance reform is the mother of *all* political issues.

Political money shapes the outcome of nearly every decision under consideration in the halls of government. And these decisions summarily determine our quality of life as Americans and our direction as a nation.

In 2016, Donald J. Trump electrified voters, shouting he would "drain the swamp" in Washington, D.C., once elected. But Trump never defined the swamp or stated how he would drain it. His followers never pressed for details. They just liked hearing the applause line. Arguably, Trump saw the swamp as the collective, calcified group of Washington denizens—politicians, bureaucrats, and lobbyists—conducting government business, indifferent to the people's needs. But he ignored the green muck, known as political cash, that feeds the swamp. These dollars ooze throughout the system, debasing those who crave it, creating a permanent, professional political class—a stasis—that remains as elected politicians transition in and out of office. Yet, inexplicably, Trump didn't see political money as the underlying problem. And he didn't see himself as part of the swamp, even though he had frequently boasted of buying off politicians throughout his career. "As a businessman and a very substantial donor to very important people, when you give, they do whatever the hell you want them to do," he told the *Wall Street Journal* in 2015.[1]

Trump often brags that he self-financed his 2016 campaign, saying it made him the only candidate in the field not beholden to special interests. But that's only partly true. While Trump self-financed his primary race with $40 million, he accepted generous handouts in the general election.

The National Rifle Association (NRA), one of the most powerful lobbying groups in the capital, spent $54 million to help
elect Trump.[2] And since becoming president, the real estate magnate's gun policies have shifted with each NRA breeze that wafts
over the Potomac to the White House.

Las Vegas casino billionaire Sheldon Adelson doled out millions of dollars to Trump's campaign in the final stretch. After
assuming office, Trump granted Adelson's longtime wish of relo-
cating the U.S. embassy in Israel from Tel Aviv to Jerusalem, a
highly volatile move that tossed a pitchfork into Mideast peace
prospects. Adelson greased the wheels by writing a $5 million
check to help pay for Trump's inauguration ceremony. It is the
largest known inaugural donation by one person in American history.[3] Then there are the Mercers. Secretive hedge-fund billionaire Robert Mercer and his daughter Rebekah Mercer, both conservative hardliners who bankrolled the right-wing Breitbart website, propped up Trump's disorganized campaign by pumping
millions of dollars into the candidate's organization. They also replaced its top managers with Mercer mercenaries Steve Bannon
and Kellyanne Conway.[4]

The point is that not even independently wealthy politicians
are immune to the corruption of political money.

It is a certainty that if Trump thinks he'll drain the swamp
without getting the money out first, it will be a farce that even
P.T. Barnum couldn't sell. The money of Washington's swamp
creatures dwarfs Trump's fortune and what he can snag in donations. He is a tiny coastal town to their Godzilla. And Godzilla
doesn't have to run for re-election. Trump won't be in power
forever, but if the muck is not drained, the swamp creatures will
be.

If you pop in the words "poll, money out of politics," or some
variation thereof, into an Internet search engine, you will find poll
after poll showing the vast majority of Americans want to "get
money out of politics." What Americans mean is that, while
money is needed to run campaigns and communicate ideas, it

should not be the deciding factor in which candidate wins office, which law is passed, or which public policy is instituted. In other words, political decisions should be based on the merits, not the money.

But when Americans are asked *how* to get money out of politics, there is little agreement.

Why?

Money, of course.

Massive business and political fortunes are at stake. It does not serve wealthy interests to have average Americans agree and act on the best and most effective method of getting money out of politics. Getting money *into* politics is how these politically sophisticated folks attained their positions of political and economic dominance in the first place.

In this book, I will illustrate how money corrupts our political system and show why campaign spending limits is the best and most effective way to get money out of politics. It is the one inevitable path for rebirthing democracy in the new millennium. I have no doubt that the country, if it is to survive, will eventually embrace campaign spending limits. I hope this book will serve to speed up the process.

Campaign spending limits is not a new idea. It's not "reinventing the wheel." Congress passed federal spending limits in 1911 (Publicity Act Amendments); 1971 (Federal Election Campaign Act or FECA), and 1974 (FECA Amendments). By 1975, 34 states had also passed laws restricting a candidate's spending in state and local elections. Many wealthy democracies including Britain, France, Israel, and Germany embrace some form of campaign spending limits.

In 1976, the U.S. Supreme Court killed campaign spending limits on all government levels in its *Buckley v. Valeo* ruling. Considering the Court's conservative trend and its hostility toward campaign finance reform, a constitutional amendment will be needed to overturn the ruling and restore the people's right to manage elections by capping spending.

Is it realistic that a campaign spending limits amendment can be ratified within a decade?

Yes.

Considering the upheaval we have seen in recent years, anything is possible.

In 1971, the Twenty-sixth Amendment lowering the voting age to 18 took just six months to pass. Average Americans overwhelmingly agreed on the issue. Today, a healthy majority of Americans agree about getting money out of politics, but have yet to rally around one proposal.

Throughout America's history, constitutional amendments have been a fairly common occurrence. After the Bill of Rights, Americans have amended the Constitution an average of once every 12 years. The Twenty-seventh Amendment (a sitting Congress may not vote itself a pay raise) is the last to be added to the Constitution. Congress proposed it in 1789 as one of 12 amendments under consideration for what became known as the Bill of Rights, but the states did not ratify it until 1992.

Somehow, today's Americans have lost the knack to periodically update our supreme law document. We have become fearful of change. It has been 48 years since America passed *and* ratified a constitutional amendment in the same period. If an amendment were passed today, it would be the second longest gap between amendments in our history. The longest gap is 61 years, from 1804 (Twelfth Amendment) in the post-Revolutionary War era to 1865 (Thirteenth Amendment) in the Civil War era.

Historically, each generation addressed the most important issue of their time by amending the Constitution for the country's betterment.

I believe "getting money out of politics" is the issue of *our* time.

There are many today who believe the Supreme Court's 2010 *Citizens United v. Federal Election Commission* ruling must be overturned by constitutional amendment to solve the corruption problem.

It is not.

This thinking presupposes that America's political system pre-2010 functioned just fine, suffering no corruption or distortion by corporations, wealthy special interests, and partisan power brokers. In fact, every Supreme Court case—including *Citizens United*—since 1976 that has slashed what is left of America's campaign finance laws stands on the shoulders of *Buckley v. Valeo*. Sure, *Citizens United* allowed corporations and unions to flood our political system with cash from their respective treasuries. But they already had the ability to corrupt our politics by channeling their billions of dollars to independent expenditure groups, political parties (via soft money), political action committees, nonprofit groups, 527 organizations, and a host of other schemes to buy what they wanted in our government. The FECA Amendments of 1974 eliminated this enormous source of corruption. It imposed a $1,000 spending cap on *all* groups and wealthy individuals that ran political advertisements advocating for or against a clearly identified candidate. If the *Buckley* Court had kept this provision intact, that spending cap today would apply to all those who manipulate and pollute our political system with their vast stores of wealth, including billionaires, Super PACs, and lobbyists. The point is—if you're going to the mat to change the Constitution, make sure you're going with the right Supreme Court case. You reverse *Citizens United*, you snip a limb off a compromised tree. You reverse *Buckley,* you rip the entire dysfunction out by the roots.

Amending the Constitution to include campaign spending limits will be harder to pass than a legislative menu of anti-corruption measures. And any effort on any level of government that would significantly or even modestly curb political corruption, such as instituting lobby reform, abolishing dark money from anonymous donors, reversing voter suppression, and many others should be applauded and pursued. Further, these measures will be needed to augment spending caps.

But make no mistake—*campaign spending limits is the only method that will truly get money out of politics.*

It is the bedrock to support all other political reforms.

Term limits won't kill Super PACs. Ranked-choice voting won't stop wealthy elites from purchasing public office. Public financing won't stop corporations from spending billions of dollars on political ads distorting issues and dividing the public. And overturning *Citizen United* won't stop candidates from begging wealthy elites for large contributions. In essence, efforts like these may slow, but won't do a blessed thing to stop wealthy elites and power brokers from buying our elections, laws, and politicians.

And just who are the "average Americans" in our country, whom I refer to in this book?

Thomas Jefferson defined this overwhelming American majority as the "general mass."[5] I would further define an average American today as a citizen who can afford to make a small political donation without the intent or expectation that it will give them sway over any election, law, or politician. To quantify this, I would say they are Americans who can reasonably afford making maximum political contributions of $1 *up to* $600, or 1% of the U.S. average income ($60,000 in 2018). Indeed, if campaign spending limits were in effect, 1% of the U.S. average income would be a fair donation limit for *all* individuals, political groups, corporations, and business associations, giving all Americans equal power in political elections as embodied in the principle of one person, one vote.

The optimist in me says the American people naturally aspire to create a better government—to "form a more perfect union." I believe there is enough discontent with the current political system to pass a constitutional amendment, although the spark of another major scandal may likely be needed to compel citizens to act. I believe that if the public is presented with good information and sound reasoning, they will understand that substantive, long-term campaign finance reform will have the unique and profound ability to positively affect every single issue and decision made in the halls of American government. I believe that curbing the overwhelming, overpowering, and utterly corrupting influence of money in American politics is the only way citizens will ever begin to trust government. I believe the collective vision of America is that of a beacon for other nations to follow—a successful example of self-governance based on openness, honesty, equality, fairness, impartiality, and integrity. Campaign spending limits can lead us to this ideal. And I believe this vision for America will sustain us over what will likely be a bitter war for the soul of this country.

The pessimist in me says the vested interests have a stranglehold on our government and are just too crafty, too resourceful, too powerful, and too embedded in the structure to root out and subdue. They're highly skilled at using their wealth to spread misinformation, fear, and division that dupe average Americans into believing that policies that will actually benefit the public will harm them. In short, they know how to exploit the distrust Americans have toward government, even though these moneyed interests are largely responsible for creating that distrust. The public will be scared away from addressing the problem and continue to grumble over the daily media spectacle of political mischief, then spasm over the inevitable mega-scandal. The public's anger and desire for a quick fix will be periodically voiced at the ballot box as incumbents are dumped in favor of fresh-faced challengers promising cleaner politics and a brighter day—only to be dumped in subsequent elections as these neophytes are co-opted into the corrupt system and the next scandal explodes.

All things considered, I choose to be an optimist.

1

WHY SHOULD YOU CARE ABOUT CAMPAIGN SPENDING LIMITS?

I T WAS THE MORNING OF April 27, 1971, and President Richard M. Nixon had a problem.

Nixon, paranoid about securing re-election in 1972, had been feverishly lining up donors to shore up his campaign war chest. His desire for another term colored nearly every decision he made. He knew the best way to secure four more years was to stockpile as much money as he could. Nixon wanted to win and win big. But he worried that his fundraising efforts were lagging.

On that morning, Nixon received Ford Motor Company chairman Henry Ford II and the company's president Lee Iacocca in the Oval Office. Ford and Iacocca needed a favor from Nixon. By 1971, media accounts of the rising number of roadway fatalities had sparked the public's demand for safer cars. Consumer activist Ralph Nader prodded much of the national discussion by raising consumers' awareness of auto safety. He vehemently demanded that Detroit build safer cars. The key part of the Nixon-Ford meeting concerned a pending federal regulation requiring automakers to install "passive restraints" in their new cars made after August 15, 1973. While passive restraints meant airbags or thick padding, the issue centered primarily on airbags.

Ford and Iacocca complained to the president that it would cost their company too much to install airbags. They wanted the feds to back off. Higher costs, they argued, would hinder American carmakers as they struggled against Japanese competitors. If Americans bought more imported cars, it would damage the U.S. economy, they warned.

Left to right: John Ehrlichman, Henry Ford II, President Nixon, Lee Iacocca, April 27, 1971. *Source*: Nixon Presidential Library

Iacocca had met earlier with Transportation Secretary John Volpe, but Volpe wasn't buying the argument. Volpe strongly supported airbags and believed they were well worth the $100 added cost per car.[1] According to a White House memo, Volpe's Department of Transportation estimated that airbags would save "600 lives and 25,000 disabling injuries this first year; 5,500 lives and 200,000 disabling injuries in the tenth year, when virtually all operating cars would be equipped . . ."[2]

Three days after meeting with Ford and Iacocca, however, Nixon ordered Volpe to kill the airbag regulation. It took 20 years before airbags finally became standard equipment in cars. In the interim, many Americans needlessly suffered—mothers, fathers, children, infants—killed, disabled, or severely injured, and their survivors shattered and grief-stricken, all because of the policy change.

So what drove Nixon's decision?

Secretary Volpe, an appointed official, weighed the facts before deciding the safety benefits of airbags outweighed the anticipated cost to install them. But Volpe didn't have to fund a re-election campaign, as Nixon did. The president's thinking was clouded by his desire for a landslide victory and a solid mandate to pass his pet policies in his second term. That meant amassing campaign donations, which meant doling out favors, calling in chits. Few would have believed the president would put his own interests above those of the public in such a crass manner.

Soon after the Watergate scandal broke, many of Nixon's aides spilled the beans on questionable White House actions, including the airbag decision. John Ehrlichman, Nixon's chief domestic advisor, intimated that campaign contributions *were* a factor in the president's decision to kill airbags. He said Nixon ordered Charles Colson, special counsel to the president, to "exploit the Ford meeting." Ehrlichman added, "I wrote a memo to Charles Colson conveying the president's wish that he hit up the Ford people for a political contribution."[3]

Throughout this period, Nixon's re-election team made the rounds to major corporations, threatening some with Internal Revenue Service audits if they didn't cough up a sizable chunk of campaign cash.

Through this extortion scheme, Nixon's operatives were awash in about $22 million in mostly secret, illegal donations. The money, most of it laundered in Mexico, not only funded the Watergate break-in and cover-up, but paid for numerous other illegal activities and political dirty tricks perpetrated on those perceived to be a threat to Nixon. The president's campaign team, for example, bribed the chauffeur of Senator Edmund Muskie (D-Maine), the biggest threat to Nixon's re-election at the time. Nixon's operatives slipped the driver $1,000 monthly payments to "photograph internal memos, position papers, schedules and strategy documents" of Muskie's campaign and deliver the copies to Nixon's top campaign managers.[4]

And just like the backing off of safety regulations that Ford Motor Company sought, Nixon paid off his other wealthy special interest donors with a slew of favors. Some of the stranger payoffs included:

- blocking legal action against Robert Vesco, a criminal and fugitive from justice, who scammed more than $200 million from investors in fraudulent schemes, but gave the Nixon campaign $200,000;

- granting permission to McDonald's to charge more for its Quarter Pounder hamburgers when other businesses were restricted by wage and price controls that Nixon had put into effect—for which McDonalds gratefully slid $200,000 into the president's campaign account.[5]

The Nixon White House is one of the more illuminating examples in the last 50 years of how unlimited spending corrupts the political system. American history is larded with many other sordid tales of ambitious politicians, drunk on campaign contributions, rationalizing their thinking, and making poor choices. It's all for the greater good, they believe. And surely there are scores of other seedy schemes that remain hidden in the murky, dark corners of American politics, past and present.

So why should you care about campaign spending limits?

Because it could be a matter of life or death, as the Nixon airbag decision clearly illustrates.

THE MONEY CHASE
Gray Line of Corruption

WHY IS OUR POLITICAL SYSTEM seemingly so corrupt?

Why do so many politicians seem like used-car salesmen—promising a shiny, dependable car to voters come Election Day, but delivering a broken-down jalopy once in office?

What is it that influences politicians to renege on their campaign pledges and cast votes that betray the people and the nation they swore to serve?

What is it that drives so many of them to take bribes, gifts, vacations, shady campaign contributions, and commit various deceitful acts in exchange for political favors sought by wealthy special interests and political power brokers? After all, these politicians are war veterans, churchgoers, community leaders, doctors, mothers, fathers, grandmothers, grandfathers. How could these seemingly upstanding American citizens get caught up in such sleazy shenanigans? What is the root of the problem?

The answer, of course, is money. It is the catalyst. It wins elections. It spawns political careers. It buys loyalty. It inflates egos. It skews judgment. It amasses power.

Corruption stems from how the money is collected and spread throughout the political system—on the federal, state, and local levels. And therein lies the flaw.

It starts with elections.

It is often said that American politics has devolved into an "arms race" for money in which the candidate who spends the most money almost always wins. And with so much on the line and no ceiling on campaign spending, the incentive is to grab every single dollar from anyone and anything with a pulse. The money often comes with strings attached. Big donors and ambitious candidates become fast friends. Relationships become entangled. Personal ethics become slippery. Political spines become rubbery. To most politicians, the next campaign dollar raised can mean the difference between political life and death. It's an *insane* pressure cooker. And it's what makes so many good people crack. It's the chink in the armor that weakens our democratic institutions.

The primary importance given to money in politics opened the door to special interests—corporations, unions, trade associations, wealthy individuals, various political groups, party power brokers—and even politicians themselves to exploit their respective stores of wealth to gain influence and power. This incentive of unlimited spending has thoroughly corrupted the system. In fact, the corruption is so deep that it seems everyone—inside and outside—is trying to buy everyone else for self-serving gain. It is a dysfunction that debases the system to its core. It's why so many citizens do not trust government and believe the system is rigged against them. Without big bank accounts, average Americans have been relegated to the sidelines, helplessly watching those with riches-to-burn call the shots that determine our quality of life and the course of the nation.

Critics readily challenge the assumption that campaign donations, gifts, and favors directly influence lawmakers' decisions by demanding evidence of this "bribery." Of course, they know this is virtually impossible without the ability to peer into another's soul to ascertain the motivation behind each decision and vote. It's perfectly legal for a lobbyist to give a campaign donation to a politician who then votes exactly the way the lobbyist wants. But it is illegal if the politician specifically promises to vote that way in exchange for money or gifts from the lobbyist. It's such a fine line that corruption could take place with a nod or wink, or even a meeting of eyes. Jack Abramoff, of the eponymous 2006 lobbying mega-scandal, said of political corruption: "When you have a system that defines the line between illegal and legal as it does, there are ways of kind of working through it," he said. "Maybe 95 percent or 99 percent of what I did wasn't really illegal."

So it is precisely this inability to peer into another's soul that makes campaign spending limits so crucial. With the temptation of millions of influence-peddling dollars wafting about, no one except the individual lawmaker may be confident whether his or her vote is tainted or not. And sometimes even the lawmaker may not know. He or she may have rationalized a bribe as a simple gift from a special interest, for example, to the charitable organization founded by the lawmaker or lawmaker's spouse. So how can citizens be confident in the integrity of their government when they can't even be confident in the fidelity of any one vote, let alone the collective votes of an entire body?

The strength of our democracy, like the strength of our monetary system, depends on public confidence. Without it, both systems lose their value bestowed collectively by the citizens, and the structures may become wobbly and eventually crash or implode. Confidence in our democracy, if measured by America's declining voter turnout, has been eroding for years.

To make the political system work, citizens are asked to place their trust in the honesty of the politician, who must toil in a fetid system. And while many politicians may start out as honest candidates, that trust has been broken time and again as they succumb to the system's pressures. The result is the upheaval of scandals big and small that rock the government on a seemingly perpetual basis. Citizens are further asked to accept the situation as a natural byproduct of conducting government business—like a dog resigned to fleas.

So who's been bought off and who hasn't? It's impossible to tell. With the endless parade of political scandals, it seems to many that all are tainted. It has become the perpetual default setting for most Americans. What *is* possible to deduce is that the system itself is tainted. It is broken and must be fixed.

So what's the solution?

The key to restoring integrity to our political system is to curb the incentive to amass money as a reliable path to political power.

INCOME REDISTRIBUTION
Special Interests' License to Steal

THE MONEY THAT FEEDS unlimited campaign spending is the ultimate tool used by a handful of wealthy special interests to tighten their grip on democracy and squeeze out what's left of citizens' political power. The result is a growing concentration of wealth among fewer moneyed interests and the creeping, constant eroding of our quality of life every single day.

Ever wonder how a small handful of mega-banks with branches in nearly every city and town in America get away with charging you 29.99 percent or more for borrowing *their* money (which is really the public's deposits) via a credit card, yet offer you a measly 1.2 percent return or less when they borrow *your* money (and make tons loaning it out) via a CD or savings account?

Or why you need a law degree and a magnifying glass to understand the terms of their credit card, loan, and other products written in the tiniest of fonts? Or why these mega-banks can slap you with
a $40 bounced-check fee for a $1.50 overdraft? Or how that overdraft occurred because the bank delayed crediting the deposit you
made days ago, while it deducted the expenses from your account
at lightning speed?

Ever wonder why you're faced with paying $4 to $5 per gallon
of gasoline every summer while companies like ExxonMobil reap
record profits of more than $45 billion per year—even through a
major recession?[6] Or why you're paying big bucks for cable TV
"bundling" packages that force you to subsidize 90 dull channels
to get the 10 you actually want? Or why you're paying $654 for
90 cholesterol-reducing Lipitor pills at your local pharmacy that
cost $65 in Canada?[7] Or why you can't afford basic health care
coverage without government assistance in a wealthy country that
forces you into bankruptcy if you suffer a serious illness or your
aging parents need assisted-living or nursing home care? Or how
your $39.99 cell phone plan turned into a $250 monthly nightmare, and you still can't get good reception? Or how the phrase
"invasion of privacy" doesn't apply to tech companies that make
billions planting spyware and other devices on your phone, computer, app, or social platform so they can track every website you
visit and sell the information to marketers? Or how politicians allow hordes of scammers to bombard your phone with phishing
robocalls, leaving you with no way to identify these culprits or
recourse to make them stop? Or how America's bankruptcy laws
allowed the corporation you helped build as a worker to slash
your pension or eliminate it altogether while its executive managers received bonuses for their handiwork? Or how your $1,800
mortgage payment ballooned overnight to $4,500 and hustled
you out of your home and your life savings? Or how it takes two
salaries now to keep an average middle-class family afloat when it
used to take just one a generation ago?

In America, average working people suffer a death of a thousand paper cuts—from parchment printed with tainted laws that slowly bleed away the value of our earnings.

Nearly everything in our lives today that is gouging our wallet or pocketbook can be traced back to a provision, rider, or amendment inserted (or killed) in some federal or state bill by a wealthy special interest working through a lobbyist—who is working through a lawmaker, who happens to be raking in campaign donations from that same wealthy special interest.

U.S. Rep. John Sarbanes (D-MD) has witnessed America's dysfunctional political system up close over his years in Congress and knows how it works against average Americans. "Maybe it's the amendment that does not get introduced in a committee because the congressman knows that it is not in sync with the desires of his money patrons," Sarbanes said. "The donation is lingering somewhere in the atmosphere. It's human nature."[8]

It's no wonder that the policies Congress pursues have led to the yawning wealth gap that exists in America. Many conservative politicians and commentators today carp about "income redistribution" whenever tax increases on the wealthy are discussed. Yet, few of them point out the income redistribution that occurred from wealthy interests hijacking our political system and passing laws that enrich themselves at the expense of average Americans.

As legendary Washington lobbyist Gerald Cassidy once observed:

> (The United States has experienced) a huge redistribution of income, and you can't blame just the Republicans, because it has happened through Democratic presidencies and through Democratic and Republican Congresses. It's just true, largely because (average Americans) have less representation.[9]

Not only do average Americans have less representation in the lobbying industry, as Cassidy pointed out, but we have less representation in Congress, as fewer working-class politicians are elected. Cassidy, by the way, founded Cassidy & Associates, one of the biggest lobbying firms in Washington, D.C. over the past 40 years. He was considered the first millionaire lobbyist and pioneered the "budget earmark" that sucked so many billions of dollars in special interest pork from the nation's budgets and contributed to our staggering national debt.

In America, through huge, unlimited campaign donations, wealthy special interests have purchased a license to steal. By co-opting government, they have legalized, legitimized, and laundered their unfair, unethical, immoral actions through lawmaking, ultimately redistributing wealth from average Americans to themselves. To those who have the power to write the laws in our country, go the spoils. It was a hostile, yet invisible takeover, using government against the people it was designed to serve.

It is self-evident that making money in our capitalist system is as American as apple pie. Unfortunately, it's not enough for these wealthy special interests to be huge winners in the capitalist game. They're also obsessed with fixing the rules—the political rules—and rigging the game in their favor.

It is decidedly un-American.

In 2016, ABC News correspondent Jonathan Karl asked Charles Koch, known as one half of the Koch brothers, whether the American political system is rigged in favor of the wealthy. Koch, with his brother David, owns Koch Industries, a Kansas-based oil conglomerate, the nation's second largest privately-held company with yearly revenues of $100 billion. The following are excerpts from Charles's response:

(Yes, it's rigged) in favor of companies like ours. It's been pointed out that, Why am I complaining about the current administration over the last decade when we've tripled our size in that period? These regulations set up a more static economy so those who are in business are protected, because we have less competition. They reduce competition and reduce innovation. Estimates I've seen out of the $15 trillion economy, probably this corporate welfare and cronyism is costing the economy about $5 trillion. The tax code alone has $1.5 trillion in special benefits and deals in it. The great majority go for the wealthy.

The truth is, we all owe many corporations, unions, environmentalists, and other special interests a heavy debt of gratitude. They employ lobbyists to provide pertinent and critical information to lawmakers in the decision-making process. The result is that we enjoy affordable consumer goods and services provided by corporations; safe bridges, roads, schools built by union labor; clean water and clean air regulations secured by environmentalists—all things that greatly add to the quality of our lives.

The majority of smaller companies are, arguably, good corporate citizens that seek to educate lawmakers and the public on how existing or proposed regulations may affect their interests. They're willing to work with Congress and the public to develop common-sense guidelines—a healthy balance that allows them to thrive, yet protects consumers' interests.

The American political system, however, is driven by money, making it extremely tempting to go beyond the task of merely educating elected officials about the issues. For some powerful special interests who possess enormous economic clout, the spillover of this temptation often leads to the manipulation of legislators and the legislative process. This elite group is composed mostly of super rich, self-serving special interests who represent many of the major industries in the country. They're used to getting their way and see Congress and the public as mere trifling annoyances.

These wealthy interests act in the best interest of themselves and their companies. They're not looking out for you, and they're not looking out for the United States. That's the job of our elected representatives. But when our leaders are corrupted by these myopic special interests, they can no longer perform this critical function. President Franklin D. Roosevelt described this wealthy, corruptive element in his annual message to Congress on January 3, 1936:

As guardians and trustees for great groups of individual stockholders, they wrongfully seek to carry the property and the interests entrusted to them into the arena of partisan politics. They seek, this minority in business and industry, to control and often do control and use for their own purposes legitimate and highly honored business associations; they engage in vast propaganda to spread fear and discord among the people—they would 'gang up' against the people's liberties. The principle that they would instill into government if they succeed in seizing power is well shown by the principles which many of them have instilled into their own affairs: autocracy toward labor, toward stockholders, toward consumers, toward public sentiment.

Roosevelt laid the blame for the Great Depression at the feet of this elite corporate league, which manipulated markets, Congress, and the public for personal gain—the country be damned. His words ring true today in assessing blame for America's most recent economic disaster a decade ago, as well as the crisis we face today defending our democratic institutions.

HOW MONEY BUYS ELECTIONS, LAWS, & POLITICIANS

IN AMERICA, POLITICAL CASH begets political access, which begets political power. It is the equation that drives the system.

In the quest to amass political cash, incumbent politicians and challengers alike naturally seek out those who donate large sums to campaigns. Unfortunately, many of these donors just happen to be corporations, unions, trade associations, and wealthy individuals—*the very entities whose interests the politicians must sit in judgment of once elected.*

America's political money chase pushes candidates to devote up to 80 percent or more of their time fundraising, which delivers them into the hands of the moneyed elite. It forces politicians into a subservient position to those footing the bill for their campaigns and political careers. Our leaders must go begging for money from those who mostly care about their own self-interest and little about the national interest.

You'll hear critics of campaign reform say that rich donors simply give money to candidates whose views they share.

Perhaps.

But with so much money and power at stake, it's not that simple. The pressure inherent in our political system squeezes a candidate to contort his or her beliefs to align with those of their wealthy donor in exchange for a large contribution. It's a process that is repeated with each wealthy donor the candidate seeks out. In addition, there are the promises made to voters that are often contradictory to those made to wealthy backers. The candidate must then walk a policy tightrope—careful not to offend anyone. It's why politicians are thought of as wishy-washy or weaselly. They have to balance all the disparate promises they've made, and are scared to death of offending their big donors. It's why you can listen to a politician talk and not know what the heck they're saying or where they really stand on any particular issue. The craftier ones can talk about the same subject, regardless of their audience's political leaning, and have them all bobbing their heads in agreement.

Is it any wonder why Americans hate politicians?

Campaign reform critics, including many special interests and the politicians they favor, believe money does not corrupt the system. They are either naïve or cynical. It's understandable, though. The system is working just fine for them. But it's not working for average Americans who understand that wealthy special interests aren't giving—*they're buying.*

This elite donor class, in return for their political "investments," gain access, seeking to cash in on the successful candidates' promises. Average Americans have little, if any, direct access to our elected officials. It is the wealthy backer's number the politician likely has on his or her personal cell. We're lucky if we can get past the first layer of a politician's interns.

Big donors use their access to zero in on party leaders and their cabals in Congress and state legislatures. They're the politicians who have amassed the most power. They control the purse strings and decide which bills live or die. They call most of the shots for the rest of the members, including appointing committee chairs. And the chances are near 100 percent that each of these party leaders and their leadership teams are highly infiltrated with special interests and wealthy "friends" who've helped them ascend the ladder of party leadership.

Using this access, wealthy interests have become experts at working our broken political system like an open cash register. The national debt routinely increases no matter which party is in power. Worse, the laws and favors the politicians dole out to their moneyed backers are often made in a vacuum, with little thought as to the cumulative effect on the direction of the country. This has often pulled America in undesirable directions and tarnished the nation's prestige as the beacon of democracy to the world.

Indeed, the money incentive to amass political power combined with politicians' dependency on moneyed special interests corrupts the cornerstone of our representative democracy—*that politicians are supposed to be independent and impartial judges when conducting the people's business.*

It is a *fatal* conflict of interest.

It is the single design flaw in our Constitution that undermines the very essence of democracy.

2

ASSUMPTION OF IMPARTIALITY

P RESIDENT BARACK OBAMA caught a few bytes in the rear in
January 2012, 11 months before Election Day.

He found himself in the middle of a raging battle between
two of his most prized donor groups—Hollywood and Silicon
Valley—over several proposed bills designed to curb online piracy of American intellectual property.

Hollywood movie, television, and music companies pushed
the bills. The primary piece was the Stop Online Piracy Act
(SOPA), which required Internet websites, search engines, and
payment processing sites to block domestic and international
websites, like The Pirate Bay, that are dedicated to illegally selling
copyrighted works.[1]

Hollywood studio executives and celebrities have been a solid,
dependable donor base for Democratic candidates and causes for
decades. But nipping on their heels are the 20- and 30-something
Internet moguls of Silicon Valley in Northern California. Companies like Google, Facebook, and Yahoo saw SOPA as a burden-
some yoke. They claimed it would repress innovation, saddling
them with the costly responsibility of policing the Internet.[2]

In 2011, Obama made statements intimating he favored the
Hollywood-sponsored bills. Entertainment executives responded
by lavishing him with $4.1 million in campaign contributions.[3]
The president's comments, however, angered Silicon Valley tech-
ies, who had given about $1.7 million to Obama.[4] They pumped

several million more dollars into his coffer to help the president see things their way. Then, on January 14, 2012, Obama shocked his Hollywood base when his administration released a statement siding against SOPA:

> ". . . we will not support legislation that reduces freedom of expression, increases cybersecurity risk, or undermines the dynamic, innovative global Internet."[5]

In response, Chris Dodd, a former U.S. senator (D-CT), 2008 presidential candidate, and then-chief lobbyist for the Motion Picture Association of America, issued a stinging rebuke: "Candidly, those who count on Hollywood for support need to understand that this industry is watching very carefully who's going to stand up for them when their job is at stake." Dodd added, "Don't ask me to write a check for you when you think your job is at risk and then don't pay any attention to me when my job is at stake."[6]

The bills were tabled.

JUDICIAL V. POLITICAL

THERE IS AN INHERENT ASSUMPTION in the American political system that lawmakers are impartial in their judgments and decision-making.

If you ask any elected official if they've ever cast votes or performed actions that were influenced or spurred by favors or campaign donations, the response will likely be a resounding "NO!" They may even be insulted that you had the audacity to ask such a question. So even the politicians themselves operate under the assumption that every vote they cast, every action they take, is impartial and not skewed to any benefactor.

There is also an assumption inherent in the U.S. justice system that judges and jury members are impartial in their judgments and decision making.

But what if defendants and their lawyers were allowed to

interact with judges and juries—as wealthy special interests and their lobbyists do with politicians at all levels of government? What if a defendant's lawyer doled out favors or gave money to the judge or jurors while the case was still open? What if the defendant arranged loans to help the judge's or jury members' business dealings or provided discounted vacations or transportation services? Or gave them Super Bowl tickets? Or took them sailing and golfing? Or took them out for a steak dinner at a fancy restaurant? Or dropped a sizable chunk of cash into a charity they run? Or found a job for their chronically unemployed son or brother-in-law? What if the defendant or defendant's lawyer met privately with the judge and each juror to plead his or her case while offering them the aforementioned favors?

If these kinds of interactions were allowed in our judicial system, would citizens have more or less faith in the verdicts? Would our system of American jurisprudence be stronger or weaker? And what percentage of Americans would fully trust our courts and those who sit in judgment of others?

Juries are, in fact, often sequestered in important or high-profile cases to prevent the perception of a tainted verdict. Even if they're not sequestered, the slightest interaction during a trial between an outside element and the jury can throw their impartiality into such doubt that the case is either thrown out or the entire jury dismissed and replaced. The slightest perception during a trial that there is anything less than 100 percent impartiality in the decision-making process frequently incites the losing party to file an immediate appeal.

So why is it okay for an influence peddler to pal around with and give money and favors to a politician whose job is to dispense impartial judgment on matters the benefactor has a personal or financial interest in? How could anyone have faith in the integrity of the politician's decisions? How could anyone have faith in the system itself?

In comparing the judicial and political systems, we see that a politician needs money to retain their office, whereas jurors and many judges do not.

So how do you protect the impartiality of politicians in a system that runs on special interest money?

You could ban private meetings between influence peddlers and politicians—as with defendants and juries. But how would you sequester 535 members of Congress and thousands of state and local legislators on a daily basis to ensure no lobbyist interaction takes place in the halls of government, lunch spots, coffee houses, bars, or elsewhere? Perhaps you could force politicians to recuse themselves from voting on matters that involved influence peddlers who have directly or indirectly given them campaign donations or favors. But there'd likely be no pols left to vote.

The problem with these proposals is that they fail to address the political system's structural flaw that forces politicians into the submissive role of chasing, begging, and groveling for every last dollar to attain the all-important money advantage and keep their political careers alive.

Sometimes, however, the roles are reversed. Money is still the prize. Corruption is still the outcome. But it's the *politicians* extracting money for legislative favors. High-ranking officials, like presidents and congressional leaders, have been accused of using tactics to "extort" money from wealthy interests who have billions of dollars at stake in legislation before Congress. "Milking," for example, is when one side is played off the other, as in the SOPA example. There is also the "tollbooth" tactic in which leaders artificially create a roadblock for the legislation in question and then solicit contributions from the bill's vested interests. When the requested contribution is received, the tollbooth arm goes up and the bill is free to proceed to the next step in the legislative process.

Perhaps one of the best chronicled examples of how money undermines impartiality in decision-making and how Washington sausage is really made can be found in the skirmish over control of the long-distance telephone industry several decades ago.

A TALE OF TWO INDUSTRIES
Democracy Sold to the Highest Bidder

IN EARLY 1995, TWO TELECOMMUNICATION SECTORS squared off in a fight over who would control the $68 billion long-distance telephone market.[7]

In one corner stood the long-distance carriers: AT&T, MCI, Sprint, and others. In the opposite corner stood the regional telephone carriers, also called the "Baby Bells": Nynex, Bell Atlantic, BellSouth, Southwestern Bell Corp., Ameritech, U.S. West, and Pacific Telesis.

For nearly 100 years, AT&T monopolized all telephone business—long-distance as well as local service. But the emergence of new technology in the 1980s inspired entrepreneurs to challenge the behemoth's dominance. They made the case that competition would provide better phone service at a lower price. In 1984, the federal government bought the argument and forced AT&T to end its monopoly. The giant divested its local phone service into seven regional companies—and the Baby Bells were born.

AT&T kept its long-distance business, which the Baby Bells were forbidden to enter. But it could not prevent challengers like Microwave Communications, Inc. (MCI) and Sprint from entering the long-distance market.

By the 1990s, the Baby Bells had acquired newer technologies like fiber-optic cables to carry voice and data. They grew more powerful and were soon ready and eager to take on AT&T and others for a piece of the long-distance pie.

The arena where the war would be fought: the halls of federal government.

The weapon of choice: campaign donations.

Jim Drinkard of *The Associated Press* followed this industry slugfest in 1995 and documented the curious connection between campaign donations and the favorable results produced for donors:

JANUARY-MARCH 1995: The AT&T group poured $68,400 of soft money (unregulated donations) into the coffers of both Republicans and Democrats. During the same period, the Baby Bells slipped a whopping $212,000 of soft money to the same recipients. The result? The Senate Commerce Committee on March 23, 1995, sided with the Baby Bells, approving a bill that allowed them quick and easy entry into the long-distance business, much to the chagrin of AT&T.

ROUND 1: to the Baby Bells.

MARCH-MAY 1995: That didn't sit well with the AT&T group. They launched a renewed offensive by showering campaign money on the House Commerce Committee and its chairman, Thomas Bliley (R-VA). The result? The committee on May 26, 1995, approved a bill favorable to the AT&T group, making it difficult for the Baby Bells to enter the long-distance market.

ROUND 2: to the AT&T group.

MAY-JULY 1995: This latest turn of events worried the Baby Bells, which counterpunched by spreading $52,000 in campaign donations to House Commerce Committee members. Then, they wisely greased the palms of House leaders, spreading $54,500 in political contributions to Speaker Newt Gingrich (R-GA), Majority Leader Dick Armey (R-TX), and Majority Whip Tom DeLay (R-TX). The Baby Bells clearly outbid the AT&T group. The result? Gingrich, on July 13, 1995, overruled the committee's bill that had been favorable to AT&T and decreed that the House would pass a bill favorable to the Baby Bells instead, giving them easier access to long-distance business. The Baby Bells group was ecstatic. Six days later, Nynex, one of the Baby Bells, dropped $100,000 worth of appreciation into the House Republican campaign committee account.

ROUND 3: to the Baby Bells.

JULY 1995: AT&T, reeling from the Gingrich broadside, regrouped and revised its strategy by pinning its hopes on the White House. They donated $103,200 to the Democratic National Committee (DNC), which was actively planning President Clinton's 1996 re-election effort. Another $50,000 was spread around to other Democratic leaders and power brokers. The result? President Clinton on

July 31, 1995, threatened to veto the Gingrich bill on the grounds it was too favorable to the Baby Bells.
ROUND 4: to the AT&T group.

JULY 1995: At this point, both the Senate and House had each passed their own telecommunications bill. Leaders of both chambers then appointed a conference committee that included House and Senate members to iron out the differences and produce a unified bill to send to the president. The conferees now became the target of industry largesse.
ROUND 5: even.

OCTOBER-DECEMBER 1995: The Baby Bells, responding to AT&T's White House strategy, stood firm hitching their wagon to Congress's star and Gingrich's bill. They poured $101,262 into the congressional campaign accounts of the conference committee members. The AT&T group countered with $160,000 in soft money donations to Clinton's re-election campaign.
ROUND 6: even.

DECEMBER 15, 1995: On this day, the conference committee announced a compromise agreement with the White House. It granted the Baby Bells entrance into the long-distance market, but gave the AT&T group concessions, including granting the Justice Department regulatory oversight of the Baby Bells to prevent any of them from morphing into a monopoly. It wasn't much of a concession, but it was something. The AT&T group showed its appreciation to the White House by funneling $190,000 to the DNC. That same day, Republican leaders publicly squawked that the compromise didn't go far enough in deregulating the AT&T group's hold on the long-distance telephone market. Days later, perhaps to quiet down House leaders, the AT&T group gave its largest campaign donation, doling out $200,000 to the Republican National Committee (RNC).

WINNER: split decision to the AT&T group, which gave more money.
LOSER: democracy.

Vice President Al Gore, disgusted at how money had influenced the decision-making process, remarked that the bill had been "sold to the highest bidder."[8]

Unfortunately, this "tale of two industries" is an accurate portrayal of how our government really works and how major legislation is routinely processed. It's the same corrupt system today as it ever was. You won't find anything like it in your child's social studies textbook.

Even conservatives agree with Gore's assessment of Washington's sleazy legislative sausage factory. Senator Ted Cruz (R-TX), a 2016 presidential candidate, stated in a speech he delivered at the conservative Heritage Foundation:

> What's happening in Washington is no accident. It is a concerted effort by corporate lobbyists and establishment politicians. Lobbyists and career politicians make up the Washington Cartel. Let me explain to you how it works: A bill is set to come before Congress, and career politicians' ears and wallets are open to the highest bidder. Corrupt back-room deals result in one interest group getting preferences over the other, although you give the other a chance to outbid them.

Is it any wonder why so many Americans believe the political system is bought and paid for and rigged against them? Is it any wonder why so many Americans tune out and refuse to vote? Is it any wonder why so many Americans hold government in such low esteem?

How low?

According to a December 2017 *Pew Research Center* poll, 18 percent of Americans trust the federal government, and only 3 percent "always" trust the government to "do what is right."[9]

A September 2015 Gallup poll revealed 75 percent of Americans believe that corruption is "widespread throughout the government."[10]

A June 2017 Gallup poll measuring the public's confidence in 16 American institutions placed Congress dead last, with a 12 percent approval rating. Internet news, television news, banks, and the medical system all ranked higher.[11] (Used car salesmen was not one of the 16.) The top three institutions, by the way, were: the military (72 percent), small business (70 percent), and the police (57 percent).

Some may ask why the U.S. Supreme Court, ranked fifth (40 percent), did not top this poll. After all, the Court's justices are appointed. They don't have to beg for money to win their jobs. Partisan politics, unfortunately, has played an ever-larger role over the past 40 years in filling the Court's vacancies. Confirmation hearings have become hyper-partisan spectacles. In recent years, sitting justices have openly hobnobbed with ideological power brokers who helped them gain their seats. This behavior may account for the lower, sub-50 percent ranking. If the poll measured the entire judiciary system, including *elected* judges in many state and local jurisdictions, the ranking may well have been near Congressland.

To average Americans, there seems to be an inverse relationship between campaign money and public confidence no matter the institution. And it follows that less money in such institutions of public trust would increase public confidence.

JUDICIAL ELECTIONS

CURRENTLY, 39 STATES ELECT JUDGES for at least one judicial level.[12] The president of the United States nominates federal judges, and the U.S. Senate confirms their lifetime appointments.

In the 1800s, states elected nearly all their judges. In the 1940s, some states grew weary of the rampant corruption caused by such elections and began adopting "merit plans" to appoint judges based on ability.

A revealing parallel to lawmakers is that the question of impartiality continues to dog popularly-elected judges. The trend in recent years has been to move toward merit appointments. Today, states still struggle with the concept of elected judges.

In 2006, *The New York Times* conducted a study of Ohio's judiciary system. It found that Ohio's elected judges routinely sat on cases that included at least one defendant or litigant who had contributed money to their election. The newspaper's review of those cases revealed that judges ruled "in favor of their contributors 70 percent of the time," and one judge favored his benefactors 91 percent of the time.[13]

Even some Ohio judges questioned the wisdom of electing judges. "I never felt so much like a hooker down by the bus station in any race I've ever been in as I did in a judicial race," said Justice Paul E. Pfeifer, a Republican on the state's supreme court. "Everyone interested in contributing has very specific interests," he said. "They mean to be buying a vote. Whether they succeed or not, it's hard to say."[14]

Sandra Day O'Connor, former U.S. Supreme Court justice and former Arizona state senator, wrote in 2008 that the election of judges in America should be phased out because it undermines the confidence Americans have in the judicial system.

O'Connor, a lifelong Republican, recounted the successful campaign of Illinois Supreme Court justice Lloyd Karmeier in 2004, when he spent more than $4.8 million to win an open seat on the bench. All candidates' combined spending in the race topped $9.3 million, making it the most expensive judicial election in American history at the time.[15] O'Connor quoted Karmeier's reaction to the spending: "That's obscene for a judicial race. What does it gain people? How can anyone have faith in the system?"[16] O'Connor then chimed in: "Good questions. When so much money goes into influencing the outcome of a judicial election, it is hard to have faith that we are selecting judges who are fair and impartial." She added, "If I could do one thing to solve this problem, it would be to convince the states that select judges through partisan elections . . . to switch to merit selection instead. Under this plan, currently used in states such as Colorado and Nebraska, an independent commission of knowledgeable citizens recommends candidates to the governor, who appoints one of them as judge."[17]

The United States is one of only three countries in the world that elects judges. Switzerland allows elections in some smaller jurisdictions, and Japan holds "retention elections" for justices serving on the Japanese Supreme Court, although those elections are usually a formality, and justices are routinely reappointed.

France debated the election of judges soon after the French Revolution. But witnessing mob justice up close, citizens decided against it in favor of a nonpolitical, impartial judiciary. Today, those seeking judgeships in France must survive a grueling four-day test just for the privilege of entering the rigorous two-year and three-month program that trains judges. The success rate for applicants can be as low as 5 percent in any year.[18]

Mitchel Lasser, a Cornell University law professor and judicial systems analysis expert, sees a lot of benefits in the French and other models, as opposed to the American way of electing judges. "You have people who actually know what the hell they're doing," Lasser said of judges who have received intensive training for their posts. "They've spent years in school taking practical and theoretical courses on how to be a judge. These are professionals." In comparing the U.S. system to others, he added, "The rest of the world is stunned and amazed at what we do, and vaguely aghast. They think the idea that judges with absolutely no judge-specific educational training who are running political campaigns is both insane and characteristically American."[19]

So, if *you* were sued in court, would you want your fate decided by a politician-judge who palled around with and received a large campaign check from the person who is suing you? Would you feel confident that the judge would be 100 percent impartial, and that you would get a fair trial? And if you lost, would you feel that the system was rigged against you?

Placed in the context of elected lawmakers, is there any reason to trust politicians when the system in which they toil undermines their independence at every turn? Would any sane person expect impartiality to flourish in American politics?

And is it any wonder that only 12 percent of Americans have confidence in the nation's primary lawmaking body?

VOTER TURNOUT
Spending Limits Abroad

SO WHY IS IT THAT AMERICANS will not tolerate any breach of impartiality in courtrooms, yet are willing to tolerate such conduct in the halls of American government?

Most Americans know the political system is corrupt to its core, yet seem demoralized and blasé about fixing it. Most just don't know what to do. The problem seems too big to solve.

A July 2015 Rasmussen poll showed 59 percent of Americans believe "most members of Congress are willing to sell their vote for either cash or a campaign contribution."[20] A January 2006 Pew Research Center poll found 81 percent of Americans believe that lobbyists commonly bribe members of Congress.[21]

Americans' contempt for the nation's politics and two-party system is demonstrated yearly by those who flee the ranks of Republicans and Democrats. Seems these citizens don't trust either party. A June 2018 Gallup poll found that more Americans identify themselves as independents (43 percent) than Democrats (29 percent) or Republicans (27 percent).[22] This movement away from the major parties continues on a slow, but steady pace across the nation. For decades, there has been a desire to form an alternative, sustainable third party, but there is little agreement on what that party should stand for—other than *not* being the Republican or Democratic Party. The trend away from the major parties shows that many citizens are deeply frustrated with the political system and view it as hopelessly corrupt. They desire change, but don't know what to do or where to begin. Lacking a major third party, many detach themselves from this "cesspool" of political iniquity and do the only thing they feel empowered to

U.S. Voter Turnout in Federal Elections
1960–2016

(Presidential election years are shaded.)

Year	Eligible Voters	Registered Voters	Voter Turnout	% Turnout
2016	250,056,000	NA	138,847,000	55.5
2014	245,712,915	NA	81,687,059	36.3
2012	240,926,957	NA	130,234,600	53.6
2010	235,809,266	NA	90,682,968	37.8
2008	231,229,580	NA	132,618,580	56.8
2006	220,600,000	135,889,600	80,588,000	37.1
2004	221,256,931	174,800,000	122,294,978	55.3
2002	215,473,000	150,990,598	79,830,119	37
2000	205,815,000	156,421,311	105,586,274	51.3
1998	200,929,000	141,850,558	73,117,022	36.4
1996	196,511,000	146,211,960	96,456,345	49.1
1994	193,650,000	130,292,822	75,105,860	38.8
1992	189,529,000	133,821,178	104,405,155	55.1
1990	185,812,000	121,105,630	67,859,189	36.5
1988	182,778,000	126,379,628	91,594,693	50.1
1986	178,566,000	118,399,984	64,991,128	36.4
1984	174,466,000	124,150,614	92,652,680	53.1
1982	169,938,000	110,671,225	67,615,576	39.8
1980	164,597,000	113,043,734	86,515,221	52.6
1978	158,373,000	103,291,265	58,917,938	37.2
1976	152,309,190	105,037,986	81,555,789	53.6
1974	146,336,000	96,199,020	55,943,834	38.2
1972	140,776,000	97,328,541	77,718,554	55.2
1970	124,498,000	82,496,747	58,014,338	46.6
1968	120,328,186	81,658,180	73,211,875	60.8
1966	116,132,000	76,288,283	56,188,046	48.4
1964	114,090,000	73,715,818	70,644,592	61.9
1962	112,423,000	65,393,751	53,141,227	47.3
1960	109,159,000	64,833,096	68,838,204	63.1

Source: Federal Election Commission

do: refuse to participate. As the chart on the next page shows, voter turnout in presidential and mid-term elections has slowly declined and remains anemic.

Turnout from 1960 to 2016 ranged from a high of 63.1 percent in the 1960 presidential election to a low of 36.3 percent in the 2014 mid-term. The 2014 turnout was the second lowest in the nation's history. Only the 1942 mid-term election 72 years earlier recorded a worse turnout at 33.9 percent.[23] The 2018 mid-term elections bucked the downward trend, registering a 49 percent turnout, the highest in 52 years. Women, Latinos, and younger Americans voted in large numbers, driven by their visceral reactions to President Trump's controversial and divisive policies and statements. Both parties ran strong get-out-the-vote efforts that also increased participation. And although turnout spiked in 2018, more than half the country's eligible voters still refused to cast a ballot.

In comparison, Great Britain's voter turnout from 1960 to 2014 ranged from a high of 78.8 percent in 1974 to a low of 59.4 percent in 2001.[24] To find a comparable American voting rate, we must hark back to 1876, when 81.8% of eligible voters participated.[25]

To put voter apathy into sharper perspective, the United States ranks 138th in voter turnout compared to 168 other countries where elections are held, according to a study by the International Institute for Democracy and Electoral Assistance, a government research group in Sweden.[26] Mexico, Uganda, Russia, Bolivia, Cambodia, France, Mongolia, Haiti, Peru, Iran, and the Palestinian Authority—all ranked higher than America. And many citizens of these countries often put their lives in jeopardy—and are sometimes killed—just for the right to vote.

Where is American exceptionalism when it comes to voting?

America is supposed to be the beacon of democracy. But what message do we send when roughly two-thirds of eligible U.S. voters in mid-term elections and half of voters in presidential years fail to exercise their most important, sacred political power granted to them by the Constitution?

The problem with shunning the voting booth is that it gives those who *do* vote more political power. It's one of the reasons why American politics today has become so hyper-partisan. Many in the middle stay home on Election Day while those on the extreme left and right vote religiously and have their voices amplified well beyond their numbers. Worse, these fringe voters are often manipulated and driven by emotional political messages, usually crafted by wealthy special interests, demagogues, and conspiracy theorists. President Harry Truman warned of voter apathy on June 17, 1948, as he spoke from a train's rear platform on his famous whistle stop re-election campaign tour across the country:

> There is just one big issue: it is the special interests against the people. And the president, being elected by all the people, represents the people. You have now a special interest Congress. You have that special interest Congress because one-third of you voted in the election of 1946, and you are getting just what you deserved. I have no sympathy with you. If you do that again, you will also get what you deserve.[27]

Many voters in other countries don't have to hold their noses to vote. They aren't subjected to the nauseating orgy of money that permeates America's politics. They aren't saturated with two-year presidential campaigns spewing endless attack ads, name-calling, fear mongering, bigotry, and outright buffoonery. In 2016, America's political discourse reached a new low. The endless string of Republican debates included a juvenile exchange between top candidates, leading to the frontrunner boasting of the size of his own penis.

Britain's election cycle is less than a month long. It begins the day Parliament is dissolved and ends 25 days later on Election Day. Britain prohibits political ads on commercial television and radio, but grants politicians limited, free broadcasting time on national television and radio.[28] In America, "the people" own the airwaves, but government auctions the airwaves off to private companies that charge exorbitant amounts for running campaign ads. British law also sets campaign spending limits on candidates, parties, and independent expenditure groups, called "controlled expenditures by third parties."

Do British spending limits violate freedom of speech? Not if the caps serve a "pressing social need," according to the European Convention on Human Rights.[29] This echoes the U.S. Court of Appeals' *Buckley v. Valeo* ruling (before it reached the Supreme Court) on campaign spending limits. The Appeals Court ruled that spending caps did not violate the First Amendment right to free speech, since the limits served to protect the "clear and compelling interest" of the nation's citizens in preserving the integrity of the election process.

Justin Fisher, a political science professor at Brunel University London, said the British view America's campaign system as the "worst of all worlds" with most candidates spending more time "raising money and not getting ideas across."[30]

Other countries share similar views that America's money-soaked, demagogic political system is excessive and unhealthy. "We are very thin-skinned when it comes to any form of propaganda," said Claas Lorenz, a 25-year-old German voter, quoted by *The New York Times*. "We had very bad experiences with it in the past," referring to Adolph Hitler and the Nazi Party.[31]

France and Israel also set campaign spending limits. Their election cycles are short as well. There's usually a few weeks of debates, speeches, and rallies before the election. Like Britain, the candidates are usually granted free air time and television ads to help get their messages out to voters. Nations like Germany, Australia, France, and Israel provide public funding for elections, which also helps parties and candidates to get their messages out to voters. This arguably translates into every European nation having a higher voter turnout rate than the United States.

The indifference of American voters in recent years has spurred some citizens to try and increase voter participation. In

Arizona, activists in 2006 tried to entice more people to vote by placing an initiative, the Arizona Voter Reward Act, on the state ballot. The measure pledged $1 million in cash to a randomly selected voter in the general election. The money would have been taken mostly from the state's unclaimed lottery account.[32] The initiative failed. It seems not even a million-dollar payday can get disillusioned American citizens to vote.

In 2015, President Obama floated the idea of compulsory voting to increase voter turnout.[33] There are about 22 countries that passed such voter laws, mostly in South America. Citizens who fail to vote may be fined or sentenced to perform community service. Obama's initiative, which didn't include fines or penalties, received virtually no support from either major party. It landed with a thud. He didn't pursue it further.

While foes of campaign spending limits grudgingly admit that voter turnout is indeed decreasing, they've come up with creative ways to explain it.

Filip Palda, libertarian author of *How Much Is Your Vote Worth: The Unfairness of Campaign Spending Limits*, pooh-poohs the possibility that low voter turnout in the United States is largely caused by citizens' disgust at the political system. Palda, a French-Canadian economist and disciple of Austrian economist and noted libertarian Friedrich A. Hayek, claims that all American voters, ideologically speaking, belong to special interest groups. All gun owners, for example, belong to the National Rifle Association (NRA), all pro-choicers belong to the National Abortion Rights Action League (NARAL), all seniors belong to the American Association of Retired Persons (AARP), etc. These groups, Palda asserts, represent all voters and bring the people's concerns to Washington's power elite, where ordinary citizens do not have access. In addition, Palda, an avid free marketer, maintains that it's the most effective and cost-efficient way for American voters to be heard. In offering his reasons for low voter turnout, Palda writes: "I suggest that fewer people vote today because the interest groups to which they belong can influence policy merely by threatening to mobilize voters . . . . By reminding politicians of their influence, these groups can get results while saving their members the bother of voting." [34]

The "*bother*" of voting?

Who knew voting was such drudgery? How horrible it must be for American citizens to walk down the street to the elementary school or church, meet their neighbors, catch up on one another and their families, discuss the issues, and cast their votes! What a hideous burden to exercise one's freedom and love of country!

Most Americans would be surprised to learn they belong to narrow-minded, special interest groups that somehow perfectly represent all their thoughts, beliefs, and opinions on the entire range of political issues.

Leave it to a French-Canadian writer relying on arcane studies by an Austrian economist to explain American democracy to Americans.

3

"REPRESENTATIVE" DEMOCRACY

" . . . there is a natural aristocracy among men. The grounds of this are virtue and talents. . . . There is also an artificial aristocracy, founded on wealth and birth, without either virtue or talents. . . . The artificial aristocracy is a mischievous ingredient in government, and provision should be made to prevent its ascendency." [1]

~ THOMAS JEFFERSON,
3rd U.S. president

AMOS SINGLETARY had heard enough.

The frail, white-haired, 66-year-old farmer from Sutton in Worcester County, rose to speak at the 1788 Massachusetts Ratifying Convention in Boston.

For weeks, Singletary, one of 370 convention delegates, patiently listened to Federalist arguments urging ratification of the document drafted by the Constitutional Convention several months earlier. But he had grave reservations. In his remarks, Singletary skewered Rufus King and Nathaniel Gorham, seated nearby, who had represented Massachusetts in Philadelphia and had signed the Constitution. They were now urging adoption. Singletary distrusted their motives:

> These lawyers, and men of learning, and moneyed men, that talk so finely, and gloss over matters so smoothly, to make us poor illiterate people swallow down the pill, expect to get into

Congress themselves; they expect to be the managers of this, and get all the power and all the money into their own hands, and then they will swallow up us little folks.[2]

Months after New Hampshire became the ninth state to ratify, thus securing the Constitution as the law of the land, King moved to New York and won election as one of the state's first two U.S. senators.[3]

Gorham, a merchant by trade, got rich swindling Native Americans out of their property rights. The new U.S. government made this possible by ratifying a long-stalled compact between New York and Massachusetts, allowing a Gorham-led syndicate to pay Massachusetts $1 million for the right to negotiate with the Iroquois nations. Gorham convinced the Native Americans to accept $5,000 in exchange for clear title to 2.6 million acres of their land. Gorham then made a fortune selling chunks of the huge tract to settlers.[4]

Singletary was, perhaps, one of the first Americans to lay the philosophical groundwork for campaign spending limits—i.e., intimating that some mechanism or brake would be needed to prevent the wealthy class from using the new political system to dominate or "swallow up" average Americans, as he put it. There was a loophole in the document, and Singletary and his fellow yeomen knew it. The problem would linger if not corrected.

Singletary's warning of the wealthy class dominating government was quite prescient. A 2012 study[5] by the National Constitution Center, a nonprofit created by Congress to educate the public on the Constitution, compared the composition of the first Congress to the 112th Congress:

1st U.S. CONGRESS (1789–1791)

91 voting members: 65 representatives; 26 senators

- 34 lawyers
- 15 soldiers

- 12 planters/farmers
- 11 businessmen/merchants
- 6 clergymen
- 5 statesmen/career politicians
- 4 physicians
- 3 teachers
- 1 diplomat

112th U.S. CONGRESS (2011–2012)

535 voting members: 435 representatives; 100 senators
(Note: some members listed more than one occupation below)

- 209 business people
- 208 public servants/career politicians
- 200 lawyers
- 81 educators
- 34 agricultural professionals
- 32 medical professionals
- 17 journalists
- 9 accountants
- 9 scientists
- 9 social workers
- 9 military reservists
- 7 law enforcement officers
- 5 ministers
- 4 pilots
- 4 Peace Corps volunteers
- 2 professional football players
- 2 screenwriters
- 1 firefighter
- 1 astronaut
- 1 documentary filmmaker
- 1 comedian

Note the rise in white-collar professionals. Business people, for example, represented 12 percent of the 1st Congress and 39 percent in the 112th Congress. Throw in lawyers and the representation increases from 50 percent in 1791 to 76 percent in 2012. Make no mistake—these business-politicians today aren't mom-and-pop shopkeepers and country lawyers. They're mostly wealthy corporatists and company executives. This white-collar demographic is getting wealthier and continues to increase its outsized representation in Congress. Also noteworthy, professional politicians comprised 6 percent of Congress in 1791, rising to nearly 40 percent in 2012. A curious, recurring theme among some of these career politicians today is how they ascend to office, then accumulate far greater wealth *after* taking office.

The percentages of other occupations have remained roughly the same. Physicians, for example, comprised 4 percent of the 1st Congress and 6 percent of the 112th. But only 20 of the 32 "medical professionals" in 2012 were actually doctors. One notable change in Congress's composition today is the advent of sports stars and entertainment professionals.

In sum, the numbers show a shift over the years toward white-collar professionals and away from blue-collar laborers like Amos Singletary.

AMERICA'S MILLIONAIRE CONGRESS

SINCE AMERICA'S FOUNDING, the moneyed class has dominated the nation's politics. Over time, their ability to exploit and manipulate the political system gradually concentrated wealth and political power in fewer and fewer hands.

When one considers America's worsening income inequality problem, it's pretty clear where the country is headed. The affluent continue to amass political power and pull the country in directions that do not reflect the consensus and will of the American populace.

It's no secret that the wealthy dominate U.S. elections. They dominate by financially backing entrenched incumbents or pliable neophytes to do their bidding. And in recent years, they often run for office themselves, as independently-wealthy candidates, posing as—*ahem*—populists! They try to win over average Americans by claiming their vast wealth insulates them from special interest corruption. You see them every election. These elites morph overnight, from wearing dark business suits to casual shirts, jeans, and baseball caps once they hit the campaign trail. If there were a Chutzpa Hall of Fame, they'd be in it.

Since the adoption of the Constitution, the Senate has always been a rich person's game. But now the House, which is supposed to be more representative of the people, is becoming an exclusive club as well.

In 2013, for the first time in the nation's history, the majority of congressional members were millionaires. There were 268 of the total 535 members in the House and Senate who possessed an average net worth (assets minus liabilities) of at least $1 million.[6] Of these 268, 70 percent served in the Senate and 45 percent served in the House. Yet, according to the U.S. Census, only 3 percent of U.S. citizens have a net worth of at least $1 million (10.1 million of 320 million total population). So in a truly representative democracy, only 3 percent of those seated in Congress should be millionaires. And average Americans, who make up the vast majority of the country, should dominate. But that's not today's political reality.

A 2018 study by Roll Call, a newspaper and website that tracks Congress, showed many of the wealthiest members occupying leadership posts. Among the top 50 richest were: Senate Majority Leader Mitch McConnell (R-KY), then-House Minority Leader Nancy Pelosi (D-CA), eight Republican committee chairs, and four ranking committee Democrats. Ten of the top 50 sat on the House Committee on Ways and Means or Senate Committee on Finance, panels that write legislation cutting taxes on the wealthiest Americans.[7]

Every election, the wealth gap grows wider between members of Congress and the citizens they represent. The median net worth of the 94 *freshmen* ($1,066,515) in this first millionaire-majority Congress in 2013 was $100,000 more than the median net worth of *all* 535 members ($996,000).[8]

And what happened to the median net worth of all Americans during the Great Recession from 2007 to 2013? Well, an American household during that period *lost* a third of its median net worth—while Senate members' net worth *rose* 22 percent and 19 percent for House members.[9] A 2015 study showed that the median net worth of congressional members was $1,029,505, compared to $56,355 for the average American household, making a congressional member's median net worth 18 times more than the average.

As Congress fills with wealthier members, average Americans today feel more detached from their government than ever. Many of us no longer see ourselves in, or identify with, our elected representatives.

It shouldn't be any surprise.

According to a study by Nicholas Carnes, author of *White-Collar Government: The Hidden Role of Class in Economic Policy Making*, blue-collar workers in Congress are extremely rare. In his book, Carnes writes that only 13 of 783 members (roughly 2 percent), serving between 1999 and 2008, held down blue-collar jobs for more than 25 percent of their working lives.[10] Carnes, a Duke University public policy professor, found a sliver of that 2 percent ascended to Congress directly from manual labor jobs, such as construction, factory, farming, retail, or service work. Yet, about 54 percent of U.S. households are considered blue-collar.

Carnes' research revealed the work history of the typical member of Congress serving between 1999 and 2008:

> Before being elected to Congress, the average legislator in my sample spent more than 30 percent of his working life in politics; more than 20 percent in law; substantial percentages in service-based

professions, business ownership or management, other business employment, and technical professions—and spent just 2 percent of his pre-congressional career in blue-collar work.[11]

Further, Carnes' data showed that members of Congress tend to vote in a manner that benefits their own class.

Millionaire politicians, Carnes found, tend to vote favorably on issues they profit from—directly or indirectly. These issues are closer to their experiences, such as tax cuts for the wealthy, tax breaks for corporations; and deregulation of Big Business. Conversely, these members tend to vote unfavorably on issues they have little personal experience with, such as unemployment insurance, minimum wage, social services, affordable health care, and affordable housing. Not all wealthy politicians, of course, fit the mold. As Carnes points out, "The FDRs and Kennedys of the world are the exceptions."[12]

In contrast, Carnes found lawmakers who had worked with their hands for long periods tend to vote favorably on issues not profitable to themselves, but beneficial to working- class families. Carnes noticed the same voting tendencies concerning wealth status for state and local politicians, although to a lesser degree than members of Congress.

What America has on its hands, unfortunately, is a political class that has rarely, if ever, known financial hardship. They've rarely experienced being one paycheck away from homelessness. In fact, the candidates we see today are often bereft of a gripping personal narrative for their campaigns, considered imperative by political managers to win votes. Usually, they have to reach back to tell the rags-to-riches tales of their parents or grandparents to convince average American voters that they understand their concerns and are "one of them." Here's a sampling from the 2016 class of presidential candidates:

- Senator Ted Cruz (R-TX) waxed on the campaign trail about his father who came to the United States with nothing but a small bit of cash stuffed in his underwear.

- Governor Chris Christie (R-NJ) told audiences about his father putting himself through college by working at an ice cream factory in Newark, New Jersey.

- Senator Marco Rubio (R-FL) pulled at voters' heartstrings with the story of his parents, whom he said emigrated from Cuba with little money, poor education, and limited English skills.

- Former secretary of state and former senator Hillary Rodham Clinton (D-NY) recounted stories of her grandfather, who worked in a factory at age 11; her father, who was a hard-working small businessman; and her mother, who suffered through an abusive childhood and left home at age 14 to work full time.[13]

What?

No "Everyman" anecdotes of celebrity-soaked Georgetown cocktail parties, soirees with the Koch brothers, $300,000 Goldman Sachs speaking fees, and limousines that have "prevented" them from actually driving a car for more than a quarter century?

Let's face it. We are represented by people who wouldn't have us over for dinner. We won't see them shopping at the local grocer or standing in line at the bank. They're in a higher social stratum than we are. They chum around with Oprah, Warren Buffet, Clint Eastwood, George Clooney, Bono, lobbyists, tech billionaires, and lesser-known business moguls. We chum around with—each other.

They don't face many of the same problems we do.

When they run for office, they have to ask us what issues we confront in our lives—as though they're anthropologists curiously observing some type of Cro Magnon sub-species. "Underwater mortgages, you say? Crushing student loan debt, you say? Disappearing pensions, you say? Mounting health and prescription drug bills, you say? This is all very interesting! Something must be done about this!"

Perhaps the quintessential illustration of how out of touch wealthy politicians can be occurred in February 1992, when President George H.W. Bush sought re-election.

Bush's campaign staff thought the president, born into an extremely wealthy, upper crust Yankee family, could connect with average voters if he visited the exhibition hall of the National Grocers Association convention in Orlando, Florida. During the tour, the president stopped to observe a modern grocery checkout lane. According to *The New York Times*, "(Bush) grabbed a quart of milk, a light bulb, and a bag of candy and ran them over an electronic scanner. The look of wonder flickered across his face . . . as he saw the item and price appear on the cash register screen." Bush asked, "This is for checking out?"[14] Observers said he was absolutely amazed at the technology. The president's aides apparently forgot to inform him that grocery scanners had been in use for 16 years.

There is another reason why our elected officials grow distant from the people they were elected to represent.

Once in Washington, lobbyists descend on them, offering connections to high rollers who regularly donate large pots of money for incumbent re-election campaigns.

The average U.S. House member is told he or she needs to raise an average of $10,000 per week to fend off challengers. This dependence on deep-pocketed political power brokers weakens an incumbent's reliance on constituents back home for campaign funds. A typical incumbent then ends up spending most of his or her time with their new Washington "friends," tending to *their* needs and not those of their constituents back home.

Worse, the temptation to climb the social ladder and live the high life with their new friends often ends in kickbacks, misappropriation of campaign funds, and sex scandals that have snuffed out more than a few promising political careers.

Then these ex-politicians turn to the only thing that can keep them in Washington, remaining in the game, and living in style: lobbying.

A RIGGED SYSTEM
Incumbents' Protection Plan

EVERY TWO YEARS, ALL 435 U.S. HOUSE SEATS are up for election, yet incumbents since 1964 have won about 94 percent of the time.

Either Congress is doing a good job or the system is rigged.

A 2018 Gallup poll found 21 percent of Americans believed Congress was doing a good job—up from 9 percent in 2013.[15] Most of Congress's poll numbers over the past six years fall within

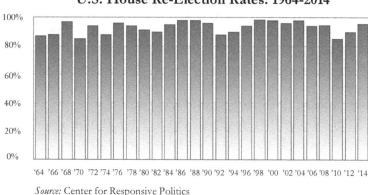

U.S. House Re-Election Rates: 1964-2014

Source: Center for Responsive Politics

that bandwidth.[17] And aside from a few blips, such as polling after the September 11, 2001, terrorist attacks, Congress's approval rating has been sliding steadily since the 1960s. This pretty much eliminates good job performance as the reason for high re-election rates.

So is the system rigged?

Well, special interest money, particularly from major corporations seeking to ease regulations, flows to those in power because they control the levers of government. Those in power are incumbents. And with the near guarantee that the candidate with the most money wins, it's understandable why incumbent re-election rates are in the mid-90 percent range.

This link between unlimited campaign spending and high

incumbent re-election rates is arguably a rigging of the system. It's no shock that congressional incumbents are in no rush to pass any legislation that would give challengers a better chance to win. If elections were fair—like a coin toss—incumbents would win about 50 percent of the time. That's overly simplistic, of course, since there are a number of variables that influence elections, including the money disparity.

As former Senator Dale Bumpers (D-AR) once observed: "Nothing illustrates what afflicts our democracy so well as this: 94 percent of candidates who spend the most money win."[16]

ONE CITIZEN, ONE VOTE

ALTHOUGH THE "ONE CITIZEN, ONE VOTE" concept is central to American democracy, it was not written into the Constitution. It is derived mainly from the Fourteenth Amendment's Equal Protection Clause.

One citizen, one vote involves the issues of redistricting and reapportionment. As stated in the Constitution's Article I, Section 2, Congress determines the number of representatives for each state after the census is taken every 10 years. The states then draw the boundaries for congressional and state legislative districts, taking into account the population change.

Historically, state legislators, particularly in the South, have drawn a number of district lines that intentionally gave more representation to white citizens at the expense of black citizens, who had gradually concentrated in urban, manufacturing areas. Blacks sued, contending they were being swindled out of their constitutional voting rights.

A trio of U.S. Supreme Court decisions settled the issue and formed the basis for one citizen, one vote.

The Court, in *Baker v. Carr* (1962), ruled that federal courts had the authority to decide reapportionment cases. It prompted more than 30 lawsuits accusing states of unconstitutional reapportionment schemes.[17]

The Court first used the phrase "one person, one vote" in deciding *Gray v. Sanders* (1963). The case involved the state of Georgia's use of a "county unit system" as a basis for counting votes in a Democratic primary. The Democrats were the dominant party at the time, and the party's power brokers virtually appointed the state's elected officials. Black citizens accused the state of using the voting system to grant outsized representation to whites in rural areas like Echols County while marginalizing the voting power of blacks in urban areas like Fulton County, which includes the city of Atlanta. There were small numbers of black citizens residing in rural areas, but not many were registered to vote. In urban areas like Atlanta, however, there were significant numbers of registered black voters.

According to the state's formula, Fulton County comprised 14.11 percent of Georgia's population, but received only 1.46 percent of the state's political representation. In contrast, Echols County accounted for 0.05 percent of the population—the lowest in the state—but received 0.48 percent of the state's political representation. Put into context, one "unit" of voting power in rural Echols County "represented 938 residents, whereas one unit of voting power in urban Fulton County represented 92,721 residents."[18]

The Court ruled against Georgia and its fraudulent vote counting system. Writing for the majority, Justice William Douglas reasoned:

> The conception of political equality from the Declaration of Independence, to Lincoln's Gettysburg Address, to the Fifteenth, Seventeenth, and Nineteenth Amendments can mean only one thing—one person, one vote.[19]

The following year, the Court's one citizen, one vote hammer cracked down again on another Southern state accused of robbing black citizens of their voting power. In *Reynolds v. Sims* (1964), the Court used the Constitution's Equal Protection Clause to declare Alabama's legislative districts unequal, unfair, and discriminatory. The case hinged on the legislature's refusal since 1901 to change the boundaries of legislative districts. In doing so, it ignored the dramatic population shift over 60 years from rural to urban areas, where a sizeable number of African-Americans had relocated. By purposely neglecting the district lines over time, voter representation gradually became more imbalanced and discriminatory. By 1962, rural Bullock County's 13,462 mostly white citizens, for example, were apportioned *two* seats in the Alabama House, while the 314,301 mostly black citizens of urban Mobile County were granted only *three*.[20] That translated into one seat per 6,731 people in Bullock County; and one seat per 104,767 people in Mobile County.

In deciding the case, the Supreme Court justices again drew from the principles embedded in the Constitution concerning the election of U.S. representatives. Chief Justice Earl Warren wrote in the majority opinion:

> . . . we decided that an apportionment of congressional seats which 'contracts the value of some votes and expands that of others' is unconstitutional, since the Federal Constitution intends that, when qualified voters elect members of Congress, each vote be given as much weight as any other vote. . . . We concluded that the constitutional prescription for election of members of the House of Representatives 'by the People,' construed in its historical context, means that, as nearly as is practicable, one man's vote in a congressional election is to be worth as much as another's.[21]

HOW "FREE SPEECH" DOLLAR VOTES DILUTE CITIZENS' BALLOT VOTES

LET'S APPLY CHIEF JUSTICE WARREN'S RULING by comparing democratic principles with free market principles as it pertains to the concept of "money equals free speech."

According to conventional wisdom, speech is communicated thought; money is property.

But the Supreme Court ruled in the 1976 *Buckley v. Valeo* case that the freedom to spend money in an election is an act of communicating political thought, therefore speech.

One could also derive from that statement that the freedom to cast a vote in an election is communicating a political thought, therefore speech. But each eligible citizen is constitutionally *limited* to only one vote—so we all theoretically possess equal power in an election. Yet we are not limited to how much money we may possess. So if spending money is freedom of speech, then wealthier citizens have much more freedom of speech than average Americans. And the vast majority of Americans who are middle to low income have far less, if any, of this freedom. So when wealthy special interests flood the political system with hundreds of millions of dollars to elect their favored candidates, they are casting votes to show their preferences. And when these "dollar votes" are mixed together with ballot votes—the one vote allotted to each citizen in an election—the most important power of the people is diluted and usurped.

In our democracy, arguably the most important political right granted by the Constitution to citizens is the power to vote. This right is supposed to be *equal* for all, whether a citizen is wealthy and living in a mansion or poor and living in a cardboard box. It is democracy's great equalizer.

There is a reason the Constitution's Framers at the 1787 Constitutional Convention decided to limit each citizen to one vote: to ensure that no citizen or cabal had an undue influence or advantage concerning all matters in the public arena. In other words, the Framers sought to protect the integrity—some would say the impartiality—of the democratic process, so that *all* public decisions would truly reflect the consensus and will of the people. And the public would have faith and confidence in its democracy.

But if wealthier citizens can use their money, that is, their stores of free speech to buy elections, laws, and politicians—and even court decisions—then, our democracy is, in large part, a farce.

In essence, wealthy special interests and political power brokers today are basically doing to average Americans what Southern whites have been doing to black urban voters for generations—using their wealth, power, and position of political dominance to expand their voting power at the expense of others with lesser means. Thomas Jefferson warned of the usurpation of political power by the wealthy class, many of whom distrusted average Americans holding and wielding the supreme power granted to us by the Constitution. Jefferson declared:

> I am not among those who fear the people. They, and not the rich are our dependence for continued freedom. [22]

Many of the Framers, of course, were wealthy and excluded wide swaths of the population from voting. But if they had intended the wealthy to ride roughshod over average Americans, they would have enshrined such a doctrine into the Constitution granting "weighted" votes to citizens according to wealth. They could have allotted citizens one ballot vote per one thousand dollars of wealth, for example, giving a person who has $1 million 1,000 ballot votes. Or they could have weighted citizens' ballot votes to the acreage of property owned.

But they didn't.

The Framers—knowing that granting weighted votes would have given *themselves* more power—did not want any single wealthy person (like a monarch) or group (aristocracy) to have an outsized influence over the workings and decision-making of government.

Surely, their vision of American democracy was not one of domination by the wealthy, as we see today. This country was born from a revolt against the concentrated wealth and power of a monarchy and the arrogance of an out-of-touch Parliament filled with wealthy aristocrats.

The Declaration of Independence does not proclaim the ultimate power of America to be the consent of the "Divine One" or the "wealthy few," but of *the governed.*"

All of this is predictably lost on some wealthier Americans.

Billionaire venture capitalist Tom Perkins made headlines in 2014, squawking that those with more money who pay more taxes should have more votes to cast in elections. Perkins, participating on an interview panel at the Commonwealth Club in San Francisco, California, was asked by Fortune magazine's Adam Lashinsky to name one idea that would "change the world." Perkins, whose net worth was $8 billion when he died in 2016, replied: " . . . what I really think is, it should be like a corporation. You pay a million dollars in taxes, you get a million votes. How's that?"[23]

Perkins apparently saw himself as a higher form of human being deserving of special privilege because of his wealth, not unlike an eighteenth century British monarch or parliament lord.

There are others like Perkins who view democracy as unfair or even a threat to the rich.

From 2005 to 2006, Citigroup, the multinational investment bank, covertly circulated a trio of strategy memos to its richest investors, detailing profitable schemes exploiting income inequality in America and warning of democratic protections that could prevent this exploitation.

In the memos, the bank's investment researchers referred to the U.S. economy as a "plutonomy"—an economy "driven by massive income and wealth inequality."[24] Strategies to capitalize on these inequalities included investing in the growing number of businesses that service the rich and stifling wage growth by fighting minimum wage legislation. The researchers, using such memo headings as, "Rising Tides Lifting All Yachts," and "Riding the Gravy Train," predicted the wealth and income inequality gaps to grow well into the future: "Our own view is that the rich are likely to keep getting even richer, and enjoy an even greater share of the wealth pie over the coming years."[25]

And what did the researchers warn was the biggest threat to the "new managerial aristocracy" riding the crest of America's plutonomy?

The vote.

The one political right and power granted by the U.S. Constitution to citizens.

Under the headings "Risks—What Could Go Wrong?" and "Is There A Backlash Building," the Citigroup folks wrote:

> Low-end developed market labor might not have much economic power, but it does have equal voting power with the rich. . . . Whilst the rich are getting a greater share of the wealth and the poor a lesser share, political enfranchisement remains as was—one person, one vote.[26]

One person, one vote.

The most important protection of democracy.

It's why the one person, one vote principle is so critical and why it's constantly under attack from the wealthy elite and dominant social classes.

It's the one cornerstone that keeps the foundation of our democracy together, keeping it from sliding into a plutocracy, dictatorship, or worse.

VOTER SUPPRESSION

TODAY'S CONSERVATIVES and their moneyed backers remain hostile to the Supreme Court's past decisions establishing the one person, one vote precept. They have launched numerous efforts over the years to discourage voting—mostly along racial lines—to weaken this most vital element of democracy.

Today, as more Latinos populate Southern states and gain political power, Southern conservatives fight to contain them and preserve white social and political dominance. Similar battles are taking place in many Midwestern and other red states.

Various methods to discourage minorities from voting are being deployed, such as: onerous identification requirements, restrictions or bans on early voting, reduction or removal of polling places in minority areas, and cleansing of "undesirables" from voter rolls for technicalities like misspelling on registration forms.

Some old methods have never died, such as permanently denying voting rights to people with criminal records who have completed their sentences. States passed many of these laws in the 1800s to deter blacks from voting who, like today, were disproportionately incarcerated.

When the Constitution went into effect on March 4, 1789, Southern conservatives wanted slaves included in the population census, which determined the number of seats in Congress and electoral votes. They fought hard to broker a compromise with Northerners to include a constitutional provision that would count each slave as three-fifths of a person in the decennial census, even though Southerners viewed slaves as property, not fellow humans. This increased the number of Southern congressional seats and amplified the Southern political voice. And after the Civil War, Southern whites couldn't wait to include freed blacks in the full and total population numbers for the same reason—to pump up the white Southern political voice—even though they had no intention of welcoming black people as equal partners in democracy. The scheme backfired when blacks, protected by federal agents during Reconstruction, began running and winning elections in Southern states.

The agents worked for the Bureau of Refugees, Freedmen, and Abandoned Lands, commonly known as the Freedman's Bureau, created in 1863 during the war. The agency carried out "social reconstruction," protecting freed black slaves and helping them assimilate into Southern white society. During this period, blacks embraced their newfound freedom and American citizenship, becoming pillars in the community as landowners, teachers, doctors, and political office holders.

To say many Southern whites were seething at blacks' economic and political successes would be a gross understatement.

Whites, fearful of losing their social and political dominance, fought back by instituting the Black Codes and Jim Crow laws. They also formed terrorist groups like the Ku Klux Klan to intimidate blacks from exercising their civil rights, including voting and serving in elected office.

Then came the Compromise of 1877—Congress's severe and disgraceful blow to blacks' blooming democratic freedom. The 1876 presidential election was a close race, ending in a dispute over the electoral vote count. According to the Constitution's Article II, Congress decides the winner in such disputes. But in a secret meeting, Northern Republicans and Southern Democrats struck a compromise, giving Republican Rutherford B. Hayes the presidency. In exchange, the Republicans agreed to pull the federal agents out of Southern states, leaving black citizens unprotected.

Congress approved the deal.

As soon as the agents left, the Southern white backlash began, and it was furious. White government officials nullified the elections of duly elected black politicians, physically dragging some off state house floors and imprisoning them on phony charges. Black-owned stores were boycotted or set ablaze. And then they came after blacks' ultimate political power—their votes.

Since the Compromise of 1877, conservatives have used every means at their disposal to discourage blacks from voting, including murder, physical and psychological intimidation, literacy tests, and other tactics.

Southern whites also charged a special tax for voting to discourage large numbers of poor blacks from participating in elections. These egregious laws outraged the majority of Americans, leading to the 1964 adoption of the Constitution's Twenty-fourth Amendment abolishing "poll taxes."

Today's conservatives, particularly in Southern states, eager to "conserve" the white status quo, have continued the work of their forebears, seeking to contain the surging political power of non-whites, who often vote Democratic. The latest U.S. Census projection that whites will be the minority population by 2045 has acutely heightened conservatives' anxiety.

What to do?

Conservatives decided the solution is to utilize the government levers they control and double down on the old playbook: suppress the vote.

In 2013, the Supreme Court dealt a huge blow to the one person, one vote tenet by gutting the Voting Rights Act of 1965. In *Shelby County v. Holder*, the Court eliminated the requirement that certain historically racist states and jurisdictions—mostly in the South—were forced to gain federal approval, or "pre-clearance," before making changes to their voting laws. Shelby County in Alabama was one of those jurisdictions covered by the Act.

Chief Justice John Roberts, who wrote the *Shelby* 5-4 majority opinion, agreed the 1965 voting law made "great strides" in combating racism at the polls.[27] But, he offered, the country had "changed dramatically" in the nearly 50 years since the law went into effect.[28] As proof, he repeatedly pointed out that minority voter registration and turnout had increased since 1965 and that minorities held elective office at "unprecedented levels."[29] With this proof, Roberts deduced that racist and discriminatory conditions no longer existed to warrant the pre-clearance process, and that it was unconstitutional for the federal government to treat these designated pre-clearance states and jurisdictions differently than other parts of America. Roberts wrote:

> In 1965, the states could be divided into two groups: those with a recent history of voting tests, and low voter registration and turnout, and those without those characteristics. Congress based its covered formula (pre-clearance) on that distinction. Today, the nation is no longer divided along those lines, yet the Voting Rights Act continues to treat it as if it were.[30]

Roberts dismissed the pleas of civil rights advocates who asserted that increased minority voter participation was the result of the Voting Rights Act remaining in place.[31] And he chose to ignore the unmistakable hyper-partisan divide growing in America. To no one's shock, except maybe Roberts and his majority, the former pre-clearance states rushed to enact new voter laws as soon as his gavel came down concluding *Shelby*.

North Carolina's Republican-led legislature nearly fell over itself, hurriedly crafting a new voting law that discouraged black citizens from voting. The Republican governor wasted no time in signing it into law. Civil rights groups, activists, and a small group of churches fought a three-year court battle against North Carolina's state government before upending the law in July 2016. The U.S. Fourth Circuit Court of Appeals' three-judge panel ruled the North Carolina law unconstitutional, citing its blatant racism. Judge Diana Motz wrote:

> Before enacting that law, the legislature requested data on the use, by race, of a number of voting practices. Upon receipt of the race data, the General Assembly enacted legislation that restricted voting and registration in five different ways, all of which disproportionately affected African Americans. . . . The new provisions target African Americans with almost surgical precision.[32]

Noting that the bill passed in only three days, Motz added:

> Indeed, neither this legislature—nor, as far as we can tell, any other legislature in the country—has ever done so much, so fast, to restrict access to the franchise.[33]

Before Justice Roberts and his conservative colleagues in 2013 took an ax to established congressional law, more than 3,000 discriminatory state voting laws had been blocked by federal justice officials during the nearly 50 years the Voting Rights Act of 1965 remained in full force.[34] Since *Shelby*, dozens of new state laws tacitly restricting minority access have been passed. More are in the works.

Arizona's recent voter suppression gambit is an example of a common tactic used since the *Shelby* ruling. For Arizona's March 2016 primary election, Maricopa County Recorder Helen Purcell, a Republican, decided to slash the number of county polling places by 70 percent—from 200 in the 2012 election to 60. She claimed it was a cost-cutting measure. The heart of Maricopa County is the city of Phoenix, the state's largest city and its capital. Phoenix's majority population is non-white and largely votes Democratic. Purcell's action translated to one polling place per 21,000 voters in Maricopa County, as opposed one polling place for every 2,500 voters in the other mostly white, Republican parts of the state.[35] On Primary Day, anger spilled over as Maricopa County voters waited up to five hours in long lines to cast their votes. Many took time off from work to vote. Some had to return to work without voting because of the long delays. It was reported across the state that large numbers of minorities were dissuaded from voting. The 1965 Voting Rights Act included Arizona as one of the states required to submit new election laws and practices for federal review. Had the Supreme Court not gutted the law, Purcell's plan likely would have been voided.

Today, half the states—nearly all of them Republican-controlled—have passed voter ID laws, perhaps the most common ruse to deny minority voters their constitutional right to vote. The proponents claim massive voter fraud is threatening America's democracy by skewing election outcomes. The only way to stop it, they claim, is for voters to show a government-issued photo identification card to local election officials before registering to vote. There remains, however, no credible evidence that shows voter impersonation—a person fraudulently casting a vote at the polls under a fake identity—is even remotely a problem.

Kansas is a good example of conservatives' voter fraud farce. The state has been exceptionally pernicious in denying minority citizens the right to vote, led by its secretary of state, Kris W. Kobach. The conservative Republican boasted on his campaign website that "Kansas voters elected him by a wide margin on a platform focused on stopping voter fraud."

In 1993, Congress passed the National Voter Registration Act (NVRA), also called the Motor Voter Act, to increase voter participation. The federal law requires state governments to offer voter registration to citizens seeking a driver's license at offices of motor vehicles. The law accepts voter registration information given by the applicant as true, under penalty of perjury. But soon after Kobach took office in 2011, he authored the Secure and Fair Elections (SAFE) Act, requiring people to show proof of U.S. citizenship with a government-issued photo ID card before they could register to vote at the department of motor vehicles. Within months, Kobach's bill sailed through both Republican-controlled houses and was quickly signed by Republican Governor Sam Brownback.

In 2016, a U.S. District judge appointed by President George W. Bush halted Kobach's law, citing violation of the NVRA that requires only "minimal information" to register.[36] In America, the two main forms of ID are a driver's license and a passport. But many urban, poor minority voters rely on public transportation and cannot afford a car or travel abroad. According to the Brennan Center for Justice at New York University, 25 percent of blacks and 16 percent of Hispanics in the United States, who are eligible to vote, do not possess these voting-required photo IDs. Only nine percent of whites do not possess these documents.[37]

The court also debunked Kobach's claim of massive voter fraud in the state. Its review of Kansas elections showed that only three non-citizens had fraudulently voted in federal elections and only 14 non-citizens had tried, but were prevented from voting at the polls in the 18-year span between 1995 and 2013.[38] Put into context, Kobach's new law in 2016 culled 32,000 Kansans— the vast majority of them minorities—from the rolls, and placed their voting status in limbo. All this to address an "epidemic crisis" of 17 fraudulent voters over nearly two decades. A federal judge later placed an injunction on Kobach's law, restoring voting power to 18,372 of that group, roughly half, who had registered through the so-called "motor-voter law."[39]

Was Kobach done?

Hardly.

In July 2016, just over a month after the federal court ruling, Kobach rammed through a new rule allowing those 18,372 people to vote in *federal* elections, but would void their votes in state and local races.[40]

Kobach, acting as the state's lawyer, appealed the initial federal ruling. He lost. The judge dressed down Kobach at the case's conclusion, citing his repeated violations of disclosure laws by unlawfully withholding documents from opponents in advance of the trial. The judge ordered Kobach to attend six hours of continuing legal education for evidentiary rules.[41]

On May 11, 2017, President Donald Trump rewarded Kobach's voter suppression work by naming him vice chairman of the Presidential Advisory Commission on Election Integrity. The panel's mission was to ferret out voter fraud nationwide, particularly the three to five million voters Trump claimed voted illegally in 2016, giving a majority of the popular vote to his opponent, Hillary Clinton. Vice President Mike Pence chaired the commission, but Kobach lead its investigation.

Trump failed to make the commission a true bipartisan effort, appointing only four Democrats to the 11-member panel. The president's voter integrity commission soon faced an onslaught of accusations attacking *its* integrity. Critics claimed the members began the exercise with a conclusion of voter fraud and worked backward, searching for data to support it. The Republican members refused to share 8,000 documents of the commission's work with its four Democratic members, who sued to acquire them.[42] Kobach released the material eight months after the commission disbanded in early 2018. The documents showed partisanship permeating the commission, including an email sent by Republican member Christy McCormick directing staff to recruit a certain Department of Justice statistician to analyze commission data. McCormick wrote she was "pretty confident that he is conservative (and Christian, too)."[43]

When the media pressed Kobach for proof of widespread voter fraud after the commission concluded its eight months of work, Kobach pointed to studies by two conservative think tanks, The Heritage Foundation and the Government Accountability Institute (GAI), to back up his claims.

The Heritage Foundation's study catalogued a range of organized, partisan, dirty-tricks schemes from buying votes to ballot tampering by public officials. But it ran afield of the original intent of proving widespread fraud of individuals voting at the polls under another's identity, hence the supposed need for stricter voter ID laws.[44]

The GAI study, written by Trump alt-right strategist Steve Bannon, a GAI co-founder, claimed it detected 8,400 fraudulent voters nationwide after analyzing 75 million voters from 21 states. Experts pilloried GAI for misleading practices employed to reach its conclusion of such a large data set. "There is a lot of sloppiness in the records," Max Hailperin, professor emeritus at Gustavus Adolphus College in Minnesota, said of the study.[45] Hailperin specializes in mathematics, computer science, and statistics, and has worked for years on Minnesota's electoral system. For a study of such a large set of numbers to be credible, Hailperin said, there should have been a calculation rate accounting for and weeding out false positives, or human errors. "When other vigilante-matching projects akin to this one have been followed up on by law enforcement authorities, generally what they find is that a very, very small proportion of these apparent red flags actually turn out to be anything real."[46]

On January 3, 2018, President Trump shuttered the Presidential Advisory Commission on Election Integrity as it began— with a Tweet. He claimed the commission's work had been thwarted by both Republican and Democratic states refusing to allow access to sensitive voter information, such as Social Security numbers, individual voting histories, names, birthdates, political affiliations—information that many states do not divulge because it is frequently targeted by online hackers for identity theft.

Despite the president's commission failing to provide proof of massive voter fraud, Trump plowed ahead calling on states to pass strict voter ID laws. Kobach by this time was running for the Kansas governorship in 2018, which he lost.

What is new and alarming today about conservative efforts to suppress minority voting is the advent of sophisticated computer technology to assist their efforts.

In 2016, the aforementioned Steve Bannon brought voter suppression into the modern era. He had been working as vice president for Cambridge Analytica, a British political consulting and data-mining company partly owned by right-wing hedge-fund billionaire Robert Mercer and daughter Rebekah. After stepping down to help run Trump's campaign, Bannon hired his old company to cull psychological data from the Facebook accounts of 30 million Americans, without their knowledge. He sought to politically weaponize the information by building an arsenal of divisive, digital programs to deploy on the population—mostly to keep minorities away from the polls, according to Christopher Wylie, a former Cambridge Analytica worker. Wylie said Bannon particularly targeted black citizens with "voter disengagement tactics" that were used to "discourage or demobilize certain types of people from voting."[47] Some of these tactics included sending doctored video clips and messages to social media accounts of black people via mobile devices, suggesting Hillary Clinton and other Democratic candidates were racists.[48] The company sold its services to a slew of conservative politicians, including Senator Ted Cruz (R-TX). Shortly after the company's scandal broke, it shut down operations.

Republicans say voter fraud is a national problem, but they have presented little to no evidence to prove their claims. There *was* evidence, however, of Republican voter fraud that did surface.

In 2012, Nathan Sproul, former head of the Arizona Republican Party and former executive director of the Arizona Christian Coalition, managed a consulting firm that conducted voter registration drives in five states. Authorities in four of those states: Florida, Colorado, Nevada, and North Carolina charged Sproul and his crew with "registering dead people, altering and faking registrations, and other abuses . . . ."[49] Another Sproul tactic was to change party affiliations of unsuspecting voters from Democrat to Republican. According to campaign finance records, Republican activist groups, including Karl Rove's Super PAC American Crossroads, had paid Sproul nearly $18 million during the 2012 election cycle to discourage certain Americans from voting.[50]

It seems conservatives are so desperate to hang on to their position of social and political dominance that they are willing to work voter suppression from every possible angle.

As for liberals, a cynic would say their crusade against voter suppression is a phony ploy for more votes from constituencies that usually vote Democratic.

Perhaps.

But it is undeniable that expanding rather than suppressing the franchise has been in liberals' DNA for generations, including their push for the Nineteenth Amendment granting women the right to vote. And much of the suffragists' energy was borne out of the liberal abolitionist movement freeing blacks from slavery.

DIXIECRATS AND THE LINCOLN LIE

THERE ARE REPUBLICANS TODAY who blame Democrats for voter suppression. It is a cynical ploy intended to muddy the political waters and confuse Americans. And it begs clarification.

To be accurate and clear, voter suppression since the Civil War has always been a *conservative* endeavor. It's true that Democrats dominated the Southern states after the Civil War, while Republicans dominated the Northern states (Abraham Lincoln represented Illinois). But within the Democratic Party, Southern conservatives dominated over the fewer and more liberal Democrats in the Northern states.

The two major parties' ideologies flipped after events over six decades, resulting in conservatives dominating the Republican Party and liberals dominating the Democratic Party:

- Democratic President Franklin Roosevelt's New Deal program in the 1930s that helped many blacks, irritating Southern white Democrats;
- the 1948 Democratic nominating convention that wrote a number of progressive civil rights planks into its platform, resulting in Southern Democrats bolting from the hall to form their own party, known as the Dixiecrats;
- the Democrats' embrace of the 1960s civil rights movement, outraging Southern white Democrats;
- Richard Nixon's 1968 Southern strategy that exploited racial hostility to energize more Southern white voters, bringing them into the Republican Party fold;
- the 1980 election of Ronald Reagan that galvanized Southern white evangelicals; and
- the refinement of conservatives' racist dog-whistle politics through the 1990s that turned the South solidly Republican.

Through all of this muddle, Republicans today giddily claim ownership of President Lincoln, the first Republican president. But the liberal abolitionists that drove the Republican party in 1860 bear almost no resemblance to conservatives that drive the Republican Party today. In 1860, Republican Northern liberals espoused civil rights, leading the fight against slavery, while the party's Southern conservatives fought to keep, or "conserve," their peculiar institution intact. These 1860 Southern conservatives are the political ancestors of today's conservative Republicans.

So for Republicans to claim Lincoln, who was a liberal abolitionist, as their own, is to assert Lincoln embodied the ideology of today's Republicans.

This is a lie.

To illustrate, the late U.S. Senator Strom Thurmond began his political career in South Carolina as a Democrat and was a staunch racist and segregationist. He served in the state legislature and eventually became governor. Thurmond, a delegate to the 1948 Democratic Convention, led the Southern revolt and left the hall when strong civil rights planks were inserted into the party's platform. He was so outraged he decided to lead his own party, the States' Rights Democratic Party, known as the Dixiecrats, and stood as it presidential nominee. In an infamous speech during that campaign, Thurmond told supporters, to great applause:

> There's not enough troops in the Army to force the Southern people to break down segregation and admit the Negro race into our theaters, into our swimming pools, into our homes, and into our churches.[51]

In 1964, Thurmond, then a U.S. Senator, switched parties to become a Republican, inspired by the party's presidential nominee, U.S. Senator Barry Goldwater of Arizona. Goldwater's rigid states' rights ideology resonated with Southerners. Thurmond and his brethren saw states' rights as a brake on federal power—a means to preserve the status quo—the white dominance of the Southern power structure. And through all of Thurmond's party changes, through all his years in public service, his conservatism and racism never wavered.

So, just as conservative Democrats in the 1800s fought to "conserve" the South's white political power structure, so do today's conservative Republicans through voter suppression and other tactics.

In essence, voter suppression is conservatives' bread and butter as much today as it has ever been.

And while conservative states like Arizona and Kansas seek to exclude "undesirable" voters, states like Oregon and California seek to include *all* voters. These two Western states automatically register a person to vote in all elections when they get a driver's license, ID card, or other document at the department of motor vehicles. The American Dream should be for all, not just for those deemed desirable by partisan power brokers seeking political power for themselves and their race.

With more voter suppression shenanigans likely to occur in America's future, average citizens should ask the following questions in response to the conservatives' strategy:

- Why don't Republicans take the democratic approach and develop policies that actually appeal to minority citizens rather than discourage them from voting?
- Why not *include* rather than *exclude*?
- Why pass discriminatory measures like voter ID laws that are in stark opposition to American ideals?
- Why purge voter rolls, curtail early voting, and end same-day (Election Day) voter registration, that are just cynical schemes to discourage the poor, elderly, and minorities from voting?
- And why is this being done while overall voter turnout in America is declining?

After implementing these discriminatory policies, conservatives are then dumbfounded that their victims vote Democratic. They deny their actions are racist, claiming they are just rooting out voter fraud to instill trust in the democratic process.

History will not be kind to them.

THE GOLDEN RULE OF DEMOCRACY

ALL CAMPAIGN FINANCE RULES, including campaign spending and donation limits, should codify an even playing field for all Americans, regardless of wealth, social status, race, sex, or anything else. It may be hard for someone like Tom Perkins or Kris Kobach to understand, but America will be a healthier and stronger nation when we are all equal in our democratic process.

And whatever rules come to pass, they will always work best if they are imbued with the simple, decent, American principle of "one citizen, one vote."

It is the Golden Rule of democracy.

4

CAPITALISM & DEMOCRACY
An Uneasy Balance

APITALISM built America.

Capitalism is a large part of who and what we are as a nation. In the beginning, America was mostly settled by monarchies and European joint-stock companies sending adventurers to exploit America's natural resources. These business-minded settlers greatly outnumbered those seeking religious freedom in the New World.

Capitalism built America's phenomenal economic system, spurring incredible engineering, medical, cultural, and technological advances. It provided strong tax revenue to help build America's infrastructure, education system, and military.

Capitalism is the engine that drives America.

But it is our democracy that steers the way.

America's marriage of capitalism and democracy unleashed the potential of human creativity and innovation that allowed the country to take root and prosper.

But it has always been a stressful marriage.

The interests of all citizens are best served when both capitalism and democracy work together in a vigorous synergy and do not infringe on the boundaries of the other.

It is a delicate balance.

For the most part, they must co-exist as equals, yet are fused with conflicting dynamics.

Capitalism is, in essence, survival of the fittest. It is not supposed to be fair or equal. It's a system that creates winners and losers. Democracy, on the other hand, was designed to create fairness and equality for all, whether citizens are winners or losers in the capitalist game.

Democracy was designed as a check on the baser elements of capitalism. The very meaning of democracy embodies an inherent code of ethics. It was created to protect the rights of all citizens, their quality of life, and the nation's natural resources. Capitalism, if left unchecked, will flatten anyone who gets in its way and will consume natural resources without restraint or conscience.

Capitalism has no inherent allegiance to a country or its citizens. And as American corporations grow ever larger and more global in scope, the only allegiance many executives have is to their companies. The oil and gas giant ExxonMobil was founded in the U.S. about 125 years ago. It is headquartered in Texas and is one of America's most storied and richest corporations. Lee Raymond, ExxonMobil chairman and chief executive from 1993 to 2005, was once asked by a fellow energy executive why he wouldn't build more refineries in America to protect against gasoline shortages caused by foreign suppliers. Raymond replied, "I'm not a U.S. company, and I don't make decisions based on what's good for the U.S."[1]

Sure, capitalism built America, but its boundless energy must be moderated and channeled for the good of the people. Allowing capitalism to overwhelm democracy and dictate our course as a nation is utter folly.

If capitalism's power is left unchecked, America as we know it will cease to exist.

We cannot rely on capitalism to protect America.

That is democracy's job.

And the only way to ensure our well-being as a nation is to build and maintain a stronger and more resilient democracy that can withstand the excesses and fecklessness of capitalism.

Money fuels capitalism, but corrupts democracy.

CAPITALISM IS NOT FREEDOM
A Perspective on China

IT IS OUR DEMOCRACY, NOT CAPITALISM, that allows us to live free. If you doubt this, then take a look at communist China. It employs a virtually unchecked strain of capitalism that has catapulted the Asian nation into an economic powerhouse, capable of overtaking the United States.

A handful of Chinese capitalists have become billionaires. A middle class is developing in and around urban areas. Without democracy, however, the people's consent cannot give the country proper direction. China has a constitution, but it gives citizens few rights and little recourse to challenge the power structure. Wealth in China is hyper-concentrated in a small number of hands, and many of these hands hold government posts. According to *The Economist* magazine, "the 50 richest members of China's National People's Congress are collectively worth $94.7 billion—60 times more than the 50 richest members of America's Congress."[2] This unsavory nexus of government and wealth has produced an endless stream of scandals, replete with rampant payoffs and greedy get-rich-quick schemes. And if anyone—government official or wealthy corporatist—crosses the wrong higher up, they could disappear into the ether.

Since 2015, a spate of Chinese billionaires have been snared in the government's anti-corruption investigation into the country's finance industry. Guo Guangchang, worth $6.9 billion and known as the Chinese Warren Buffett, went missing after police targeted him for questioning.[3] Guo is the chairman of the Fosun Group, one of the country's biggest conglomerates. It owns the Club Med resorts and the Cirque de Soleil entertainment enterprise. A month before Guo's disappearance, Yim Fung, chairman of one of China's largest brokerage firms, vanished.[4] Scores of others in the probe have been jailed without formal charges or simply went missing, including Zhang Yun, president of the Agriculture Bank of China, one of the country's four largest banks; and Poon Ho

Man, CEO of China Aircraft Leasing Group.[5] In January 2017, Chinese agents arrested Xiao Jianhua, one of the richest billionaires in China, who many say served as the personal banker to top Communist Party officials. Chinese operatives whisked him away from his Hong Kong hotel suite to the mainland. The Chinese government gave no reason for his "disappearance." There is speculation that his enormous wealth threatened some Party elites, fearing he might play kingmaker as new members were being appointed to the Politburo Standing Committee, the nation's top political panel. Agents were also rounding up hundreds of Xiao's employees.[6]

Then there are the government scandals. The purging of officials at all levels seems to be a regular sport in China. And don't bother seeking justice through the courts, particularly if you're an average citizen. You may get a trial, you may not. It depends on who you know and who you've offended. Courts, particularly in rural areas, are generally at the mercy of the latest strongman in the territory. Yes, China is making plenty of money, but anyone's freedom can be revoked in a Shanghai minute without any formal charges, *habeas corpus*, or other civil rights protections. Citizens have few rights when seeking the return of a disappeared loved one. And one more thing—while a Chinese resident may own the physical building that is their home or business, they do not own the land beneath the structure. The state owns all the land in the country, except for some rural areas that are owned by farming collectives. Citizens must lease the land from the government, usually in 20- to 70-year increments.

Want to practice Christianity in China? It's a good bet you'll be practicing in jail. China's communist government is officially atheist and views religion as subversive to the government. There are some "state-approved" religions, but churches are under regular supervision by state agents. In 2016, government officials in Zhejiang Province removed or burned the crosses of about 2,000 churches.[7] Such acts are common in China. Worshippers are also randomly jailed. It's why millions of Chinese Christians meet in secret family churches away from the watchful eyes of government spies. In 2016, President Xi Jinping clamped down on property owners (structures, not the land), threatening to fine them if found to be harboring these churches on their premises.

Want to protest for better wages or civil rights? In November 2018, 10 young activists in Beijing did just that. They "went missing" after government thugs beat them, tossed them in cars, and took them to parts unknown.[8]

Chinese women arguably suffer the most invasive breaches of personal liberty. Since the 1980s, China stepped up the policing of its "one-child" policy. A Chinese woman who just gave birth to her first child could expect a knock on her door from a Communist Party official. The law required the new mother be fitted with an intrauterine device (IUD), preventing her from bearing another child.[9] In 2014, China abandoned the one-child policy.

Yes, capitalism is great, and it's thriving in China. But without democracy, would you want to live there?

Get-rich-quick capitalist thinking in any country will recklessly sow future problems prohibitively expensive to address. China's three decades of raging, unchecked capitalism consumed and polluted the country's natural resources at an alarming clip. Unregulated waste generated by rapid industrialization poisoned its lakes, streams, groundwater, and air.

In 2016, the Chinese media reported a study by Dabo Guan of the University of East Anglia in Britain that showed more than 80 percent of groundwater wells in Northern and Central China were polluted by factories and industrial farming. The water, full of heavy metals, manganese, and other contaminants, is unfit for drinking and bathing.

China's air, pumped full of greenhouse gases from coal-powered energy plants, is so fouled, citizens wear surgical masks just to breathe. The smog can make noon look like night, burning the eyes and leaving an acrid taste in the back of one's throat.[10] In November 2015, Beijing issued its first-ever "red alert" for air pollution. The city warned citizens of air toxicity that measured

40 times higher than the highest level considered safe by the World Health Organization.[11]

The research group Berkeley Earth estimates that 4,000 people die every day in China from air pollution-related illnesses.[12] The smog's toxins, the group said, are equivalent to every person in the country—man, woman, and child—smoking 1.5 cigarettes every hour. Along with respiratory illnesses, cancer and other disease rates in China have skyrocketed.

China faces a massive health care cost in future years, placing a drag on economic growth. The problem will be compounded by a massive productivity crisis, as younger people get sicker earlier, reducing their lifetime work output.

To keep its economy chugging, China's live-now-pay-later philosophy favors development over most all public safety concerns. But citizens are starting to push back. Some outraged residents in recent years have protested the building in their towns of new factories that pollute without consequence and generate jobs that pay poverty wages. They have been jailed for speaking out, since they are not granted freedom of speech. Citizens know many of the facilities are dangerous and lightly regulated by government safety officials. In the past two years, a series of chemical factory and warehouse explosions killed scores of people in their homes. In response, entire towns have blockaded their boundaries, physically preventing the building of new chemical factories in their midst. The government has countered by ordering the military to attack these towns and quell the uprisings.

China's unchecked capitalism has also created a burgeoning homeless population, as swarms of rural inhabitants seeking jobs have flooded into urban areas. And since citizens have no land rights, reckless profiteering has exacerbated the problem. Chinese investors working with government officials sweep entire communities out of their homes with little or no remuneration to inhabitants, because these people happen to live in the paths of proposed development projects.

If you visit Shanghai, the wonders of capitalism are on full display. The city is erecting shiny skyscrapers faster than most any city in the world. They are often adorned with 20- to 30-story digital product advertisements. Many citizens pull out laminated menus of items for sale, thrusting them in the faces of tourists walking about.

It's all capitalism, all the time.

But it hides the gritty reality of life without freedom.

Without democracy, we are China.

THE BASER ELEMENTS OF CAPITALISM

CHINA IS JUST ONE EXAMPLE of capitalism's dark side.

Just how dark can it get? How low can humans go in the pursuit of profit?

Slavery, which still exists today in parts of the world, is the ready answer. But the recent the saga of Martin Shkreli provides a better clue. He's an example of how contemporary American culture has mainstreamed some of the baser elements of capitalism—greed and psychopathy.

Shkreli, a 32-year-old Wall Street hedge fund "genius," made national headlines in 2015 when he jacked up the price of Daraprim, a drug that helps certain HIV and cancer patients, and pregnant women stave off blindness and death. Shkreli, through his shell company, Turing Pharmaceuticals, purchased the drug's patent and quickly hiked the price from $13.50 per pill to $750. Patients' costs suddenly rose to hundreds of thousands of dollars overnight. Shkreli claimed the increase was needed to fund improvements to the drug. There was, however, no scientific evidence that the 62-year-old drug needed improvement.

A huge media backlash ensued.

Shkreli was defiant. He relished antagonizing the public with his indifference to patients' suffering by posting pictures of himself online flaunting the millions of dollars he made in his business endeavors.

In a December 2015 interview at the Forbes Healthcare Summit, Shkreli said he regretted *not* raising Daraprim's price even higher than $750 per pill, insisting his primary loyalty was to his stockholders. "No one wants to say it, no one's proud of it, but this is a capitalist society, capitalist system, and capitalist rules," he said. "My investors expect me to maximize profits, not to minimize them, or go half, or go 70 percent, but to go to 100 percent of the profit curve that we're all taught in MBA classes."[13]

Shkreli's comments prompted some pharmaceutical professionals to label him a psychopath.

This begs the question: Is there a link between capitalism and psychopathy? There are, of course, many ethical business people. But what ethics, if any, are inherent in a corporation? It's well-known that an individual's mentality, behavior, and decision-making capacity can drastically change when joining a group or mob. The same kind of groupthink regularly occurs in corporations. This has serious political consequences, since the Supreme Court's 2010 *Citizens United* ruling maintained that corporations are legal persons and have the same political rights as a citizen to spend unlimited amounts of "free speech" dollars to influence public elections and policy.

In the 2004 documentary, *The Corporation*, Dr. Robert Hare, a criminal psychology researcher and FBI consultant on psychopaths, was asked whether the modern corporation's typical behavior could be considered psychopathic. Using the World Health Organization's Manual of Mental Disorders, Dr. Hare listed the following characteristics of psychopaths:

- callous unconcern for the feelings of others;
- incapacity to maintain enduring relationships;
- reckless disregard for the safety of others;
- deceitfulness;
- repeated lying and conning others for profit;
- incapacity to experience guilt; and

- failure to conform to social norms concerning lawful behavior.

Dr. Hare's diagnosis: "They would have all the characteristics, and in fact, in many respects, the corporation of that sort is the prototypical psychopath."

In 2012, a University of California, Berkeley team led by Dr. Paul Piff explored the effects of extreme wealth on the human condition. Seven separate social experiments were conducted on 800 subjects. The data revealed wealthy individuals tended to behave more unethically than working class people. Dr. Piff's conclusion stated:

> In studies 1 and 2, upper-class individuals were more likely to break the law while driving, relative to lower-class individuals. In follow-up laboratory studies, upper-class individuals were more likely to exhibit unethical decision-making tendencies (study 3), take valued goods from others (study 4), lie in a negotiation (study 5), cheat to increase their chances of winning a prize (study 6), and endorse unethical behavior at work (study 7) than were lower-class individuals. Mediator and moderator data demonstrated that upper-class individuals' unethical tendencies are accounted for, in part, by their more favorable attitudes toward greed. [14]

Dr. Piff suggested that wealthy people are less dependent on social bonds to survive and are therefore "less likely to perceive the impact" their behavior has on others.

Sounds like a Shkreli profile match.

Several days after Shkreli's Forbes summit interview, he was arrested by federal authorities on charges of securities and wire fraud. Apparently, he was operating his hedge fund as a Ponzi scheme—using investors' funds to finance his pharmaceutical ventures instead of investing in financial securities. On December 17, 2015, police whisked Shkreli away in handcuffs from his luxury Manhattan apartment.

On February 4, 2016, Shkreli, summoned by Congress to

testify on drug pricing practices, refused to answer questions, citing his Fifth Amendment right to not incriminate himself. He smirked and stifled his laughter during the questioning. Minutes after leaving the table, Shkreli blurted on Twitter: "Hard to accept that these imbeciles represent the people in our government."[15]

When he first caught the media's attention, Shkreli tried to deflect the public's hatred that rained down on him, saying that many others in the pharmaceutical industry gouge patients at will with no compunction or humanity. On this count, according to many industry watchers, Shkreli is correct. It's not a stretch to say similar behavior permeates other large industries.

On March 9, 2018, the ever-present smirk left Shkreli's boyish face. After jurors found him guilty of conspiracy and securities fraud, a federal judge sentenced him to seven years in prison. Just before sentencing, Shkreli sobbed, tissue in hand, as he read a statement pleading for leniency. Reflecting on his actions, Shkreli said, "I look back and I'm embarrassed and ashamed."[16]

Sadly, his puddle-producing confession didn't deter some young people from making Shkreli a capitalist folk hero, worthy of emulation. There is a strain of "no apologies-f--- you" capitalism that is running in America's veins today, and this narcissistic, juvenile ethos has spilled into politics. We are living in an age where the baser elements of capitalism are surging and overwhelming the wisdom and decency of democracy.

CAPITALISM NEEDS RULES

IF YOU WANT A RESILIENT DEMOCRACY and guaranteed freedom, then rules are needed to curb capitalism's baser elements.

There are, however, many capitalists who call themselves libertarians or "free marketers." They don't believe government should regulate capitalism. They believe *government*, if left unchecked, is the real evil that will naturally extinguish our freedom. They believe the market, if left free from government interference, will eventually cleanse itself of swindlers, cheats, and general corruption. These free marketers are the same special interests who, over the past 35 years, worked to eliminate a number of common sense rules for the nation's financial markets. It was this free market mindset that brought America to its knees in the 2008 economic collapse.

If there is one person who understands the baser elements of capitalism, it is Alan Greenspan, the former Federal Reserve (FED) chairman.

Greenspan ushered in the era of financial deregulation. He was largely credited as the central figure—the "maestro"—who presided over the economic expansion of the go-go 1990s and the first half of the 2000s. His idol was Hollywood screenwriter-philosopher Ayn Rand, whom Greenspan invited to the Oval Office for his 1987 swearing-in ceremony as FED chairman. Rand, heartily embraced by today's free marketers, espoused an ideology of total laissez-faire—absolutely no regulation or government oversight of the economy. When CBS reporter Mike Wallace asked Rand in a 1959 interview to sum up her philosophy, she replied, "Let me put it briefly. I am for the separation of state and economics."

From 1987 through 2006, Greenspan put Rand's ideas into practice. He firmly believed that the government should not police the financial markets for fraudulent activity. He believed that market forces would naturally absorb all transactions, including fraudulent deals perpetrated by white-collar criminals, with no lasting ill effects.

With Greenspan at the helm of the banking system and guiding monetary policy, the U.S. economy steadily grew. But so did a lucrative market for sub-prime mortgages and two financial instruments called collateralized debt obligations (CDOs) and credit default swaps. Greenspan scoffed at raising interest rates in the 2000s that many economists believed would have prevented the market from overheating and the housing bubble from bursting. He simply didn't believe in actions and rules he thought would interfere with capitalism.

Thomas Hoenig, president of the Federal Reserve Bank (FED) of Kansas City from 1991-2001, was the lone FED voice against Greenspan's policy of low interest rates, known as "easy money." Reflecting on the causes of the collapse, Hoenig said, "I have a lot of faith in markets. However, I still need rules. And I still need a referee, because otherwise you get a chaotic environment and very bad outcomes." [17]

Think about it. Without proper rules and referees in business *and* society, there would be chaos.

What would it be like to drive on America's roadways without rules? Would there be more or fewer injurious or fatal auto crashes without stoplights, traffic signs, road lines, basic driving rules, driver's license requirements, and law enforcement to ensure safety and order?

What if there were no food safety rules and no food inspectors? Would incidences of sickness and death from food poisoning increase or decrease? Would you mind if there were rodent droppings in your meals, as long as the free market eventually ferreted out and closed down the offending food manufacturer? But how long would that take? And how would you know that same manufacturer wouldn't change its name and continue business as usual? Or whether another unscrupulous, unregulated manufacturer would take its place?

Can you picture a football game played without rules or referees? Or a baseball game? Or any other such human endeavor? Even with small amounts of money at stake in a simple, private bet, for example, rules and referees are needed to maintain fairness and order—*let alone the complexity of trillion-dollar financial markets* that tanked America's economy in 2008.

And how would our nation's campaign finance system work with few rules or referees? Unfortunately, we don't have to imagine that scenario. We live it every day.

Rules are a necessary component of business and politics. But, like capitalism and democracy, a delicate balance must be maintained. Too strict, they can impede commerce. Too loose, they can invite corruption.

Free marketers loathe government in general for its regulatory function. They claim it cuts into profits; stifles innovation. But they curiously ignore basic human nature and business organizing principles: the larger the organization, the more rules are generally needed to properly manage and maintain order. A thick binder of policies, for example, is not needed in a business that employs three people. Everybody likely knows what the other is doing. But a large multi-national corporation or a large government entity with thousands of workers needs more rules so managers and employees can work from the same page toward fulfilling the organization's mission.

It is ironic that the same corporations that bemoan government regulation crank out reams of new rules for their own workers on a regular basis. These company rules (in addition to government labor laws) regulate workers' travel, lunchtime, coffee breaks, dining, health care, pensions, and other benefits. Many of these regulations are endlessly tweaked to save the company money at workers' expense. And it all begs the question: Just how would these corporations function without any company rules to govern and manage themselves?

Not well.

Their workers would be freelancing all over the place, making deals without the knowledge of their higher ups, coming to work whenever they felt like it, selling company secrets to competing interests, and worse. It would be, in a word, chaos.

For free marketers, it seems their core principle of no regulation works best when only applied to government.

And let's be clear: deregulation, in many aspects, translates to privatizing profits while socializing risks. McDonald's, for example, takes in billions of dollars per year, pays its chief executive officer and high-level managers tens of millions of dollars annually, but pays most of its workers minimum wage. And while the burger giant spent tens of thousands of dollars lobbying Congress against raising the minimum wage, it came to light in 2013 that the Chicago-based company was actively encouraging its workers, through its McResources helpline, to sign up for government food stamps and other welfare benefits. In essence, McDonald's profits were being subsidized by taxpayers.

Corporations that pollute also routinely lobby government to loosen environmental rules. And who usually foots the cleanup bill?

Taxpayers.

It is unethical and un-American to shirk one's responsibility and harm human beings in the pursuit of wealth. All that society is asking businesses—through government rules— is to clean up after themselves and take responsibility for their actions. If a company can't make the numbers work paying its workers a living wage or producing its product and disposing its waste in a safe and responsible manner, then maybe it shouldn't be in business.

On October 23, 2008, Greenspan, who had retired a year before the recession hit, was summoned by Congress to answer questions about the economic collapse. The former FED chairman was candid in his responses. The following is a partial transcript of his testimony before the House Government Oversight Committee, led by Chairman Henry Waxman (D-CA):

> HW: You have been a staunch advocate for letting markets regulate themselves. And my question for you is simple. Were you wrong?
>
> AG: Yes. I found a flaw, but I've been very distressed by that fact.
>
> HW: You found a flaw in the reality?
>
> AG: (A) flaw in the model that I perceived is the critical functioning structure that defines how the world works, so to speak.
>
> HW: In other words, you found that your view of the world, your ideology, was not right.
>
> AG: Precisely. No, that's precisely the reason I was shocked

because I've been going for 40 years or more with very considerable evidence that it was working exceptionally well.

When Greenspan was pressed on the wisdom of allowing an unfettered free market to regulate itself, he replied:

I made a mistake in presuming that the self-interests of organizations, specifically banks and others, were such as that they were
best capable of protecting their own shareholders and their equity
in the firms.[18]

REAGAN & ANTI-GOVERNMENTISM

SELF-PROCLAIMED FREE MARKETERS today dominate the Republican Party. They espouse a hybrid mix of right-wing conservative val-ues and libertarian economic dogma that engenders anti-govern-ment thinking. But they discard the purist libertarian tenets of all-out economic freedom that include legalizing drugs, abortion, prostitution, and other activities that conflict with their conserva-tive values.

These conservative hybrids have perpetrated a fiction over the past 35 years, swallowed by many average Americans, that capi-talism can do no wrong and government can do no right.

When confronted by deregulation disasters like the 2008 eco-nomic collapse, free marketers claim such fiascos are *caused* by the weakened, toothless regulations that remained in place that they couldn't manage to kill. In that way, their philosophy, to them, will always be correct. There will always be some minor or ob-scure law or rule they can blame their disasters on. Conveniently, their model works only when there is not even one regulation interfering with market forces. This will never happen. So their philosophy, to them, will never be exposed as a hoax.

Then there is the libertarian contention, propagated by indus-trialists like the Koch brothers, that the free market will only work when crony capitalism is abolished. Crony capitalism is government intervention in the market usually at the behest of, and for the benefit of, business. But who or what entity would ensure crony capitalism would be eliminated? The libertarian free market ethos would prevent government regulation. Would the Kochs and other corporate titans, who spend billions of dollars manipulating government and politicians for profit, suddenly abide by the honor system? Would they voluntarily stay out of the public arena, leaving billions of dollars in potential profits on the table? Would they sit idly by, waiting for "pure" competition to work its magic, creating even more money?

This is, of course, rubbish. But it's *pure* rubbish.

The only way to get wealthy interests' fingers out of the public pie is for government to pass and enforce sensible regulations. There is no other way.

So how did average Americans swallow this libertarian fish tale?

First, let's be honest. Who really likes rules?

No one.

No one likes paying taxes. No one likes getting a building permit. No one likes being told they can't do something they want to do.

No one likes being told "no."

People don't even like reading the rules to play a game of Monopoly. "Screw the rules, let's just play the game." People like simple. Many also like a hint of rebelliousness. But most of us grudgingly abide by the rules because we know the game (of life) will ultimately be more safe and enjoyable for us and those around us.

So when someone of stature comes along and convincingly says: "You know what the real problem is? Rules"—it's incredibly tempting to agree. It is human nature. Now "no" becomes "yes." And we all like to hear "yes." "Yes! You can do whatever you want. You can eat as much cake and ice cream as you want, and you won't get fat."

Cut to one of the greatest pitchmen in American political

history: Ronald Reagan.

President Reagan launched his anti-government crusade—germinating in conservative circles for years—into the American mainstream in his 1981 inaugural address by proclaiming:

> Government is not the solution to our problem. Government is the problem.

It was a great sound bite that resonated with many Americans. Simple. Attractive. Appealing. And a little rebellious.

"No" to rules. "Yes" to doing whatever the heck you want, economically speaking.

To hybrid conservatives, that means, in a word:

F-R-E-E-D-O-M!

The word is the epicenter of their ideology. They use it liberally and passionately. Freedom for the individual above all else, they proclaim—as long it does not interfere with the rights of others. But libertarians' idea of others' rights can be as mushy as a Halloween pumpkin in December.

In interviews, Charles Koch has admitted there is too much money in politics, but believes the billions of dollars he has pumped into the political system are for the betterment of all Americans. He can't see that by having such an outsized voice, whether he spends with good intentions or not, is extremely harmful to democracy—one person, one vote; equality and other ideals. Koch and other libertarians share a blind spot when it comes to realizing the cumulative effect of their actions—everyone doing their own thing exactly the way they want. Their "freedom" philosophy works well if they live in the woods like Ted Kaczynski, but not so well in close quarters with other humans in a society.

So what evil is taking away their freedom by making all these rules?

Government.

But what construct is charged with protecting our democracy?

(Hint: it's not the free market.)

Reagan's assault on government would make sense if only perfect people populated the world. Then there would be no need for regulation, and by extension no need for government.

Those who blame business *or* government as the sole cause of the country's ills need to digest this simple fact: businesses and governments are composed of people—imperfect people— good, bad, and everything in between. Because of this, rules are needed. Some businesses and some governments are run well, and some aren't. Some departments *within* businesses and governments are run well, and some aren't. It largely depends on the managers, who are, by and large, humans. There are people in both business and government who exhibit tremendous talent and zeal to better this country through their work. To demonize or lionize either business or government as a monolithic whole is ignorant and shows an utter lack of insight into the human condition.

It is delusional to blindly trust capitalism alone as humankind's savior. The business pages of newspapers and magazines are choked with stories of bank fraud, stock fraud, real estate fraud, insurance fraud, medical fraud, accounting fraud, tax evasion, toxic waste dumping, interest rate rigging, overbilling, Ponzi schemes, insider trading, embezzlement, product safety violations, perjury—not to mention a yawning income inequality gap created by the wealthy, co-opting government for their private gain. These capitalists cut corners and shed morals like a snake sheds its skin just to grab a quick buck, indifferent to the harm they cause. There are surely multitudes of other white-collar crimes being perpetrated daily on average Americans that remain undetected by the media and law enforcement.

And where do people go—even the most ardent libertarians— when they've been economically harmed?

Government.

It is the aggrieved who seek redress in the courts or legislative bodies. Contrary to hybrid conservative thought, government workers don't sit around dreaming up new regulations. Our laws are mostly *private driven*—in all levels of government. If a corporation wants to stifle competition, like an oil company tamping down the rise of renewable energy businesses, a visit to their politician friends for legislation will be in order. If a business deposits its sewage in the ground, contaminating the shared aquifer feeding adjacent private property wells, you can bet the neighbors will be visiting town hall seeking water regulations. Citizen laws can also protect businesses, for example, by instilling consumer confidence that the products are safe for consumption and by ensuring there is fair competition through anti-trust and other laws.

The challenge for government, essentially, is to protect consumers, but not harm businesses trying to compete or who are good actors caught in laws designed to regulate bad actors.

In sum, we are imperfect.

We create markets.

Markets are imperfect.

Therefore, we need rules.

Spare the rod, spoil the capitalist.

CAPITALISM OVERWHELMING DEMOCRACY

DON BLANKENSHIP was angry.

As chairman, CEO, and president of Virginia-based Massey Energy, Blankenship was a man of economic power. He earned nearly $20 million per year, reportedly the highest salary in the coal industry. He was used to getting his way.

But in August 2002, a West Virginia jury found Blankenship guilty of fraud and contract tampering. It ordered him to pay $50 million in damages to a small coal company that he undermined and forced out of business. He had no intention of paying.

Blankenship didn't play by the rules. In his world, playing by the rules was for suckers. He believed that his economic power, which gave him the ability to manipulate the political system, placed him above the law.

You may remember Blankenship's Massey Energy. It's the company that owned the Upper Big Branch Mine in Montcoal, West Virginia. After racking up safety violations at 19 times the national rate, the mine exploded on April 5, 2010, killing 29 miners toiling underground. A year before the blast, the federal Mine Safety and Health Administration (MSHA) had issued a total of 2,400 safety violations to 10 of Massey's mines.[19]

Blankenship routinely put his workers' lives at risk because it was more profitable than obeying the rules. He knew how to play our broken political system. He knew it catered to moneyed special interests like himself. Blankenship routinely paid lobbyists to stonewall federal regulators. He paid more to influence congressional lawmakers to kill reasonable mining safety measures.

Things were going rather swimmingly until Blankenship decided to bully a small West Virginia coal company, Harman Mining, out of business. Harman produced a special, high-grade metallurgical coal used to make its steel. The company had contracted with a Virginia business, Wellmore Coal, which blended Harman's coal with other coal. The mixture was then sold to LTV, the nation's third largest steel maker.

But Blankenship wanted the LTV contract and sought to push Harman Mining and its coal out of the way. Blankenship's first move was to purchase Wellmore Coal's parent company in 1997. He thought he could then force LTV to buy Massey's coal. But LTV refused because it needed the higher-grade Harman coal to properly produce the quality of steel LTV's buyers expected. Rebuffed but undeterred, Blankenship then tampered with the Harman-Wellmore contract by inserting a provision that cut Harman Mining out of the agreement. Blankenship knew the loss of the contract would put Harman out of business. Blankenship then used his economic power to buy a piece of property that surrounded Harman's mine, making it unattractive to potential buyers seeking to purchase the small coal company.[20]

Next, Blankenship low-balled Harman's operator, Hugh

Caperton, with an offer to buy Harman Mining for a fraction of its real worth. Caperton refused Blankenship's offer and sued Wellmore Coal (now owned by Blankenship's Massey company) for breach of contract. Caperton won a $6 million judgment against the company.

But Caperton didn't stop there. He then filed another lawsuit against Massey charging it (and Blankenship) with fraudulent misrepresentation, concealment, and tortious interference with existing contractual relations.[21] Caperton won again. In August 2002, a jury ordered Massey and Blankenship to pay Caperton $50 million in compensatory and punitive damages.[22]

But Blankenship wasn't worried. He would fight back using his arsenal of money and connections. He headed to the arena where his weapons were almost always guaranteed to win him victory—his ace in the hole—the political system.

Blankenship set his sights on the five-seat Supreme Court of Appeals of West Virginia, which would be hearing his challenge of the $50 million judgment against him. One of the court's judges, Warren McGraw, was up for re-election. The race would be decided before the court heard Blankenship's appeal.

Blankenship, a longtime heavy donor to Republican candidates and causes, went to work. He handpicked a Republican lawyer, Brent Benjamin, to run against McGraw, a Democrat. Blankenship gave the maximum donation he could to Benjamin's campaign committee—$1,000 per individual. But he funneled about $2.5 million from his bank account to an independent 527 group called And For The Sake Of Kids, which supported Benjamin and opposed McGraw.[23] To top it off, Blankenship paid $500,000 for several TV and radio ads, mostly attacking McGraw.

In sum, Blankenship spent over $3 million to buy the appeals court seat for Benjamin—and basically, for himself as well. That amount was three times the total amount spent by Benjamin's own campaign committee and $1 million more than the combined amount spent by both campaign committees.[24]

Blankenship's donations paid off.

Benjamin won the race by 47,735 votes (382,036 to 334,301), 53.3 to 46.7 percent.

When Blankenship's appeal came before the appeals court, Benjamin refused to recuse himself from the case. The court then promptly overturned the $50 million judgment against Blankenship, with Benjamin casting the deciding vote in the 3-2 decision.[25] Caperton, outraged at Benjamin's conduct, sought a rehearing of the case.

Then, a new wrinkle appeared. After the case was decided in Blankenship's favor, pictures surfaced of appeals court justice Elliott Maynard vacationing with Blankenship in Monte Carlo on the French Riviera—while the case was still open. Maynard had voted with Benjamin to overturn the $50 million judgment against Blankenship.[26]

The lawsuit was eventually appealed to the U.S. Supreme Court. On June 8, 2009, the Court delivered a 5-4 decision in favor of Caperton, ruling that Justice Benjamin should have recused himself from the case.

Justice Anthony Kennedy wrote in the majority opinion:

> Blankenship's campaign contributions— in comparison to the total amount contributed to the campaign, as well as the total amount spent in the election—had a significant and disproportionate influence on the electoral outcome. And the risk that Blankenship's influence engendered actual bias is sufficiently substantial that it "must be forbidden if the guarantee of due process is to be adequately implemented" . . . On these extreme facts the probability of actual bias rises to an unconstitutional level.[27]

Note Justice Kennedy's phrase, " . . . as well as the total amount spent in the election—had a significant and disproportionate influence on the electoral outcome." It seems Justice Kennedy found the "total amount" of Blankenship's unlimited spending corrupted the election's outcome. By saying this, Kennedy is making the case that Blankenship's freedom of speech should have been abridged—his spending capped—to prevent corruption of the Benjamin-McGraw election.

Kennedy has been the swing vote on a string of 5-4 Supreme Court decisions over the past decade that have savaged campaign finance reform laws. In those cases, Kennedy clings to the notion of money as free speech, and that any spending cap is a violation of the First Amendment. It is a mystery how Kennedy, now retired, could reconcile his judgment in the Blankenship case with his other campaign finance rulings.

And who were the four U.S. Supreme Court justices who found *no* judicial bias or conflict of interest in Caperton v. Massey? They would be John Roberts, Chief Justice of the United States (who wrote the dissenting opinion); and Associate Justices Antonin Scalia, Samuel Alito, and Clarence Thomas.

One would think any reasonable person would immediately detect the appearance of bias and conflict of interest in such an outrageous case. After all, if you were Hugh Caperton, would you trust a court that delivered a deciding vote against you by the judge who your adversary installed on the court—just for this particular case?

Blankenship was one of the most well-connected political players in West Virginia. For five years, his money and his political wiles staved off federal prosecution for his many offenses. In 2015, he was finally brought to trial and faced 30 years in prison. A federal jury acquitted Blankenship of deceiving investors and regulators, but found him guilty on one count of conspiring to violate mine safety regulations.

Federal regulators claimed victory. But it showed how powerless they were when facing an extremely wealthy coal baron. "The fact is that we've been in this country since 1880, and this is the first time that (a conviction of a coal executive) has happened," said Davitt McAteer, former assistant secretary of labor for the Mine Safety and Health Administration, who had led the Massey investigation. "If you had asked me the question 'Could this have happened 15 years ago?' The answer is no," he said. "You wouldn't have had the willingness of the U.S attorney to accept that coal industry persons could be responsible. When coal was king, this could not have happened."[28]

Blankenship, of course, appealed immediately.

In April 2016, after Blankenship deftly used every avenue of power he could to delay court action, he was sentenced to one year in prison for conspiring to violate federal mine safety laws.

After Blankenship served his time, did he keep a low profile and lead a humble life?

Of course not!

He used his sizeable fortune to launch his 2018 candidacy for West Virginia's U.S. Senate seat. He lost, but garnered considerable support.

Only in America.

So did capitalism overwhelm democracy in Blankenship's case?

Yes.

Is this an isolated case?

No.

Blankenship is not an anomaly, an outlier. There are Don Blankenships in every state, city, and town in this country.

Wealthy. Connected. Greedy. Arrogant.

They are knowledgeable in manipulating the system to get what they want. They know the rules don't apply to them like they apply to everyone else, like the 29 average American miners who died at Blankenship's hands in the Upper Big Branch.

BUILDING A BETTER BULWARK
TO PROTECT DEMOCRACY

IN CREATING THE CONSTITUTION IN 1787, the majority of the Convention's members intended to construct a bulwark to protect democracy from unchecked capitalism for the good of the general masses, who are, in contemporary terms, average Americans.

The Framers were not seeking to protect the wealthy, even though many of the Framers themselves were rich. That is the genius of their vision.

Thomas Jefferson elaborated on this point in a March 22, 1812, letter to his friend, the Rev. Francis A. van der Kemp:

> The only orthodox object of the institution of government is to secure the greatest degree of happiness possible to the general mass of those associated under it . . . (and) unless the mass retains sufficient control over those intrusted (sic) with the powers of their government, these will be perverted to their own oppression, and to the perpetuation of wealth and power in the individuals and their families selected for the trust.[29]

In other words, if citizens do not construct a sufficient bulwark to protect democracy, the baser elements of capitalism will overrun the young nation. And the citizens will eventually become the slaves rather than the masters of their own government.

Although Jefferson and the Framers warned future generations of Americans against the baser elements of capitalism, they unintentionally left open a loophole in the Constitution that the wealthy and powerful have exploited through the years. The winners in the capitalist game have used their "free speech" dollars to control the levers of government and steal ownership of the country from the people.

If Americans today truly want to "get money out of politics," then we'd better get on with building a better bulwark to protect the nation's democracy once and for all. And the foundation for that bulwark is campaign spending limits.

5

MONEY AS SPEECH

"I want to start by thanking you, Charles and David (Koch), for the important work you're doing. I don't know where we'd be without you." [1]

~ SENATOR MITCH McCONNELL (R-KY), Senate majority
leader, speaking at the Koch brothers' 2015 donor summit

THE THIRD TIME'S THE CHARM, Mitt Romney undoubtedly thought, just days after the Republican Party's strong showing in the 2014 mid term election.

Romney hoped to emulate his hero, Ronald Reagan, who won the presidency on his third try. The former Massachusetts governor immediately put out feelers for a 2016 bid to the Republican Party's major donors. But they weren't returning his calls. The kingmakers were shopping for a new face, new blood. Within weeks, Romney packed it in and announced he would not run. Without the backing of the party's super wealthy donors, unless you're a billionaire like Donald Trump, even a mere multi-millionaire like Romney knew he was toast.

As predictable as the ocean tides and the swallows returning to Capistrano, prospective presidential candidates obediently flock to a handful of the biggest money donors before a presidential election cycle. They preen, they fawn, they coo—competing for the affections of America's present-day caesars, unleashed by the Supreme Court's *Citizens United* ruling. They sidle up to them, paying tribute for a chance to be anointed with millions of free speech "donation votes" dropped into their supporting Super PACs and a possible designation of frontrunner for the nomination.

In America today, a new "pre-primary" system has emerged that winnows out the field of presidential hopefuls. It begins well before any average American casts a vote in the Iowa caucuses or state primaries. In early 2015, Republican presidential candidates hopscotched around the country, toadying up to elite donors holding auditions, including:

- January 21: Arthur Laffer, Steve Forbes and other wealthy supply-side enthusiasts, New York City
- January 25: the billionaire Koch brothers, Rancho Mirage, California
- February 18: a return engagement with Laffer, Forbes, and supply-siders, New York City
- February 24: conservative business leaders supporting the American Opportunity Alliance, Jackson Hole, Wyoming
- February 26: wealthy supporters of the anti-tax group The Club For Growth, Palm Beach, Florida
- March 5: elite donors of the American Enterprise Institute, the premier Republican think tank, Sea Island, Georgia
- March 7: agricultural corporate executives, Des Moines, Iowa
- April 24: casino billionaire Sheldon Adelson and his Republican Jewish Coalition, Las Vegas, Nevada [2]

Every four years, the media dutifully run stories on these hand-picked presidential contenders based largely on how much money they've raised—often before these candidates have opened their mouths to say what they supposedly believe in. As the anointed candidate gathers in the dollars, the herd thins, and one or two of the less viable candidates predictably limp through the latter stages of the primary season, lucky to glom onto a few stray ideological tycoons who like to gamble on long odds.

These powerful cabals of Republican and Democratic donors have displaced voters. They usually determine who will continue on as "legitimate" contenders for president and Congress and heavily influence what issues they will run on. They decide, in effect, who will lead the country and the direction it will follow.

These cabals have always had a stranglehold on American politics, tightening their control from the Gilded Age onward. In 1913, President Woodrow Wilson observed their insidious ascendance, usurping the political power of average Americans:

> The government, which was designed for the people, has got into the hands of the bosses and their employers, the special interests. An invisible empire has been set up above the forms of democracy.[3]

So who are these political elites comprising the "Invisible Empire," pulling the strings in our political system and buying America's elections, laws, and politicians? And how many are there? A *New York Times* analysis of 2016's top money donors described them as "overwhelmingly white, wealthy, older, and male, in a nation that is being remade by the young, by women, and by black and brown voters."[4]

There are rough estimates of how many political oligarchs there are in America, since more wealthy donors are funneling—some would say laundering—their millions in "dark money" through political nonprofit groups that do not have to reveal donors' identities.

Sen. Lindsey Graham (R-SC), a 2016 presidential candidate, is at the lower end of estimating the size of America's Invisible Empire. In a stump speech in Barrington, New Hampshire, Graham noted: "It's the Wild, Wild West," referring to the nation's loose campaign finance rules. "What I worry about is that we are turning campaigns over to about 100 people in this country," he said, "and they are going to be able to advocate their case at the expense of your cause."[5]

Lending some credence to Graham's estimate is *Politico*, a

political media website popular with Washington insiders. The website's analysis of the 2014 mid-term election found that the top 100 donors spent a combined $323 million on the election, slightly less than the combined $356 million from about 4.75 million donors who gave $200 or less.[6]

Burt Neuborne, New York University law professor and legal director of the Brennan Center for Justice, which follows campaign finance issues, believes the number of American super donors is higher. Responding to the 2014 *McCutcheon v. Federal Election Commission* Supreme Court ruling that loosened contribution limits for wealthy donors, Neuborne said: "If these aggregate limitations go down, 500 people will control American democracy. It would be 'government for the 500 people,' not for anybody else—and that's the risk."[7]

The *McCutcheon* case itself points to a more solid estimate of the Invisible Empire. Wealthy Alabama businessman and Republican National Committee (RNC) member Shaun McCutcheon teamed with RNC leadership to successfully overturn one of the few limits on political donations. The Court's ruling killed the provision in the U.S. campaign finance code that limited an individual's *aggregate* political contributions given directly to candidates and political action committees (PACs). The aggregate cap is adjusted for inflation. For the 2014 federal election cycle, an individual donor like McCutcheon maxed out at $123,200 in total contributions. That included $48,600 in aggregate donations given directly to any number of candidates and $74,600 given to PACs and state or local party committees.[8] A Center for Responsive Politics study of the 2012 presidential election revealed that only 646 donors had each hit the federal contribution aggregate limit for giving money to candidates and PACs. And just 216 super-wealthy donors—likely the same folks who gave the maximum to candidates—accounted for 68 percent of all money given to Super PACs.[9] That is a dizzying amount of free speech for a very elite few who dwell in the rarified air of the Invisible Empire.

Most average Americans don't have six-figure bundles of cash lying around to spend on politicians and PACs, let alone multi-million-dollar donations to Super PACs. In fact, most don't even come close to earning six figures in an entire year. But to the Supreme Court, $123,200 is just not enough for wealthy donors like McCutcheon to skew the political system in their favor. The Court ruled 5-4 in favor of the Alabama millionaire. The aggregate cap is now $3.5 million per election cycle, limited only by other existing donation laws and the number of federal elections every two years. During arguments in the *McCutcheon* case, Justice Scalia opined, "I don't think $3.5 million is a lot of money (for an individual donor to spend in an election)." [10] Keep in mind that we're only talking about donations given *directly* to candidates, PACs, and political parties. McCutcheon already had the right to donate unlimited amounts to independent groups that supported his favored candidates.

Chief Justice Roberts, in his *McCutcheon* majority opinion, wrote:

> We conclude, however, that the aggregate limits do little, if anything, to address (corruption in the political system), while seriously restricting participation in the democratic process. [11]

And just *whose* participation was seriously restricted by the limits? Was Roberts talking about the democratic participation of 250 million average American voters who could afford to donate anywhere from $1 to $600 or so?

Apparently not.

Roberts was referring to the Invisible Empire's roughly 500 to 700 wealthiest contributors who donate hundreds of millions of dollars to buy our elections, laws, and politicians and rig the system in their favor.

It is curious why the Supreme Court even bothered to take the *McCutcheon* case. Is it really that important to rip out the last remaining campaign funding restraints to alleviate the slightest inconvenience for McCutcheon and his fellow mega-donors?

Even Republicans admit America's political oligarchy is getting out of hand. Norman Ornstein, a prominent voice at the American Enterprise Institute, a conservative-libertarian think tank in Washington, D.C., recently commented on the string of successful Republican rollbacks of campaign reform. He observed: "We're back to the Nixon era—the era of undisclosed money, of big cash amounts and huge interests that are small in number dominating American politics." [12]

Michael Malbin, president of the Campaign Finance Institute, which tracks campaign money, sharpened Ornstein's analysis by adding a more modern spin: "The question is whether we are in a new Gilded Age or well beyond it—to a Platinum Age." [13]

THE KOCH BROTHERS

THE "KOCH PRIMARY" IS THE INVISIBLE EMPIRE'S biggest presidential vetting sideshow. This "pre-primary" is run by libertarian-conservatives Charles and David Koch, owners of Koch Industries, a Kansas-based oil conglomerate.

Forbes magazine ranks Koch Industries as the nation's second largest privately-held company, with yearly revenues of $100 billion. [14] This industrial behemoth runs Koch-sponsored business operations in all 50 U.S. states and 50 countries. [15]

You may have heard of the Koch brothers. They have an unprecedented amount of free-speech dollar votes, spending billions buying what they want from our political system. *Forbes* ranks the brothers tied at seventh place on the list of wealthiest Americans. [16] If the brothers' personal wealth were combined, it would rank as the second largest fortune on earth.

Koch Industries is diversified, owning many companies and subsidiaries. It produces oil, gasoline, energy generation, paper goods for office and industry, Dixie cups, clothing, Brawny paper towels, and much more. A journalist for *The Weekly Standard* observed Koch Industries' pervasiveness in the American marketplace: "You awake to lights powered by them, walk on carpet made by them, cook and drive with gas they provide or process, and wear cool gym clothes that they make possible. You may even wipe with their Quilted Northern or Angel Soft brand toilet paper."[17]

The Kochs created an enormous political network, dubbed by pundits as the "Kochtopus," to carry out their agenda. It is so vast and well-funded that its tentacles reach from presidential elections all the way down to local school committee races. The Kochtopus funds hundreds of political advocacy groups in many forms across the country. The Kochs' main political apparatus, Americans For Prosperity (AFP), is a political nonprofit group that gobbles up dark money to fund an expansive array of conservative activities. It boasts operations in 34 states.

The Kochs also built their own intelligence operation, headed by a former Central Intelligence Agency analyst. The staff of 25 conducts espionage, which the Kochs call "competitive intelligence" on Democratic groups. Its mission is to neutralize Democratic efforts that gain traction in Congress and across America. According to *Politico*, the Kochs' spy group provides "regular intelligence briefings" to Koch network members, tracking the "canvassing, phone-banking, and voter registration efforts of labor unions, environmental groups, and their allies."[18]

The Kochs and their operatives are seemingly everywhere, yet they are invisible to most average Americans.

If you insert the name of any Republican presidential hopeful in the last few decades and the name "Koch," into a search engine, you'll see stories of Koch political donations and the posh retreats the Kochs host around the country. The events attract presidential and congressional candidates who come to audition and kiss the brothers' rings. If the candidates find favor with the brothers, they are granted a private audience with them to personally make their pitch for Koch campaign contributions.

There *are* Koch counterparts in the Democratic party as well, playing an outsized role in selecting who will carry the party

torch. But they are minnows compared to the Kochs. The combined net worth of Charles and David Koch is $87.2 billion.[19]
Forbes estimates the net worth of Tom Steyer, the highest profile
Democratic billionaire donor, at $1.6 billion.[20] Steyer and others
are trying to emulate the Koch model by networking with other
rich folks to leverage their donations, channeling them into specific political operations. They have a long way to go to catch up
to the Kochtopus.

In January 2015, the Koch brothers announced they and their
network of 450 donors would pump $889 million into the 2016
election.[21] In comparison, the Republican Party and its congressional committees in 2012 spent a combined total of $657 mil-
lion. So in today's politics, *two people* have more sway, as per funding, than the entire Republican Party's national organization.

Is this democracy?

Some Koch defenders say that the brothers are merely two
among many wealthy special interests in a political network.
Their influence, they claim, is overstated by pundits and the media. But the Kochs, by their own admission, are hands-on when it
comes to politics, controlling their network dollars with an iron
fist. The brothers decide who will receive funding and how it will
be used. They aren't benevolent givers who sow the seeds of creativity for others' ideas to blossom. The Kochs work to ensure
that every dollar funneled through their network to a political
group strictly serves the brothers' libertarian agenda. "If we're
going to give a lot of money, we'll make darn sure they spend it
in a way that goes along with our intent," David Koch told *Reason*
magazine. "And if they make a wrong turn and start doing things
we don't agree with, we withdraw the funding."[22]

Although the Koch brothers didn't achieve their goal of top-
pling President Obama in 2012, their Super PAC, Freedom Partners Action Fund, spent $23 million on the 2014 mid-terms, de-
livering an 87 percent success rate electing Republicans in close
races.[23] The Kochs don't win every fight, but their money tips the
scales in many races throughout the country, making them king-

makers with an obscene, outsized influence and direct access to our leaders. It is no coincidence that their wealth soared dramatically in tandem with the velocity of their political spending. In 1984, the brothers were each worth $375 million. In the mid-1990s, their fortunes rose to $1.5 billion apiece.[24] In 2008, they raked in $17 billion apiece. And after spending $1 billion on the Kochtopus during the Great Recession, their wealth exploded in 2015 to $42 billion apiece.

By "investing" in our democracy, the brothers receive a hefty return from their politician beneficiaries who control the levers of government. This is classic income redistribution, taking away from those with little representation in Washington to those with a lot, as legendary lobbyist Gerald Cassidy observed. In a 2011 interview, Charles Koch remarked, "The easy way to make money is to get special political privilege."[25]

As pundits and the media outed the brothers for their corrupting political activities, Charles tried recently to recast himself and David as *opponents* of crony capitalism, when Big Business gets rich rigging the political system in its favor.

It's been a hard sell.

Even with a full-on Koch public relations blitz, Charles still came across as reptilian on national TV talk shows. There's just too many politicians he's installed in office enslaved to his libertarian ideology. Too many cases of the Kochs using their money to loosen government regulations that grow the brothers' fossil fuels business. Too many behind-the-scenes scams killing government tax credits and other incentives meant to grow renewable energy businesses that would compete with Koch oil. And too many incidences of the Kochs' involvement deregulating financial markets that led to America's 2008 economic meltdown.

It's easy for Charles to call for the elimination of crony capitalism, since it would barely dent Koch Industries at this point. Charles was conspicuously silent on the issue a decade ago, when government largesse helped triple this size of his business. Charles and David are two of the biggest crony capitalists in American history.

How stupid do they think average Americans are?

Plenty.

KOCHMANDERING
Flipping America Red

THE KOCHS' STRATEGY is brilliant.

By sinking millions of dollars into state politics, they've created Republican state legislatures and turned them into a farm system for a conservative Congress. It's a major reason why Republicans have been making solid gains for the past 20 years.

While the Democrats basked in past dominance, the Kochs set up political organizations in 34 states to find and push conservative candidates who will do their bidding in Congress and in state houses across America. The brothers invested heavily in state Republican leaders to ensure that redistricting lines drawn every 10 years for congressional and legislative districts were skewed to favor Republicans with libertarian bents.

Two-party state houses across the nation were once overwhelmingly Democratic. But with the aid of Koch network dollars, Republicans turned many of them red. Democrats drubbed Republicans nationwide in the 2018 mid-terms, but the GOP still retained control of the legislatures in 30 of 49 states, or 61 percent (excluding Nebraska's unicameral legislature).[26] In 1982, Republicans only controlled 20 percent of state houses while Democrats controlled 69 percent.[27] And as for governorships, Republicans today control 27 of 50 executive offices, or 54 percent.

The Koch brothers' strategic political vision was key to Republicans' state house successes. In 2010, the Koch network seeded money to create the REDistricting Majority Project (REDMAP), a program run by the 527 group, The Republican State Leadership Committee (RSLC). REDMAP focuses on re-drawing a state's congressional and state legislative district boundaries, trying to build long-term Republican majorities in the U.S. House of Representatives and state houses. Redistricting is a major tool used by both major parties, suppressing the political power of opponents. Basically, the rigged districts allow the parties in power to capture more congressional seats while actually garnering fewer overall votes. The RSLC bragged about its exploits on its website:

> On November 6, 2012, Barack Obama was re-elected President of the United States by nearly a three-point margin, winning 332 electoral votes to Mitt Romney's 206 while garnering nearly 3.5 million more votes. Democrats also celebrated victories in 69 percent of U.S. Senate elections, winning 23 of 33 contests. Farther down-ballot, aggregated numbers show voters pulled the lever for Republicans only 49 percent of the time in congressional races, suggesting that 2012 could have been a repeat of 2008, when voters gave control of the White House and both chambers of Congress to Democrats. But, as we see today, that was not the case. Instead, Republicans enjoy a 33-seat margin in the U.S. House seated yesterday in the 113th Congress, having endured Democratic successes atop the ticket and over one million more votes cast for Democratic House candidates than Republicans.[28]

This leads to an overlooked but important point about campaign money. It doesn't take much for a billionaire to buy a congressional election, let alone a state contest. In a tight congressional race, a $50,000 Koch donation can often tip the scale to victory. And $50,000 spread among a gaggle of state candidates can upend governments.

Peanuts to the Kochs.

But to the candidate—congressional or state—it can mean the difference between political life and death. Average Americans mostly see headlines of million-dollar donations thrown around by wealthy interests to sway presidential or other high-profile races. But in the majority of lower level political campaigns, "large" donations are in the range of $15,000-$50,000. The Kochs and other wealthy special interests are experts in knowing just how much it takes to leverage their money and lock in a candidate's loyalty to do their bidding.

New Yorker writer Jane Mayer, commenting on REDMAP's success, observed: "The thinking behind it, which was very ingenious, was that the state legislative races are cheap, and if you can just put a bit of money into them and flip the state house, then you can control the redistricting process, which in turn gives the Republican Party a great advantage in putting members of Congress in the House of Representatives." Mayer, who writes extensively about the Koch brothers, added, "And most people don't pay a lot of attention to what's going on in the states. . . . But it's kind of ground zero for where politics is playing out." [29]

So how corrupt is the redistricting process?

Wisconsin provides an answer.

Wisconsin Governor Scott Walker (R) was one of the Koch brothers' favorite politicians. In 2011, then-Governor Walker and the Republican-led legislature crafted a redistricting map that scholars called the "worst gerrymandering in modern American history." [30] A group of outraged voters challenged the map.

It was revealed that Republican legislative leaders hired a law firm to draw the map behind closed doors, free from public scrutiny. Republicans signed secrecy oaths concerning the process and barred Democrats from participating. The firm hired a consultant, who used a sophisticated computer application to draw district boundaries. The program's algorithms smoothed out the rough shapes that would appear as gerrymandering to the naked eye, while packing districts to skew Republican. The consultant generated multiple maps, each one hiding any hint of impropriety, including racial discrimination. The consultant called this smoothing process "sensitivity testing." [31]

The result?

In 2012, Republican legislative candidates won 60 of 99 seats up for grabs in the Wisconsin legislature while Democrats garnered the *majority* of all votes cast in these elections.[32] Sachin Chheda, director of the Wisconsin Fair Elections Project, put the state's corrupt redistricting process in perspective: "Under the current maps, politicians choose their voters. We want a map where voters choose their politicians instead."[33]

The Democrats, of course, were guilty of gerrymandering, too, when they controlled the majority of state legislatures. From 1955 to 1995, the Democrats held a 40-year lock on the U.S. House of Representatives. Many of the same tricks Republicans employ today were pioneered by the Democrats. President Ronald Reagan, in remarks at the Republican Governors Club Annual Dinner on October 15, 1987, was particularly rankled by the "rigged" reapportionment process:

> In 1984, there were 397 congressional races contested by both parties. In the races, Republicans won half a million more votes than the Democrats, but the Democratic Party won 31 more seats. In California, one of the worst cases of gerrymandering in the country, Republicans received a majority of votes in congressional races, but the Democrats won 60 percent more races. The fact is gerrymandering has become a national scandal. The Democratic-controlled state legislatures have so rigged the electoral process that the will of the people cannot be heard. They vote Republican but elect Democrats.

Sound familiar?

It is clear neither party can be trusted with redistricting. Each seeks power at the expense of robbing average Americans of their political voice. It's why 13 states have taken steps to bypass their state politicians in favor of appointing commissions or independent citizens panels to draw redistricting maps, according to the National Conference of State Legislatures. More states are looking to change as well.

So what does this have to do with campaign spending limits?

Proper spending limits would curtail the Invisible Empire's

obscene, outsized influence in all levels of government. It would end their manipulation of redistricting, lawmaking, and elections. Properly enforced, spending limits would hand power back to the people. The Invisible Empire knows this to be true, which is why they are dedicated to eradicating any campaign finance reform law or proposal. Further, the Invisible Empire doesn't care that polls show the majority of Americans in both major parties favor campaign spending limits. The Invisible Empire designed the Republican REDMAP strategy to grow and protect their power. They are confident their hand-picked pols, weaned on large contributions and libertarian ideas, will not cross them.

If some of their politician farmhands defect and side with average Americans on spending limits, the Invisible Empire will simply use its trump card, running million-dollar ad campaigns making their case that getting money out of politics is not an anti-corruption solution, but an anti-free speech scam. Except they'll never tell average Americans that the only people whose free speech would be curtailed are America's donor class members, also known as the 700 or so who comprise the Invisible Empire.

2020 CONSTITUTIONAL CONVENTION?

WHAT IS GENUINELY ALARMING about the Koch REDMAP strategy, relaunched recently as REDMAP 2020 for the next redistricting cycle, is that it portends a possible, ominous constitutional crisis.

Under the Constitution's Article V, there are two methods to propose amendments:

1. *Legislation*: A member of Congress must introduce a bill in the House or Senate; the bill is then passed by a two-thirds majority vote in each house.

2. *Constitutional convention*: Congress calls a constitutional convention if two-thirds (34) of the nation's state legislatures vote to submit an "application" to Congress to hold a convention.

The United States has never used the latter method. Congress passed legislation to propose all 27 amendments that have been ratified and added to the Constitution.

But with the Republicans' state dominance, the Koch brothers have joined other wealthy conservatives to fund efforts seeking a constitutional convention to propose highly partisan amendments, perhaps as early as 2020. This cabal includes: the Walton family ($130 billion net worth), Koch brothers ($87.2 billion net worth), DeVos family ($5.5 billion net worth), and the Coors family ($4 billion net worth). These Invisible Empire caesars are funding the State Policy Network, a band of 64 conservative think tanks around the country, tasking it with pumping out policy papers and marketing materials to politicians, media, and social media urging a constitutional convention.[34]

There are several other groups targeting state legislatures to invoke a constitutional convention.

The Balanced Budget Amendment Task Force (BBATF), a conservative nonprofit, is closest to invoking a convention. According to its website, the group has signed up 28 state legislatures, only six shy of the 34 required to invoke a convention. And there are six Republican-controlled state legislatures that have not yet taken up the issue. The BBATF hopes to reach its goal of 34 states by 2020.

The Convention of the States (COS) is a group of former Tea Partiers pushing for three amendments: federal balanced budget; limits on federal power; and term limits for members of Congress. So far, 12 states have joined their cause. The COS is confident it can sew up 34 states by 2020. But there is also talk of the group piggy-backing on the BBATF, forcing their two extra amendment proposals onto the agenda.

At the other end of the political spectrum, Public Citizen, a liberal think tank and advocacy group, is leading a coalition to overturn the Supreme Court's *Citizens United v. Federal Election Commission* ruling that allowed corporations and unions to use their treasuries for political spending, leading to the creation of

Super PACs. The group has 19 states signed up for its cause and needs 15 more to invoke a convention.

There are other nascent efforts underway with a wide range of amendment proposals, but they have yet to secure a significant amount of state support.

Here's where it gets interesting—and a little scary.

Although the legislatures voted on specific issues, like a balanced budget amendment, on which to base a constitutional convention, delegates are not bound only to those issues. Organizers could quickly lose control and the convention could become a runway train with delegates proposing all sorts of amendments.

Why?

Because Article V gives no instructions on convention protocol. The Constitution is silent on such questions as: Who would preside over the convention? Would states that did not support the convention be allowed to participate? How many votes would each state get? Would all votes be decided on a simple majority or super majority?

With no set rules, it is highly plausible that amendments could be proposed in secrecy, substantially changing the Constitution or junking it altogether. It's already happened in our history. America's political leaders convened the 1787 Constitutional Convention in Philadelphia to amend the Articles of Confederation. But the delegates, once assembled, decided to toss the Articles and write an entirely new document from scratch—the Constitution. Liberal opponents of a "balanced budget" constitutional convention fear that conservatives could pass amendments on a number of issues, including banning abortion and gay marriage; suppressing the minority vote; curtailing civil rights; curbing labor rights, and dismantling Social Security and Medicare. Conservatives fear liberals may wrest control of the convention and abolish the Second Amendment, the Electoral College, and institute comprehensive campaign finance reform.

According to many constitutional experts, a constitutional convention could very well be a black hole, absent any formal rules. Michael J. Gerhardt, a University of North Carolina law professor and scholar in residence at the National Constitution Center, observed: "Once you have a convention, then in some respects it becomes a free-for-all. All bets are off."[36] Harvard University constitutional law expert Michael J. Klarman also believes a convention would have no boundaries. "I think a convention can do anything they want—re-establish slavery, establish a national church. I just don't think there's any limit."[37] According to David Super, a Georgetown University law school professor, there is no force or mechanism in the Constitution that can override what a convention may do.[38] Laurence Tribe, noted Harvard University constitutional law professor, said of the many questions surrounding a constitutional convention, ". . . there is no agreed upon process for coming up with definitive answers to any of these unknowns."[39]

Congress *could* issue guidelines, but once the convention is convened, there is nothing stopping the delegates from junking those rules and drawing their own, as did the delegates to the 1787 convention.

The president cannot set the rules because the Framers excluded the executive branch from playing a role in the amendment process.

And the Supreme Court? In 1939 the Court refused to involve itself in a question concerning amendment ratification, thus setting the precedent that the amendment process is a "political question," reserved for elected government.[35]

The Constitution does provide one backstop to a runaway convention: any amendment approved still needs to be ratified by three-quarters (38) of the state legislatures. For partisan amendments, this means that to achieve ratification, some legislatures with divided control between the parties will be needed.

Then, there is the nuclear option to worry about. There is nothing to stop the convention from changing Article V itself, for example, by requiring a lower number of states to ratify an amendment. The Constitutional Convention of 1787 did this too, requiring ratification by only nine states, as opposed to the Articles of Confederation's unanimous requirement by all 13 states.

This book advocates for a constitutional amendment, but by using the same approach—proposal by legislation—that has been used for all the Constitution's amendments.

In sum, as a consequence of the corrupt, partisan redistricting process in most states, America is in danger of falling into a serious constitutional crisis. To appropriate the immortal phrasing of Vice President Joe Biden (D), redistricting is a big f-----g deal.

REACH OF THE KOCHTOPUS

THE KOCHS' POLITICAL MASTERY is undeniable. The Kochtopus's reach is absolutely stunning. It is virtually everywhere.

Sure, the Kochs' wealth buys them federal and state political dominance. But they wisely partake in local politics as well. The Kochs invest in local elections and issues by reaching into the tiniest American hamlets, paying locals to set up "grassroots" political groups. They also pay to set up "astroturf" groups that hire outside people to pose as homegrown activists, creating the illusion of local support for candidates and issues.

The Kochs believe in vertical integration, dominating all levels of political activity. They've invested heavily setting up conservative think tanks that churn out studies, data, and position papers, propping up their libertarian philosophy and serving as policy resources for their candidates. They've funded the American Legislative Exchange Council (ALEC), a group that secretly meets to draft conservative-libertarian bills. ALEC then matches Koch-approved legislation with thousands of national and state politicians, who file these bills in Congress and their respective state legislatures.

The American City County Exchange (ACCE), another Koch group, is patterned after ALEC as a forum that matches Koch legislation with local officials to peddle in their respective chambers.

In a shrewd and cynical move, the Kochs financially backed the Libre Initiative, a project that lures Latinos to "freedom schools" or special events designed to mold their thinking to libertarianism. The brothers did this partly to counteract the damage President Trump has inflicted on the Republican Party's relationship with Latinos, including Trump's racist remarks against Mexicans, his separation of children from mothers at the U.S. border, and his lackluster response to aiding Puerto Ricans in the aftermath of Hurricane Maria in 2017. The Kochs also know the U.S. Census projection of a "minority white" America by 2045 does not bode well for Republicans. So the Koch network never slows down. They keep churning. They are out in front of this issue, just as they were with redistricting.

Another ambitious Koch initiative involves infiltrating higher education, which to conservatives leans liberal. Since 1980, the Kochs funneled $200 million of their free speech dollars to university research institutions, dictating what issues should be studied and in what manner.[40] They've funded scholarly programs in 238 institutions of higher learning across America to spread their libertarian gospel.[41] Charles Koch often refers to this scheme as building a "Republic of Science" that preaches academic freedom. This freedom, of course, centers around shilling the libertarian creed of free markets and limited government regulation. It is the Kochs' religion, so to speak. Students and activists, however, rose up to push back on the Kochs' ambitious plan. "We really see higher education as the first cog in their political machine," said Kalin Jordan, a co-founder of UnKochMyCampus, which fights against Koch corruption of academic autonomy. "They see themselves as creating the next generation (of libertarian thinkers), and in creating a next generation, they're really pushing out any other thought on campus."[42]

Several years ago, in another vertical integration effort, the brothers tried to buy the Tribune Company, a media syndicate that includes some of the most prestigious newspapers in the country: the *Los Angeles Times*, *Chicago Tribune*, *Baltimore Sun*,

Orlando Sentinel and *Hartford Courant*. They failed. In 2017, though, they gained a toehold in national publishing by financially backing the Meredith Corporation in a deal to purchase Time Inc., publisher of *Time* magazine. There will surely be more such purchases in the future to help propagate their agenda.

Whatever cranny the Kochs can exploit in our political system to buy America's elections, laws, and politicians—they're there.

Already camped out.

Their network is marbled in the sinews throughout the body politic, and it is highly impressive.

As it grows, our political power shrinks.

LOCAL KOCH

THE MORE MONEY THE BROTHERS PUMPED into the Kochtopus, the further its reach grew—from international to local politics.

Nothing is too big or too small for the Kochtopus.

In 2014, the Kochs' bulls-eye landed on the Kenosha Unified School District (KUSD) school committee race in southeastern Wisconsin. The district is the state's third largest, with about 22,500 mostly low-income minority students. The Kochs sought to defeat several school committee candidates who fought against Governor Scott Walker's slashing of funding for local schools. The cuts fell particularly hard on the KUSD and other less affluent school systems.

The Kochs' political nonprofit and political education arm, AFP, descended on the school district and immediately inserted its influence on the race. Outside money supporting local conservative groups began pouring in. The Koch group backed Tea Party candidates in the KUSD election with foot soldiers knocking on neighborhood doors, campaign workers writing negative ads against their opponents, and a $1 million television commercial that aired hundreds of times in the tiny media market.[43] Citizens were unaccustomed to the level of nastiness, misinformation, and mudslinging that rained down on them.

The school district, by the way, just happened to be located in U.S. Rep. Paul Ryan's congressional district. Ryan, the 2012 Republican vice-presidential nominee and former House Speaker, is an avowed libertarian and was supported by Koch funding.

The town of Coralville, Iowa, also made it onto the Koch hit list. This small town of 20,000 was another local jurisdiction to run afoul of the Kochs' libertarian ways. The cry had gone up in the Koch network that the town's mayor and council voted to borrow tens of millions of dollars to redevelop a blighted area of riverfront property. Some of the Tea Partiers in town didn't like the idea of the elected officials spending money to retain private property for the benefit of the citizens.

An army of Koch soldiers swarmed Coralville streets before the election, helping Koch-minded candidates defeat the mayor and vie for three council seats. Instituting the astroturfing technique, Koch troops dressed and posed as locals, knocked on doors, posted flyers, ran radio ads, and basically conducted an all-out campaign to overturn the local government.[44]

Tim Phillips, the Kochs' political strategist and AFP president, says the reason the brothers "fight local issue battles is because they result in good policy outcomes, generally promoting economic freedom via less taxes, less government spending."[45]

In other words, there is no election, no town too small for the Kochs to assert their will.

To ensure the Kochs' grip on American politics far into the future, the AFP created the Grassroots Leadership Academy to groom succeeding generations of conservative-libertarian activists and politicians. The mission is to mobilize trained bands of partisan troopers and deploy them anywhere, anytime to support Koch-minded, conservative candidates contending in the presidential election all the way down the ballot to local races.

The Kochs' end game is to build a perpetual farm team to fill openings in state legislatures and Congress when they occur.

The Koch brothers *are* plutocracy in action.

THE LIBERTARIAN WAY

AFTER WALL STREET TANKED THE ECONOMY in 1987, the Kochs fought against government regulation designed to prevent similar disasters from occurring.

Charles and David, like then-President Ronald Reagan, saw government as the enemy. The brothers worked successfully through their political nonprofit group, Citizens For A Sound Economy, to defeat sensible financial regulation. They pushed hard—shoulder-to-shoulder with big banks—to pass the Financial Services Modernization Act of 1999, also called Gramm-Leach-Bliley, repealing the Glass-Steagall Act. President Bill Clinton signed the 1999 measure into law. Congress had passed Glass-Steagall in the Great Depression's aftermath after banks recklessly speculated with depositors' hard-earned savings. Crushing this law in 1999 made billions for the Kochs and their friends. But it savaged millions of average Americans nine years later when the lack of protection Glass-Steagall had provided led to the 2008 financial collapse. Bankers once again rolled the dice with average Americans' earnings. Commercial banks originated predatory subprime mortgages, subsequently selling them to investment banks. Goldman Sachs, the biggest of the investment banks, then bundled these toxic loans and sold them to unsuspecting investors. The resulting Great Recession lasted the better part of a decade.

So has America learned anything from the greed, recklessness, and unwavering libertarian-conservative belief in the power of the unfettered free market to regulate itself and the resulting devastation it wrought in the Great Depression and Great Recession?

Of course not.

The Koch Brothers have been busy watering down the Dodd-Frank law since it passed in 2010 and killing other sensible measures to avoid another financial collapse.

Why?

Because it always works out for them and their network of

wealthy friends. The game is rigged. The people who caused the Great Depression and Great Recession made out just fine. They fixed the capitalist game by buying our government. So no matter if the economy rises or tanks, they'll make money. It doesn't matter to them what happens to average Americans and the country. Their libertarian philosophy rejects empathy with their fellow citizens. They are willing to die for liberty (their own), regardless of the consequences to others. That is not their problem. They will enjoy their freedom as never before. What is good for them individually, they believe, *must* be good for everyone else.

In August 2015, Charles Koch addressed an exclusive gathering of his wealthy friends in Dana Point, California, to strategize a plan of attack for the 2016 election. In his speech, he compared his libertarian fight to dismantle government regulations to black America's struggle for civil rights. That is, he equated his "struggle" to make more money with blacks' struggle for basic human dignity and equality. Coincidentally, Charles Koch recently befriended Michael Lomax, president of the United Negro College Fund (UNCF). Lomax became the UNCF's president in 2004. The following year, the Kochs bought the paper and chemical company, Georgia-Pacific, which had been a longtime UNCF contributor. Thus a Koch-Lomax connection was made. Charles later donated $25 million to the UNCF, with $18.5 million of the gift going toward creating a Koch Scholars Program.[46] Charles will help decide which professors teach the program and the development of the curriculum. Koch money allows Charles the "freedom" to shape the minds of young black students toward his way of thinking.

Meanwhile, Charles was exercising a more familiar brand of Koch "freedom" in Crossett, Arkansas, as it relates to black people.

A Koch-owned Georgia-Pacific plant in Crossett had dug a system of long, wide ditches to dispose of the factory's wastewater. This putrid flow of dark sludge, containing formaldehyde, a known carcinogen, and a cocktail of suspected carcinogens, flowed downstream near low-income residential neighborhoods. A toxic steam rose from the sludge and blew into the yards and houses of residents, who were mostly low-income black citizens. Those who lived on Penn Road suffered the most. Many experienced headaches, dizziness, muscle weakness; and eye, nose, and throat irritation.[47] In a few years, 11 of 15 households on the street suffered a cancer-induced death.[48]

Koch Industries ranks consistently among the heaviest polluters in the United States. Aside from ExxonMobil and American Electric Power, it is the only company that ranks among the top 30 in air pollution, water pollution, and greenhouse gas emissions.[49] There is a long list of Koch Industries' environmental violations, including 312 oil and chemical spills across America.[50] For decades, Koch plants treated the Mississippi River like an open sewer, illegally polluting it with ammonia-laced wastewater and upping the discharge when not monitored on weekends. In the 1990s, they dumped 600,000 gallons of jet fuel into the river's surrounding wetlands.[51] Summing up the Kochs' arrogance and indifference toward their neighbors' desire to enjoy clean land, water, and air, federal Environmental Protection Agency Administrator Carol Browner remarked of the Kochs: "They simply did not believe the law applied to them."[52]

It follows, then, from the Kochs' sense of entitlement that a large share of Koch political money goes to fund candidates who weaken federal and state environmental laws, which the Koch brothers view as a form of government tyranny. Their libertarian idea of freedom works for them because their money allows them to buy freedom from government regulation. But their self-serving view of freedom also buys other freedoms. For example, it buys average Americans the freedom to live in or near areas polluted by Koch companies; the freedom to get sick and die from Koch effluent and carcinogens; and the freedom to waste what little money they have suing the Kochs and their government friends for damages.

Back in Crossett, Koch money had been spread liberally

throughout Arkansas state government. So it was no surprise that Georgia-Pacific and the state's environmental agency were in lockstep, maintaining that the plant's discharge met all state requirements. In 2011, a documentary entitled *Koch Brothers Exposed*, highlighted the elevated cancer rates of the Penn Road neighborhood. Two years later, a study verified the existence of carcinogens emitted from the plant.

No action has been taken.

The Kochs' money gave the brothers the freedom to buy Arkansas government and pollute in Crossett, among many other areas in America, regardless of the human cost. What matters to the Kochs is that their profits are banked instead of being spent on proper waste disposal. You see, the free market isn't really free. It's like saying public education is free. The free market is not free if it infringes on another's rights or pollutes the air, water, and earth. Someone has to pay to clean it up. But the Kochs don't see it that way. They believe the free market's negative externalities are a cost of doing business, and everyone, somehow, profits from business. So, to them, it's a wash. They believe they aren't infringing on others' rights.

Call it the Immaculate Profitization.

It is the libertarian way.

But to Penn Road's black residents, the libertarian way smells a lot like the stinking, steaming sludge oozing behind their backyards.

The sickened residents had little money to fight back and therefore very little "freedom of speech."

The Kochs won their "civil rights" battle in Crossett.

Black residents lost theirs.

ENHANCING POLITICAL VOICE

WEALTH BUYS "FREE SPEECH" POLITICAL ADVERTISEMENTS distributed in mass communication formats, such as television, radio, newspapers, magazines, websites, smart phones, billboards, robocalls, leaflets, and junk mail.

Wealth buys "free speech" access to influential politicians, policymakers, and appointed officials in all levels of government, including judges and district attorneys.

Wealth buys "free speech" access and power to pass laws that decriminalize practices of some corporations, such as polluting or robbing average Americans of their disposable incomes.

Wealth buys "free speech" access to state legislative leaders who draw the redistricting lines every ten years, influencing which party will control Congress and the legislatures.

Wealth buys local "free speech" by reaching into the smallest of America's hamlets to set up phony grassroots political groups that pose as homegrown entities.

Wealth buys "free speech" to corrupt university research institutions, dictating what issues should be studied and in what manner.

All this "free speech" purchased by wealthy elites enhances their own political voices while diluting those of average Americans. As Senator John McCain (R-AZ) once observed:

> If money is free speech, the big interests are sitting in the front with megaphones, and the average citizens are sitting in the back.

The Supreme Court's conservative justices, however, view it differently than McCain. They've relied on the following *Buckley v. Valeo* passage for 40 years to validate their evisceration of campaign reform laws:

> . . . the concept that government may restrict the speech of some elements of our society in order to enhance the relative voice of others is wholly foreign to the First Amendment . . .

But that would mean the Nineteenth Amendment and others embodied a concept wholly foreign to the First Amendment. By granting women the right to vote, did it not *enhance* the female voice at the expense of diluting or restricting the male voice? Did the Fifteenth Amendment granting black people citizenship not *enhance* the black voice while diluting or restricting the white voice? Did the Twenty-sixth Amendment that lowered the voting age to 18 not *enhance* the younger voice at the expense of diluting or restricting the voice of older Americans?

Critics also warn that a campaign spending limits amendment abolishing the concept of "money as speech" would be the first to *take away* rights granted to the people.

But many of the Constitution's amendments have been passed in the pursuit of freedom, equality, and the common good. And depending on a person's perspective, the same amendments could be viewed as taking away rights as well. A person could say the Sixteenth Amendment took away a citizen's right to keep his or her earnings instead of sending a portion to the government in the form of federal income tax. There are some states that may believe the Twenty-fourth Amendment that banned poll taxes to discourage black and poor voters took away their right to manage their own elections. Perhaps, there are even a few white Southerners today who would say the Thirteenth Amendment robbed them of their competitive advantage by stripping them of their right to own slaves.

It is self-evident that the common thread running through all these amendments is that Americans were making sacrifices for the common good: taking away the rights of some—usually those accustomed to positions of outsized monetary, political, or social dominance—and granting rights to others to make things more equitable for all.

It is the *same idea* behind campaign spending limits.

Further, free speech is not absolute in America. There are many existing laws that in some way abridge a person's right to free speech. A citizen isn't free to yell "fire" in a crowded movie theater, blast his or her stereo at 3 a.m. in a residential neighborhood, run naked down Main Street, interrupt a public meeting by shouting through a bullhorn, deface public or private property with graffiti, or any number of activities that could be argued as exercising one's free speech.

And as for political speech, a citizen or politician is rarely allowed unlimited quantities in the public arena. The amount of time citizens may address elected bodies such as a city or town council or board of supervisors or selectmen, particularly during public comment, is almost always abridged or restricted, often to five minutes or less. The political speech of elected officials is abridged when they address legislative committees or full legislative bodies that place restrictions on speaking. Political speech is also restricted for candidates in political debates, where responses to complicated questions are often limited to one or two minutes. Political speech in general is abridged so everyone has a fair and equal say. What would our democracy look like—what would your city or town look like—if the time to speak in a public forum to address elected officials were sold to the highest bidder—usually the wealthiest person in town—with little or no time left for you or anyone else to be heard on issues that affect the entire community? While these are examples of political speech abridgement, the Constitution allows them as "time, place, manner restrictions," backed by several Supreme Court cases.

So like other constitutional amendments, campaign spending limits seeks to redistribute the rights and power of some—roughly 700 citizens comprising the Invisible Empire—to the many—250 million average American voters, to serve the common good and make things more equitable for all.

It's called democracy.

6

LOBBYING

The Fourth Branch of Government

ENGINEER DOUGLAS BROWN busied himself on the night of April 20, 2010, monitoring the control panel of the Deepwater Horizon, a rig situated above BP's Macondo oil well about 52 miles off Louisiana's coast.

All seemed normal. Workers went about their night-shift routines while day workers settled in for a good night's sleep.

Just before 10 p.m., Brown noticed a hissing sound coming from somewhere in the rig. Minutes later, the gas alarms began ringing. Pressure monitors spiked, as the engines that supplied the entire structure with power began wildly revving up on their own. Suddenly, a violent explosion ripped through the platform's core and flung Brown smack into the control panel. The bomb-like concussion blew a hole in the floor, sucking him down to the level below. Brown was dazed and covered with debris. Then, a second blast collapsed the rest of the ceiling and control room floor on top of him.[1]

A series of explosions followed.

Huge fireballs and flames shot into the darkness and engulfed the rig. Smoke and soot permeated the air, making it hard to breathe. Workers scurried up from the living quarters below, scrambling around the mud-splattered deck, grabbing belongings and trying to find their way to a lifeboat. Some desperate workers, cornered by searing flames, dove 60 feet from the platform into the blackness of the Gulf of Mexico.[2] Brown survived, but 11 of his crew members did not.

The Deepwater Horizon, irreparably damaged, sank into the Gulf two days later.

For nearly six months after the disaster, the well spewed more than 210 million gallons (4.9 million barrels) of crude from the ocean floor. It was the worst oil spill in American history. It leaked 20 times more oil than the 1989 Exxon Valdez tanker disaster in Alaska's Prince William Sound, the second-largest spill.

The residue from the Deepwater Horizon debacle continues to harm the environment and the health and livelihoods of many coastal residents.

BP, a British-owned company, had an abysmal safety record leading up to the catastrophe. A fatal explosion in 2005 at its Texas City, Texas, oil refinery claimed 15 lives and injured 180 workers. The company raised eyebrows with a spate of other mishaps, including a major oil spill in 2006 at BP's poorly managed pipeline in Prudhoe Bay, Alaska.

During the two years before the Gulf spill, BP shelled out $32 million to deploy an army of former U.S. government officials to lobby Congress, the White House, and 14 federal agencies. The oil giant's goal was to further its business interests by sanitizing its safety record.[3]

By all accounts, BP's lobbying offensive succeeded. It bought a pass from government regulators who looked the other way. They ignored the company's history of poor safety and greenlighted the Macondo oil well. BP's lobbyists also persuaded officials to loosen offshore drilling regulations, reducing federal supervision of the project. In sum, BP's lobbying money allowed the conglomerate to virtually regulate itself.

Freed from most government oversight, BP employed slipshod engineering and lax safety practices on the Macondo well to save the company time (the project was six weeks behind schedule) and money (the well was $58 million over budget) to artificially prop up the company's stock value for investors.[4]

In January 2011, the National Commission on the BP Deepwater Horizon Oil Spill and Offshore Drilling, a panel convened by President Obama, concluded the disaster was preventable. It cited a laundry list of blunders and ill-advised cost-saving measures by all involved: BP, the oil well's owner; Transocean, the oil rig's owner; and Cameron and Halliburton, the project's subcontractors. The commission said the lack of regulation leading to the explosion was the consequence of the "industry's resistance to more effective oversight." It added, "The result was a serious, and ultimately inexcusable, shortfall in supervision of offshore drilling that played out in the Macondo well blowout and the catastrophic oil spill that followed."[5]

The commission's findings fell on deaf ears.

Thanks to the handiwork of oil industry lobbyists, Congress failed to take steps or pass legislation that could prevent similar disasters from occurring.

In October 2011, the Obama administration gave BP approval to restart its drilling operations in the Gulf of Mexico.

In January 2013, BP reached a plea bargain with the U.S. Department of Justice concerning the Gulf spill, agreeing to pay $4 billion in fines and penalties—the largest settlement in U.S. history. BP also pleaded guilty to 14 counts of criminal wrongdoing, including felony manslaughter and obstruction of Congress. The obstruction charge stemmed from an unnamed "senior executive," who withheld documents, manipulated figures, and lied to Congress, claiming that 5,000 barrels of oil per day were spewing from the ocean floor when the actual number was 60,000 barrels per day.[6]

In April 2016, a judge approved a final $20 billion settlement against BP over civil charges stemming from the Gulf spill. The judge awarded the money to the federal government and five Gulf states harmed in the disaster. Experts estimated, however, that BP will be able to write off $15.3 billion of that total, including payments for natural resource damage.[7] Translation: taxpayers will pick up the tab.

BP is the entity overseeing the Gulf cleanup, which is kind of like putting Pretty Boy Floyd in charge of bank security.

For six years, while BP dragged out its protracted legal battle, it steadfastly maintained that its cleanup effort was a remarkable success, and that the Gulf was back to normal. You may have seen the oil giant's slick TV ads featuring smiling actors pretending to be diligent cleanup workers. They wore shiny, spotless BP hard hats and BP logoed shirts while woodenly selling the story that the company was working tirelessly to clean and rebuild the area. The ads claimed BP spent millions of dollars on the cleanup and was absolutely committed to Gulf coast residents. "Safety is at the heart of everything we do," was a frequent tag line.

But behind the scenes, BP stuck to a different script.

Behind the actors, makeup, lighting, soothing music, and pristine coastal backdrops, the company had undertaken another kind of cleanup job. BP spent millions of dollars on lobbyists and lawyers to minimize the amount of cleanup work required and the amount of money paid out to spill victims.

Sure, BP was correct that fisheries rebounded, but it's not back to normal for all. Some fishing areas have been slow to recover, and others have vanished completely. BP also patted itself on the back when it announced that nearly all the oil on the water's surface had been skimmed off. But it failed to mention the sea of crude that sank to the bottom—a dormant ghost from 2010 that periodically rears its head.

In August 2012, Hurricane Isaac hit the Gulf area and kicked up batches of that oil, re-soiling parts of the Louisiana coast.

In June 2013, a giant 40,000-pound blob of tar mixed with sand and shells washed up on an island off the Louisiana coast.[8]

In May 2015, the National Oceanic and Atmospheric Administration issued a report showing a link between the spilled petroleum and the masses of bottlenose dolphins dying from lung and adrenal lesions off the shores of Alabama, Louisiana, and Mississippi.[9]

In 2018, researchers found thousands of "sand patties" made of sand and oil traced to the Macondo well disaster continuing to wash ashore, fouling Gulf beaches. Although microbes have eaten some of the oil residue on the Gulf's bottom, it will still take several decades before shrimp and other life forms return to the spill area.

More incidents will surely follow.

BP's Macondo oil well project—the $32 million special interest lobbying gift that keeps on giving.

LOBBYING'S RETURN ON INVESTMENT

THERE IS ONLY ONE REASON corporations, unions, and trade associations spend billions of dollars each year to influence legislation—swarming Congress, state legislatures, city councils, and their respective staffs with policy briefs, research reports, marketing, polls, etc., as well as lavishing them with campaign donations, gifts, meals, vacations, and promises of future employment:

It works.

They wouldn't waste their money if it didn't.

The three branches of American government are the executive, legislative, and judicial. They are the three-legged stool designed by the Founding Fathers that comprises our government's system of checks and balances, ensuring no one branch can run roughshod over the country and destabilize our democracy.

But there's another branch not mentioned in the Constitution that many believe rivals, and some say exceeds, the power of the other three. It's referred to as the lobbying branch—or the "fourth branch" of government. It's comprised of the Invisible Empire, other wealthy special interests, and the massive armies they deploy to influence elected officials in the lobbies and halls of American government.

Wealthy interests are guaranteed a great return on their lobbying investments because they understand the hunger, lust, and need politicians have for campaign donations to keep their jobs. It is standard lobbying practice to approach newly elected members of Congress before they've even taken the oath of office and offer to organize their re-election fundraisers. They know how to get their hooks in early. In 2006, the *Wall Street Journal* published Federal Election Commission records showing 71 members of Congress had hired registered lobbyists to serve as treasurers for their re-election campaigns or political action committees.[10]

The candidates' driving thirst for campaign money has fueled the rise of the influence-peddling industry, growing by leaps and bounds over the past decades. Special interests have been pumping more cash into their lobbying efforts because the rate of return has been increasingly higher. The $4 trillion federal budget is such an easy target for special interests that they've come to rely on it as a huge and fertile profit center.[11]

It's not hard to drum up examples of lobbying power. Author Steven Brill, writing for *Time* magazine, tracked the lobbying dollars spent by the Private Equity Council (PEC), a business trade group that invests large pools of money in privately-held companies, and what the group received in return. From 2009 to 2010, the PEC joined a coalition seeking a special tax break for their industry members. The group spent about $15 million on lobbying to get Congress on board. The PEC chipped in about $4.8 million for its share of lobbying expenses.[12]

The result?

A $10 billion kiss from lawmakers over 10 years.[13]

Not a bad investment: $15 million to get $10 billion in lower taxes. Lawmakers opposing the tax break simply wanted the companies' income to be taxed the same as workers' wages. Supporters of the tax break insisted the corporate windfall would create jobs.

Perhaps.

But average Americans are quite capable of creating jobs too, especially with the aid of huge tax breaks. Indeed, more average Americans could start businesses and hire employees with a little windfall-seed money spread around the 50 states. And most likely, these businesses would hire local workers and contribute directly to local economies as well.

In 2006, Michael J. Cooper of the University of Utah and Huseyin Gulen and Alexei V. Ovtchinnikov, both of Virginia Tech, authored a study, *Corporate Political Contributions and Stock Returns*, to gauge the effect of political money. Their research found most corporations profited enormously from doling out campaign donations to congressional candidates. The professors tracked corporate political action committee (PAC) donations to congressional candidates made from 1979 to 2004. PACs are groups set up by special interests (corporations, unions, business associations) that funnel cash in limited, regulated $10,000 or $15,000 increments directly to their favored candidates. The professors compared the PAC donations to how well each corporation's stock performed. They found that the stocks of politically-active corporations outperformed those of other firms by about 6 percent, or an extra $150 million in returns for each politically-active firm. The trick, according to the authors, was that "the more candidates a firm supports, the higher are its next year's raw and abnormal returns."[14] The authors concluded: "Thus, our results imply that firms participate in the political system not from the standpoint of consuming a patriotic consumption good . . . but rather from the standpoint of creating positive net present value investments."[15]

There are, of course, similar academic studies that have reached different conclusions. A 2002 MIT study touted by anti-reformers concluded that PACs receive little if any return on their political contributions and do not view them as investments.[16]

There is, however, an abundance of anecdotal evidence to the contrary. And it is particularly persuasive since it comes from those who have actually worked in the lobbying industry.

Howard Marlowe, formerly a U.S. Senate staffer and Senate Finance Committee counsel, bemoans the "mutual addiction" of money and influence that lawmakers and lobbyists have for each other. "We need to take the dollar sign out of the legislative process," Marlowe urges. "That's the only way that the public will begin again to have faith in the political process."[17]

He should know.

Marlowe later worked as a Washington lobbyist for more than 30 years, founded his own successful lobbying firm, and served two terms as president of the American League of Lobbyists.

Former *Washington Post* campaign finance reporter Jeffrey Birnbaum offered this explanation of lobbying's burgeoning profitability: "One reason behind this growth is the lobbying industry's simple-yet-dazzling economics. For a relatively small investment in a lobbying campaign, corporations can receive a gargantuan return." Birnbaum added, "The Carmen Group Inc., a mid-size firm, has calculated that for every $1 million its clients spend on its services, it delivers, on average, $100 million in government benefits. A yield that immense, common in federal lobbying, is unheard of anyplace else."[18] Birnbaum subsequently left the newspaper to work as public relations president for the lobbying firm Barbour, Griffiths & Rogers.

A 2009 study by professors from Washington and Lee University and the University of Kansas showed that $220 could be earned for every dollar invested in peddling political influence.[19] Strategas Research Partners, a New York City-based investment research firm with offices in Washington, D.C., created a lobbying index, using this study as inspiration. The Strategas index includes 50 companies that spend the most on influence peddling as a percentage of their assets. The biggest spenders hail from the financial and health care sectors. Not surprisingly, the index's return on investment has outperformed the Standard & Poor's 500 Index (S&P 500) by 11 percent for the past 15 years.[20] It registered a 17.4 percent return compared to S&P 500's 6 percent.[21] It is a stunning yield.

Warren Buffet, billionaire investor and the third richest person in the United States, also recognizes the incredible returns that can be gained not just from lobbying, but from seeding money to politicians.[22]

In a *New York Times* column, Buffet, worth $82 billion, according for *Forbe*s magazine, wrote:

> For five decades, I've looked for undervalued stocks. But if I'd been interested in the biggest bargain around, which I wasn't, I would have bought political influence. For many a year, it was far cheaper than anything to be found in the stock market. A relatively modest contribution—say, $25,000—was enough to make the donor a V.I.P. in the political world. And really big amounts? As a fundraising senator once jokingly said to me, 'Warren, contribute $10 million and you can get the colors of the American flag changed.' [23]

Lobbying is, in fact, so lucrative that it was one of the few economic sectors that actually expanded during the depths of the Great Recession. Lobbying firms broke industry revenue records in 2009 while the rest of the nation struggled with suffocating debt, a tight lending market, and high unemployment rates. "Lobbying appears recession-proof," said Sheila Krumholz, executive director of the Center for Responsive Politics, a nonprofit that tracks campaign spending. "Even when companies are scaling back other operations, many view lobbying as a critical tool in protecting their future interests, particularly when Congress is preparing to take action on issues that could seriously affect their bottom lines." [24]

Record spending by lobbying firms over the past 10 years begat record lobbying employment, which begat record expansion of the Beltway economy. The Washington, D.C., metropolitan area during that period—right through the recession—added 21,000 households to the nation's top 1 percent of earners. [25] This growth, fueled by influence peddlers and federal contractors plundering the nation's treasury, far outpaced any other metropolitan area in the nation. A U.S. Bureau of Labor Statistics study in September 2014 showed Washington, D.C., had eclipsed both New York City and San Francisco as America's most expensive place to live, as measured by housing costs. [26] A Tiffany & Co.

store, Tesla dealership, and other upscale merchants catering to
the nouveau riche have sprouted around the nation's capital.[27]

These developments should set off alarm bells in every corner
of America, waking citizens to the fact that our democracy is not
in good health. The heart of our nation, our capital, is clogged
with excesses of opulence and fast money.

It is failing.

THE U.S. BUDGET
Carving up & Carving Out

CAPITALISM IS SUPPOSED TO THRIVE on competition. But many in the
Invisible Empire are competition averse. If they cannot quash up-
start competition, they buy it up—or they go to Congress for help
to either quash it or neutralize it. They ensure their schemes succeed by paying their lobbyists millions of dollars to persuade politicians to either kill proposed legislation—like an oil conglomerate seeking to kill tax incentives for renewable energy companies—or, more commonly, insert "friendly" bill provisions that
benefit their own companies.

The financial industry is a good example.

In the spring and summer of 2010, an army of about 2,000
investment and bank lobbyists infiltrated Congress (that's almost
four lobbyists per lawmaker), which was hammering out the Wall
Street reform bill. These high-paid influence peddlers successfully
larded the bill with special language, known as "carve-outs," that
benefit their corporate clients. The final bill ballooned to 2,319
pages. In contrast, the 1914 law that created the Federal Trade
Commission totaled eight pages. The 1935 Social Security Act
comprised 28 pages.

Brill, the aforementioned *Time* writer, monitored the negoti-
ations between Congress and Wall Street lobbyists leading up to
the reform bill's 2010 adoption. He offered this observation:
"Complexity is the modern lobbyist's greatest ally." Noting the

hefty size of the bill, he added, "And on almost every page there were dozens of phrases—typically framed in near unintelligible legalese—whose wording could mean millions or billions to some company or industry."[28]

Brill then links the overwhelming success of lobbying to unlimited campaign spending by writing: "Beyond the resources lobbyists can deploy, there's the campaign money they can supply. The average winning congressional campaign in 2010 is likely to cost about $1.5 million, requiring the incumbent to raise roughly $15,000 a week. Lobbyists not only contribute on their own, but are the most important fundraisers in the money grind, because they serve as lawmakers' links to the most promising donors: those with business interests related to each member's committee assignments."[29]

Many reform critics, however, say the answer to improving our government is not fewer lobbyists and more restrictions, but more lobbyists and fewer restrictions. They believe more lobbyists, operating under little or no regulation, will bring more light—that is to say, more information to the process.

Perhaps.

But who would be funding these extra battalions of lobbyists and what information would they be armed with? Would average Americans foot the bill, directing lobbyists to supply lawmakers with unbiased information from different perspectives so the best decisions will be made for "We, the People?"

Not likely.

It would be the usual suspects shelling out big money to influence peddlers to provide sanitized, biased information from one perspective to lawmakers.

Actually, you can already see the effect of an increased number of lobbyists. Thumb through the 2,319-page Wall Street reform tome, and you'll get the picture. Just don't drop it on your foot, or you'll have to go the hospital. Then, you'll have to wade through the 2,409 pages of President Obama's 2010 Affordable Care Act to navigate the changes in the health care system.

America does not need more lobbyists. Our political system is already inundated with them in numbers that overwhelm our elected leaders. These shills are seemingly everywhere. Special interest groups pay lobbyists to monitor every movement of Congress, state legislatures, and to a lesser degree, municipal bodies. From the air, these influence peddlers perch like hawks on treetops waiting for prey to pop out of a hole in the ground. When a bill (usually regulatory in nature) is spotted that would harm one of their clients, they swoop down and attack—immobilizing and often killing it before it sees the light of day. From the ground, they worm their way into the inner sanctums of congressional and state leaders, planting carve-outs and writing vast swaths of legislation that benefit their corporate clients.

This is how it works.

Nothing is left to chance.

We elect politicians to represent, serve, and protect us. But we're not protecting *them* from a fetid, corrupt system that overwhelms and undermines them at every turn.

Average Americans need to step up.

ROGUES GALLERY

WHERE TO begin?

Teapot Dome? Abscam? Watergate? Iran-Contra? Abramoff? Cambridge Analytica? Russian collusion?

A virtual smorgasbord of corruption.

A whimsical deli owner could coin a million witty sandwich names based on the scandals in American politics.

While mega-scandals like Watergate garner most of the attention, the real story of American politics is the many incidences of corruption—big and small—that occur every day in the shadows of American government. As you read through this book, consider this: If you take the hundreds of well-known scandals (most of them federal), then add them to the thousands of scandals documented in state, county, city, and town governments across America where unlimited campaign spending is just as prevalent, you start to understand the magnitude of the corruption that has overtaken the entire body politic.

Then think about this: *these are only the scandals that have come to light.*

And nearly all of the corruption can be traced back to the single flaw in our system: the intense pressure created by the money incentive to amass political power.

The corruption is not solely endemic to the United States. You'll find nearly identical stories in the history of any country that allows unlimited fundraising and spending. And until governments enact laws limiting campaign spending, you will see these stories here and elsewhere—again and again. Only the names and dates will change.

JACK ABRAMOFF SCANDAL

THE VOLUME OF POLITICAL SCANDALS big and small are too numerous to cite here. They are well cataloged in other works.

Instead, it will be illustrative to focus on the most recent mega-scandal, which conveniently showcases how the lust for money and power leads to mischief, abuse, and corruption. It also reveals many of influence peddlers' tools of the trade. This scandal erupted in 2006 and found super lobbyist Jack Abramoff at its epicenter.

Abramoff, a life-long Republican operative and former College Republican National Committee chairman, had friends in high places when he was barely out of college. His close buddies Ralph Reed, future leader of the Christian Coalition; and Grover Norquist, future president of Americans for Tax Reform, a right-wing anti-tax group, were fellow conservative activists who rose through the ranks together. Abramoff rubbed elbows with President Reagan and was familiar to many of the president's aides.

After spending time in Hollywood as a struggling screenwriter and movie producer, Abramoff returned to politics, earning a reputation as a major fundraiser for Republican candidates and causes.

When Republicans took control of Congress in 1995, Abramoff transitioned from fundraiser to lobbyist, believing his talent to influence politicians could better serve the conservative agenda. As he steadily rose in the lobbying ranks, his access to political money—and his own wealth—rose as well.

By the 2000s, Abramoff's web stretched far and wide, spreading fraud and corruption to everyone and everything he touched. His "lobbying shop" featured his own Washington, D.C., restaurant, Signatures, as well as a luxury skybox at the city's MCI Center—home to a pro basketball team, pro hockey team, and venue for major concerts and other events. Frequent Abramoff guests included House Majority Leader Tom DeLay (R-TX) and his staff. According to a top GOP leadership aide, DeLay staffers were such frequent flyers in Abramoff's MCI luxury skybox, they started to feel like they owned it. "Jack was sort of like a drug dealer," the aide said. "He'd give them a taste, then get them hooked."[30]

Aside from bribing a slew of elected officials and their staff members in exchange for votes and favors, Abramoff excelled at hustling wealthy, naïve clients far removed from Washington, and he couldn't resist bragging about it. Hushed accounts of his exploits ricocheted around town. Eventually, these stories caught the ears of regulators. Soon, Abramoff and his house of dirty cards came crashing down, a victim of his own hubris. In 2004, the Senate Indian Affairs Committee got wind of Abramoff's schemes and called him to testify. It was revealed that Abramoff and his partner, Michael Scanlon, had worked as a tag team, bilking six Native American tribes for more than $82 million over several years.

The tribes operated casinos and sought lobbying help to prevent other Native American tribes from starting casinos nearby. The six tribes approached Abramoff for political advice and consulting services. Abramoff advised them to hire Scanlon's company, Capital Campaign Strategies, LLC, which provided grass-roots campaign and public relations support. Abramoff and Scanlon charged the tribes exorbitant fees while pretending to work tirelessly for them. Scanlon amassed nearly $40 million in profits from the hustle. Without the tribes' knowledge, he kicked back $20 million to Abramoff.

It wasn't enough that these two scam artists were getting rich defrauding their Native American clients. They felt compelled to denigrate them as well. In one email, Abramoff mocked tribe members as "monkeys" and "morons" because of the ease with which he could separate them from their money.[31] In another email, Abramoff bragged that he secured the help of J. Steven Griles, U.S. Interior Department deputy secretary, to block a rival Native American tribe from opening a casino that would have taken business away from Abramoff's client, the Saginaw Chippewas. Abramoff gloated that he was close to tempting Griles, a former lobbyist, to rejoin the ranks of influence peddlers for much more than he was earning at the Interior Department.[32] In June 2007, a federal judge sentenced Griles to 10 months in prison for lying to a U.S. Senate panel about his dealings with Abramoff.[33]

On January 3, 2006, Abramoff fittingly donned a black hat and black trench coat for the perp walk into U.S. District Court in Washington, D.C., to face corruption charges. He confessed his guilt in bribing members of Congress and their staffs with gifts, meals, sporting event tickets, vacations—and, of course, campaign donations. Abramoff also confessed to charges of fraud and tax evasion.

The Department of Justice's criminal charges gave an example of how Abramoff and Scanlon operated. The following is a sample of their lobbying activities:

Bribes: Scanlon and Lobbyist A (Abramoff), together and separately, provided a stream of things of value to an official described as Representative #1 (Bob Ney, R-OH) and members of his staff, including, but not limited to, a lavish trip to Scotland to play golf on world-famous courses, tickets to sporting events and other entertainment, regular meals at Lobbyist A's upscale restaurant (Signatures), and campaign contributions for Representative #1, his political action committees and other political committees on behalf of Representative #1.

Graft: At the same time, and in exchange for these things of value, Scanlon and Lobbyist A (Abramoff), together and separately, sought and received Representative #1's (Ney's) agreement to perform directly and through others a series of official acts, including but not limited to, agreements to support and pass legislation, agreements to place statements in the Congressional Record, meetings with Lobbyist A and Scanlon's clients, and advancing the application of a client of Lobbyist A for a license to install wireless telephone infrastructure in the House of Representatives.[34]

Abramoff, by the way, was a carveout master. Some say he perfected the technique. The super lobbyist had members of Congress at his fingertips, ready to insert a surreptitious rider, clause, or unintelligible legal phrase that would make his clients millions of dollars.

Neil Volz, an Abramoff staffer and Ney's former chief of staff, once approached Ney to insert a secret bill provision, authored by Abramoff, granting a controversial, but highly lucrative casino license to one of the super lobbyist's Native American clients. The following are excerpts from a *60 Minutes* broadcast on November 6, 2011, with Lesley Stahl interviewing Abramoff and Ney about the carveout:

JA: So what we did was we crafted language that was so obscure, so confusing, so uninformative, but so precise to change the U.S. Code.

LS: Here's what you tried to get tacked on to this reform bill: Public Law 100-89 is amended by striking section 207 (101 stat. 668, 672).

JA: Right. Now isn't that obvious what that means? It was perfect. It was perfect.

LS: So that's what you tried to get inserted?

JA: Yes.

LS: And that was going to provide for a casino?

JA: Yes.

LS: And who on earth is going to know that?

JA: No one except the chairmen of the committees.

LS: Who stuck it in there?

JA: Yes.

LS: And it was deliberately written like that?

JA: Precisely. Yes.

LS: And that's done a lot?

JA: Members don't read the bills.

LS: (to Ney) You didn't even know what it was for?

BN: Had no idea.

LS: Well—why didn't you know what it was for?

BN: I didn't– –I didn't care.

While Abramoff feverishly wrote carveouts akin to traders issuing bid orders on the floor of the New York Stock Exchange, he worked many other scams and had his hands in a lot of pots, as do other high-profile lobbyists. He was a registered foreign lobbyist and used the credential to prey on a number of international firms.

In one of his brasher schemes, Abramoff had planned to burnish his international reputation by representing Naftasib, a Russian oil conglomerate that reportedly supplied oil to the Russian military.[35] His goal was to impress the Russian government so they would hire him to lobby Congress and other U.S. officials on their behalf. Naftasib set up an obscure Dutch firm, Voor Huisen, to funnel money to Abramoff. His ruses involved assisting Voor Huisen to secure U.S. taxpayer dollars to finance private housing in Russia, as well as issues "pertaining to defense and security."[36] To help launder the piles of cash he was accumulating, an Abramoff colleague set up a nonprofit in the United States called the U.S. Family Network, which was supposed to raise funds for evangelical Christian charities. It was, however, another shell operation that funneled money from Russian investors and others to Abramoff.[37]

Perhaps most odious of all was that while Abramoff was helping companies drain the U.S. treasury of taxpayer dollars, he was using his cunning to kill legislation that would bar American companies from receiving federal contracts if they located their offices in foreign countries to avoid paying taxes. Scandal-plagued Tyco, which had relocated its headquarters to the tax haven of Bermuda, a British territory, paid Abramoff over $3.2 million, including $1.5 million to design and run a grassroots campaign attacking the measure's supporters.[38] But the campaign never materialized. Tyco cried foul and sued when it realized that Abramoff had duped them into funneling the cash to a shady nonprofit, Grassroots Interactive, that did nothing but re-route the money to other Abramoff projects.[39]

Although Abramoff was a lifelong high roller and trusted Republican insider, when the feds nabbed him, his friends and beneficiaries scattered like rats in a tenement fire. "Jack who?" they asked in befuddlement. Soon after the scandal broke, the White House moved to contain any fallout by signing a hushed agreement with the Secret Service declaring the White House visitors log off limits to the press and public.[40] You may remember it was the visitors log that revealed Monica Lewinsky's many curious visits to the Oval Office. Undaunted, a House committee pieced together Abramoff's billing records and emails and determined that the super lobbyist made contact with White House officials at least 485 times over a three-year period.[41] Despite repeated statements of innocence, President Bush's longtime political advisor, Karl Rove, and Rove's executive assistant, Susan Ralston, were caught lying about the closeness and frequency of contact they had with the disgraced lobbyist.

Ralston, a former Abramoff employee, had served as an efficient conduit between Rove and Abramoff. She set up meetings between the two men to discuss presidential appointments and Abramoff's business deals. In one email, Ralston schemed with

Abramoff to help him exploit the terrorism threat to American citizens by plotting to help Abramoff "capitalize on the 'rush to get lucrative government contracts' being awarded by the Department of Homeland Security."[42] White House emails also showed Ralston soliciting Abramoff for free gifts, including tickets for the Washington Capitals hockey team, Baltimore Orioles baseball team, and tickets to a Bruce Springsteen show. In 2001, she emailed Abramoff: "Can we get the row A seats for the 12/22 Caps game?"[43] In 2002 she emailed: "Need 4 for O's on 8/23 and 4 for Springsteen if possible."[44] The White House denied any wrongdoing. But when Congress investigated her actions, Ralston stepped down from her post in October 2006.

In March 2007, as Abramoff sat in a minimum-security jail cell in Cumberland, Maryland, on charges of wire fraud to buy a fleet of Florida casino gambling boats, federal prosecutors suspiciously worked to reduce his six-year sentence.[45] Incidentally, the owner of the casino fleet was mysteriously gunned down in a gangland-style hit just after he sold his business to Abramoff and his cohorts. Apparently, the fleet owner believed he was swindled and had sought to regain ownership of his floating casinos. Abramoff, then known as inmate number 27593-112, was further sentenced to four years in prison for his illegal lobbying activities.[46] He served his sentences concurrently and was released from jail in 2010.

Since regaining his freedom, Abramoff has been busy rebuilding his public image. He released a tell-all memoir of his super lobbyist days and embarked on hundreds of TV and radio appearances to promote the book and himself. According to *The New York Times* in 2012, Abramoff was "on the paid speaking circuit, has a Facebook game application, is talking about a reality TV show, and is trying to get back into the movie production business."[47]

In 2017, Abramoff resurfaced as a registered lobbyist representing the Republic of Congo's president, who was seeking a meeting with President Trump.[48]

Only in America.

7

THE REVOLVING DOOR
Mr. Smith Goes to K Street

S O YOU'RE A CLOSE, PERSONAL FRIEND of the president and a
generous donor to his campaigns.

And now it's paid off.

You've been rewarded with a plum government job paying a
healthy six-figure salary. Let's say the job is director of the Federal
Emergency Management Agency (FEMA), even though you're a
lawyer by profession and have scant experience in emergency services. And let's say an unexpected Category 5 hurricane hits a
major city on your watch. But you're unskilled and unprepared
to protect this city and its millions of inhabitants. Not only do you
botch the preparedness planning, but the aftermath as well. You
accomplish this by instituting a disaster relief program with an ex-
traordinarily inept accounting system. It has so many loopholes
that nearly $2 billion is lost to scam artists and ghoulish oppor-
tunists, including 1,100 inmates in Gulf Coast jails, who simply
called into FEMA, lied, and collected an aggregate of more than
$10 million in disaster relief assistance.[1]

And let's say your name is Michael Brown, and you're exposed
as a negligent incompetent in discharging your duties as FEMA
director—and you lose your job.

What do you do?

Become a lobbyist of course!

You set up an office on K Street in Washington where most

lobbying shops are headquartered and work as a consultant on emergency preparedness and disaster relief issues, trading on your high-level government contacts. A *St. Louis Post-Dispatch* editorial commenting on Brown's career change said it best: "After you hire Brownie, you might want to hire Typhoid Mary to help you avoid infectious diseases."[2]

The upshot?

Clients actually lined up to hire Brown. He crowed that he would be making "significantly more" in his new consulting business than his $148,000 FEMA salary.[3] Since his sacking, Brown continues to rake in money, shilling for a slew of special interests, including technology companies that specialize in disaster relief, emergency services, and anti-terrorism and security screening programs. Much of his time is spent lobbying the Department of Homeland Security and his former agency, FEMA.

And what job did Brown have prior to his FEMA stint that prepared him to be its director? He served as an International Arabian Horse Association commissioner for 12 years. He was sacked there, too.

Every year, hundreds of public officials seeking riches spin through the revolving door from public service to lobbying. It seems that if you're well-connected, like Michael Brown, it doesn't matter how bad you've screwed up in the past. In fact, Lobbying World is one of the few places in the universe where disgrace and incompetence can pay off big time.

LIST OF LEADERS-TURNED-LOBBYISTS

IN 2018, THERE WERE 429 former U.S. House and Senate members working as lobbyists in the nation's capital.[4]

There are 535 sitting members of Congress. Does that tell you how strong the money incentive has become in our political system? Here is an abbreviated list of high profile public-servants-turned-lobbyists:

- *Dick Cheney* (R-WY): vice president, 2001-2009
- *Rick Santorum* (R-PA): senator; 2012 and 2016 presidential candidate
- *Christopher Dodd* (D-CT): senator; 2008 presidential candidate
- *Joe Lieberman* (D/I-CT): senator; 2004 presidential candidate; 2000 vice presidential nominee
- *Phil Gramm* (R-TX): senator; 1996 presidential candidate
- *Bob Kerrey* (D-NE): senator; 1992 presidential candidate
- *Dennis Kucinich* (D-OH): congressman; 2004 and 2008 presidential candidate
- *Tom Daschle* (D-SD): Senate majority leader
- *Trent Lott* (R-MS): Senate majority leader
- *George Mitchell* (D-ME): Senate majority leader
- *Tom DeLay* (R-TX): House majority leader, indicted on criminal charges of conspiracy to violate election law, later acquitted
- *John Ashcroft* (R-MO): senator; U.S. attorney general for President George W. Bush
- *William S. Cohen* (R-ME): senator; secretary of defense for President Bill Clinton
- *Robert Torricelli* (D-NJ): senator (resigned after scandal for accepting illegal campaign donations)
- *Larry Craig* (R-ID): senator (arrested in 2007, for propositioning a male undercover police officer in a Minneapolis-St. Paul International Airport restroom)
- *Bob Packwood* (R-OR): senator (resigned in 1995 after years of sexually harassing female members of his staff and female lobbyists and writing about it in his diary)
- *Tom Foley* (D-WA): House Speaker
- *Newt Gingrich* (R-GA): House Speaker; 2012 presidential candidate
- *Dennis Hastert* (R-IL): House Speaker (sentenced on April 27, 2016, to 15 months in jail for child molestation)
- *Richard Gephardt* (D-MO): House minority leader; 1988 and 2004 presidential candidate

- *Dick Armey* (R-TX): House majority leader
- *Norman Mineta* (D-CA): congressman; former secretary of transportation; former secretary of commerce
- *John Doolittle* (R-CA): congressman; (did not seek re-election in 2008 after entanglement in Jack Abramoff scandal; no charges were filed against him)
- *Anthony Weiner* (D-NY): congressman; resigned after pleading guilty to sexting (texting) obscene material to a minor; now a registered sex offender
- *Patricia Schroeder* (D-CO): congresswoman
- *Joe Walsh* (R-IL): congressman
- *Allen West* (R-FL): congressman
- *Joseph McDade* (R-PA): congressman; Appropriations Committee vice chairman

The last politician on this list, former Congressman Joe McDade, is an interesting case. Perhaps, the most "overexposed" congressman in history, this former high-level Republican beat a raft of federal bribery charges while in office only to be caught years later with his pants down putting on a little show at a posh island resort in Florida.

McDade, elected in 1962, served 36 years in the House, rising to vice chairman of the Appropriations Committee. He also chaired several Appropriations subcommittees. McDade endured an eight-year federal investigation into charges he accepted bribes, mostly from United Chem-Con Corp., a defense contractor McDade persuaded to relocate to his Pennsylvania district. The illegal gifts included: "$10,250 in 'sham campaign contributions' from United Chem-Con and its employees; numerous trips on United Chem-Con's jet; a Masters Golf Tournament jacket; an all-expenses-paid trip to Jamaica in 1985; and a free vacation at United Chem-Con's beachfront condo in Delaware."[5] The case against McDade hinged on a deal he reportedly made with Chem-Con president James Christian in March 1983 to exchange campaign contributions and gifts for McDade's help securing lucrative

Navy contracts for the company.

On August 1, 1996, McDade beat the rap. Days later, supporters threw him a lavish poolside party at the San Diego Hilton Beach & Tennis Resort in Mission Bay, California—3,000 miles away from his district and constituents. Companies, politicians, and power brokers lined up to sponsor the event, including: QVC Network, Rockwell International, General Dynamics, TRW, Union Pacific, Michael Baker Corp., Frank Fitzpatrick, Martin G. Hamberger, Plato Marinakos, Tenneco, GDE Systems, Tracor Inc., and U.S. Rep. Curt Weldon (R-PA)."[6]

McDade retired from Congress in 1998 and kept a low profile as a lobbyist until 2007, when the 75-year-old was charged with indecent exposure in Sanibel, a resort island near Fort Myers, Florida. Witnesses said the former pol openly masturbated 10 to 15 feet away from several female guests as they lounged near a hotel pool. That same day, McDade was spotted pleasuring himself on a nearby beach in front of a married couple. The woman told police that when she got up from her beach chair, McDade "followed her to a boardwalk that leads to the hotel and masturbated while he watched her wash her feet under a shower."[7]

In 2008, a Florida judge declared McDade incompetent to stand trial for the offenses. His attorney convinced the court that McDade's Parkinson's disease medication caused him to act out sexually and erase any memory of the incidents. The drug's side effects, though, didn't seem to affect McDade's ability throughout this sordid episode to function as chairman of Ervin Technical Associates, a high-powered Washington lobbying firm. For years, McDade continued to pull down a salary exponentially higher than his congressional pay, until he died in 2017.

THE POWELL MEMO

FOR YEARS, THE REVOLVING DOOR between Capitol Hill and K Street has been accelerating at warp speed.

Lobbying has become so lucrative that election to the Senate or House—or any state legislature for that matter—is now seen by many as a mere stepping-stone to accruing riches as a lobbyist.

Robert L. Livingston, a former Republican congressman from Louisiana, House Speaker designate, and subsequent founder of the Washington lobbying firm, The Livingston Group, summed up the situation: "Companies need lobbying help (from former congressmen and senators). There's unlimited business out there for us."[8]

It has not always been the case.

In 1974, about 3 percent of members leaving Congress became corporate lobbyists. Today, it's jumped to about 50 percent of senators and 42 percent of representatives.[9]

Congressional historians say the revolving-door trend took off in the 1980s. Before that time, most members of Congress looked down their noses at K Street and former colleagues who joined lobbying's ranks. The genesis of the trend, however, began in 1971 with a memorandum written by Lewis Powell, an obscure Virginia corporate lawyer and future Supreme Court justice. Powell tapped into the groundswell of corporate resentment against the 1960s' wave of liberal regulation of industries. He convinced Big Business to switch gears from playing defense— batting away environmental, consumer protection, and other regulations, to playing offense—writing and pushing deregulation bills and viewing Congress and the budget as a fertile profit center. The memo galvanized America's business titans.

The U.S. Chamber of Commerce's top brass had approached Powell to write the memo, seeking direction on how to stem its string of legislative losses.

Powell titled his memo: "Attack on American Free Enterprise System."

It was a passionate call-to-arms, dripping with militaristic terms—a fiery, free-wheeling, highly political, shot across the bow to the "sources of the attack" against the free enterprise system. The memo culminated in a Machiavellian-like plan of guerilla warfare, neutralizing the enemy's legislative successes and energizing Chamber members and other business interests to win the lobbying war in the halls of government. Powell lamented that the "American business executive is truly the 'forgotten man.'"[10]

The Powell Memo eerily reads like a paranoid manifesto suited to any number of extreme right-wing entities and ideologues today, including Fox News, Breitbart, the Mercers, the Koch brothers, Steve Bannon, and radio and web show hosts. Powell describes the enemy, or "sources of the attack," against capitalism:

> The sources are varied and diffused. They include, not unexpectedly, the Communists, New Leftists and other revolutionaries who would destroy the entire system, both political and economic. These extremists of the left are far more numerous, better financed, and increasingly are more welcomed and encouraged by other elements of society, than ever before in our history. . . . The most disquieting voices joining the chorus of criticism come from perfectly respectable elements of society: from the college campus, the pulpit, the media, the intellectual and literary journals, the arts and sciences, and from politicians.[11]

In another passage that resonates today, Powell cited a poll of 12 college campuses that showed "almost half the students favored socialization of basic U.S. industries."[12]

After taking a few pot shots at perceived enemies, including consumer activist Ralph Nader, whom Powell described as the "single most effective antagonist of American business," he urged Big Business to fight back.[13] Powell bemoaned business leaders' timid support of Congress's tax breaks and loopholes that benefitted large industries. By responses of "appeasement, ineptitude and ignoring the problem," Powell wrote, business allowed liberal politicians to portray such corporate benefits as class warfare—political corruption by the rich exploiting the poor.[14]

Powell then envisioned the Chamber as the leading force and

emboldened it to unify business interests under its roof and plan and execute far-reaching strategies to wrest power away from common enemies:

> In all fairness, it must be recognized that businessmen have not been trained or equipped to conduct guerilla warfare with those who propagandize against the system, seeking to insidiously and constantly to sabotage it. . . . But independent and uncoordinated activity by individual corporations, as important as this is, will not be sufficient. Strength lies in organization, in careful long-range planning and implementation, in consistency of action over an indefinite period of years, in the scale of financing available only through joint effort, and in the political power available only through united action and national organizations. . . . The role of the National Chamber of Commerce is therefore vital.[15]

Powell finishes by laying out an expansive plan to permeate every corner of American culture in a vertical organization structure, putting a stranglehold on American politics: newspapers, radio, television, books, liberal arts education, business schools, speakers bureaus, marketing, publishing, scholarly journals, books. It reads like a blueprint of the Koch brothers' Kochtopus.

The Chamber, armed with the Powell Memo's game plan, saw its fortunes rise dramatically with the 1980 election of Ronald Reagan. The former California Governor and Hollywood actor ushered in the ascendancy of anti-government, business-friendly conservatism. Reagan flipped the script, extolling business and denigrating government. He sent a signal throughout Washington that corporate lobbying was now considered honorable (not to mention, profitable) and should be encouraged. The White House and congressional Republicans put out the welcome mat for influence peddlers. It was a dream come true for lobbying firms. They swiftly opened the spigots and flooded former members of Congress and their aides with job offers at whopping salaries.

The melding of government and lobbying reached its apex between 1995 and 2006 when Republicans controlled both houses
of Congress for the first time in 40 years. Anti-tax activist Grover
Norquist and House Majority Whip Tom DeLay (R-TX) crafted
an idea they thought would keep the Republicans in power indef-
initely. They dubbed the infamous scheme the "K Street Project."

After so many years of Democratic rule, Norquist and DeLay
chafed that lobbying firms were top heavy with Democrats. It
needed to change, and fast. The scheme's basic idea involved bul-
lying these firms, mostly located on K Street, to fill top lobbying
jobs with high-level congressional staffers, fiercely loyal to the
Republican Party and its cause. Senator Rick Santorum (R-PA)
and DeLay threatened the firms with restricted access to leadership offices if they did not comply. But DeLay pursued a larger
plan than just lobbying parity with Democrats. He envisioned the
Republican Party co-opting the entire corporate lobbying industry into an overwhelming, seamless political power base fueled by
unlimited special interest money. If successful, Republicans could
steamroll their conservative agenda through Congress for years to
come. Santorum teamed with DeLay to push the project in the
upper house. Santorum chaired twice-monthly meetings in a Capitol Hill conference room with a handpicked group of about two
dozen Republican lobbyists and a smattering of Republican senators.[16] The meetings, off limits to Democrats and the press, added
a member of President George W. Bush's staff in 2001.

Jack Abramoff's influence peddling shop, by the way, became
a prime landing spot for these budding Republican aides-turned-
lobbyists, particularly DeLay staffers. In 2005, DeLay resigned
from office after being indicted for violating Texas election laws
in 2002.

No problem.

While fighting his case, DeLay founded a Washington lobbying firm, First Principles, LLC. In 2011, a Texas state judge sentenced him to three years in prison for illegally funneling corpor-

ate political donations to Texas legislative candidates. Two years later, DeLay successfully appealed the decision.

In 2006, Pennsylvania voters tired of Santorum and tossed him out of office.

No problem.

Santorum immediately found employment as a lobbyist. He later ran unsuccessfully for president in 2012 and 2016.

Conservatives mothballed the K Street Project.

Although Santorum disavowed his role in the scheme when running for president, Norquist seemed proud to have created it, even attempting to trademark the name "K Street Project."[17]

In retrospect, DeLay's power grab was an updated version of Mayor Daley's Chicago Machine or Boss Tweed's Tammany Hall—but on a national scale.

One would be hard-pressed to find a more influential memorandum than the Powell Memo that still reverberates today throughout our politics.

SHAMELESS
Cashing In on Homeland Security

THERE ARE FEW (IF ANY) ISSUES more important to the nation's citizens since 9/11 than national security. Our collective consciousness was changed instantly and forever by those heinous attacks.

In response, the government created the Department of Homeland Security (DHS) to tackle the sacred mission of restoring confidence and a sense of security to the American public. But the DHS was hastily organized. It was burdened with a bulky management structure and an unclear mission as to how it would function with other law enforcement agencies like the Federal Bureau of Investigation (FBI) and the Central Intelligence Agency (CIA).

Since its inception, mismanagement within DHS abounds. Billions of dollars have been squandered on deceitful and incompetent private contractors. Sloppy DHS accounting practices have wasted billions more. In fact, the tens of billions of dollars Congress continues to pour into DHS remain a vulnerable target for wily profiteers and scam artists.

And who would know how best to exploit the department's weaknesses for profit? Former DHS managers, of course.

Within five years after its creation, 90 DHS officials, including two thirds of its top managers, followed the agency's first secretary, Tom Ridge, a former Pennsylvania Republican governor and congressman, through the revolving door to lobby their former employer, DHS, on behalf of defense companies.[18]

Their new employers paid them exorbitant salaries beyond government pay scales because they knew these former DHS officials—through their institutional expertise and access to former DHS colleagues—could readily direct billions of dollars in government contracts their way. Even lower-rung managers cashed in. Carol DiBattiste, a deputy administrator in the department, saw her income jump from $155,000 to nearly $1 million when she joined ChoicePoint, a database contractor lobbying DHS.[19]

Worse, these former DHS managers even re-wrote the department's rules, while still with the agency, to transition more easily to lobbying. They did it to circumvent the federal "cooling-off period" that bans former government workers from lobbying their former agencies within one year of leaving their jobs. They accomplished this by getting the Office of Government Ethics to approve the splintering of DHS into seven different segments.[20] The one-year ban only applied to DHS employees-turned influence peddlers seeking to lobby the same segment in which they had worked. Michael J. Petrucelli, the agency's acting director of citizenship and immigration, for example, began lobbying within months after leaving his post. His new employer, GridPoint, sold its products to the Coast Guard. Petrucelli was able to lobby DHS before the cooling-off period expired because the Coast Guard had been placed in a different DHS segment than his former division of citizenship and immigration. The obvious problem, however, is that the "segment" policy is nearly impossible to enforce because there is overlap among the agency's many different offices.

Would this lobbying exemption pass the smell test for anyone living outside the nation's capital? Clark Kent Ervin, a former DHS inspector general who left the agency to join a nonpartisan think tank, said of DHS's revolving door: "People have a right to make a living," he said. "But working virtually immediately for a company that is bidding for work in an area where you were just setting the policy—that is too close. It is almost incestuous."[21]

SHILLING FOR FOREIGN CLIENTS

FOREIGN SPECIAL INTERESTS hiring former U.S. officials to lobby for them is a recurring, common thread in the modern tapestry of Washington influence peddling.

As previously noted, British-owned BP spent $32 million to hire a small army of former U.S. government officials as lobbyists to gain approval for BP's ill-fated Macondo oil well project. These shills were a mélange of the Republican-Democratic party elite.

BP's lobbying troops included:

- *Ken Duberstein*: President Reagan's chief of staff
- *Jim Turner*: Democratic Texas congressman
- *Mike Berman*: Carter administration official
- *Eric Ueland*: former Republican Senate Majority Leader Bill Frist's chief of staff
- *Tony Podesta*: brother of John Podesta, who served as President Clinton's chief of staff and advisor to President Obama
- *Daniel Meyer*: President George W. Bush's legal aide
- *Michael LaRocco*: Interior Department official
- *David Marin*: House Oversight and Government Reform Committee (under Republican control) investigator
- *Various Capitol Hill staffers*: aides to former Senators Mary Landrieu (D-LA) and John Breaux (R-LA), and former Congressman Jim McCrery (R-LA) [22]

Indeed, there are many high-profile U.S. leaders who have lobbied Congress and administration officials on behalf of foreign governments and business interests.

Former Senator Bob Dole (R-KS), the 1996 presidential nominee and 1976 vice presidential nominee, lobbied for several Chinese firms.

The late Senator Fred Thompson (R-TN), a 2008 presidential candidate, lobbied for a number of foreign interests, including the deposed government of Haiti.

Richard Gephardt (D-MO), a former House minority leader and presidential candidate in 1988 and 2004, founded his own lobbying firm soon after leaving office. In January 2010, Gephardt proudly trumpeted the signing of a new client, Georgia, formerly a Soviet Union republic, that paid $430,000 to retain the firm. After landing the contract, the Gephardt Government Affairs posted on its website: "Gephardt's ties to Democrats and the Obama administration could be helpful to the Georgian government, which wants U.S. support for its effort to join NATO and U.S. support against Russia."

Gephardt earned millions of dollars over the years representing Taiwan, South Korea, El Salvador, and Turkey. It seemed his only allegiance was to money. As a congressman in 2003, Gephardt co-sponsored a bill requiring the U.S. to recognize the Armenian Genocide, in which the Turkish government slaughtered about 1.5 million people between 1915 and 1917. Gephardt passionately fought for the measure year after year in Congress. But in 2015, nearing the 100-year anniversary of the mass killing, *lobbyist* Gephardt, with Turkey's $8 million lobbying fee tucked in his suit pocket, worked to defeat the same measure he championed for years as a congressman.[23] According to the *St. Louis Post-Dispatch*: "Records at the Justice Department show scores of Gephardt meetings, email exchanges, arranged visits on Capitol Hill with Turkish diplomats and contacts with the highest officials of the Obama administration, including former Secretary of State Hillary Clinton."[24] Many were furious at Gephardt's sellout. "It really impairs having credibility on human rights issues when we pick and choose the genocides we recognize," said U.S. Rep. Adam Schiff (D-CA).[25]

There are many other former U.S. leaders with lower profiles who shill for foreign governments. Some of them are backbenchers who never attracted the large special interest dollars while in office, but quickly scooped up the big lobbying bucks once they left. The story of Tommy Robinson (R-AR), a former low-level congressman, is a common narrative.

Robinson forged an interesting path from sheriff of Arkansas' Pulaski County in the mid-1980s, to congressman in the late 1980s and early 1990s, to liquor store owner in the mid-1990s, to lobbyist in 2006 for the Democratic Republic of the Congo.[26] The former congressman works mostly on oil deals for his clients.

Interesting transition—liquor store owner to foreign lobbyist.

Folks, if it's this easy for former public servants like Robinson to get rich selling out America to foreign interests, then you know the system is rotten to the core.

Most average Americans would be shocked to learn how many foreign nations hire Washington lobbyists to manipulate Congress and the White House. These foreign interests often abscond with gobs of taxpayer dollars that would otherwise be spent on Americans.

In 2007, for example, a group of Iraqi clients spent nearly $17 million hiring 18 Washington lobbyists to press their agenda, mostly seeking government funds.[27]

In 2013, Iraq's post-Saddam Hussein government officially hired its first Washington lobbying firm, the Podesta Group, headed by BP lobbyist Tony Podesta, mentioned earlier, to fish for money and favors.[28]

Even factions *within* Iraq have their own Washington lobbyists. The regional government of Kurdistan in northern Iraq retains five Washington lobbying firms to push its interests. In May 2016, their lobbyists secured $415 million in U.S. taxpayer dollars to arm and equip the Kurds' Peshmerga militia force.[29] In January

2016, a coalition of Iraqi Sunni exiles opened a Washington lobbying office to fish for American taxpayer largesse.[30] A month
later, a former governor of Iraq's northern Nineveh province paid
$90,000 to retain a Washington lobbyist, seeking U.S. taxpayer
funds to prop up his 4,000-strong military force outside of Mo-
sul.[31]

There are many more countries, and factions within those
countries, buying lobbyist representation in our nation's capital.

Why?

Because most everything is up for sale in the United States political system—and they know it.

LIKE FATHER, LIKE SON

ANN EPPARD had impeccable timing.

The day after the Republicans ended Democrats' 40-year rule
in Congress in the 1994 election, Eppard left her job as chief of
staff for U.S. Rep. Bud Shuster (R-PA) to open Ann Eppard Associated, Ltd., her own Washington lobbying firm. Days later,
Congressman Shuster was named chairman of the House Transportation and Infrastructure Committee, a post notorious for doling out billions in pork barrel projects involving highways,
bridges, tunnels, overpasses, airports, railroads, and riverways.
During her 22 years in Shuster's employ, Eppard became his close
friend and confidante. It was a fact that did not escape transportation companies, which threw millions of dollars at her feet to do
their bidding on Capitol Hill.

House rules actually barred Eppard from lobbying Shuster directly for one year, but she could still lobby his aides and committee staff in the interim—workers she supervised for years.
Within no time, she signed up major clients, including Federal
Express, Union Pacific, and the Outdoor Advertising Association
of America.[32]

While Eppard lobbied the Transportation Committee, she

kept her paying job as Shuster's political fundraiser and her non-paying job as his political advisor. The arrangement raised many eyebrows in Congress. Although Shuster had run unopposed since his 1984 victory, Eppard continued to rake in hundreds of thousands of dollars for his campaign coffer. Shuster spent a good chunk of the campaign money on wining, dining, and other questionable personal expenses.

To congressional observers, Eppard and Shuster were so intertwined, it was hard to tell where one began and the other ended. According to *Time* magazine, Eppard's influence with Shuster regularly spilled over into his official duties: "At a conference committee on highway legislation last fall (1995), Shuster rankled some in the Senate by tying up talks for weeks with his demands to loosen the federal restriction that keeps billboards off scenic roadways. The billboard industry was both an Eppard client and leading Shuster contributor."[33]

For several years, both Eppard and Shuster were thriving in their new jobs. Eppard's client list grew, adding Amtrak, Contrail, The Pennsylvania Turnpike Commission, and Metropolitan Washington Airports Authority to her portfolio. And as Eppard's bank account swelled, Shuster's power and campaign coffer grew accordingly.

But by 1998, the wheels started to come off.

The U.S. Attorney in Boston, Donald Stern, launched an investigation of Eppard stemming from her days as Shuster's aide overseeing Boston's Big Dig, the nation's most expensive transportation project at the time. Stern charged Eppard with accepting $230,000 in bribes from a lobbyist representing two Boston businessmen seeking to keep their land from an eminent domain taking for the project.[34] Stern also accused Eppard of stealing $27,500 from Shuster's campaign account.

In 2000, the House ethics committee charged Shuster with "serious official misconduct," stemming from his relationship with Eppard. Shuster narrowly escaped a House censure, receiving a mild rebuke instead. The ethics committee slapped him with a "letter of reproval," for allowing Eppard to remain his paid fundraiser while she lobbied him and his committee. Other charges included: accepting illegal gifts from Eppard clients, spending campaign funds for personal use, and directing some of his staffers to work on his re-election campaigns while on the government clock.

Stern accepted Eppard's guilty plea to one charge of taking bribes, and she quickly resumed her lobbying career. Shuster resigned from Congress in January 2001 to work as a transportation lobbyist. In a fitting end to their legacy of government service, Eppard threw Shuster a party—a "fare-well salute" honoring him for his public service. The lavish party was predictably paid for by transportation lobbyists and their clients.[35]

And who took over Shuster's vacated congressional seat?

His son, Bill Shuster.

And what panel was the younger Shuster (R-PA) immediately assigned to?

The Transportation and Infrastructure Committee.

It didn't take him long to find trouble.

In 2010, House Minority Leader John Boehner (R-OH) chastised the married, younger Shuster for regularly partying with female lobbyists. In 2013, Boehner believed Shuster had mended his ways and appointed him to committee chair, formerly held by Shuster's father.

Several years later after divorcing his wife, the younger Shuster began dating lobbyist Shelley Rubino, a vice president for Airlines for America (A4A), the country's largest airline trade group, representing virtually every major airline and cargo carrier in the nation. It's no small coincidence that Shuster's committee oversees nearly every facet of the $160 billion airline industry. Shuster also became close, personal friends with Rubino's boss, Nick Calio, president and CEO of A4A. Calio had also been a close, personal friend of Shuster's father, when the elder Shuster ran the transportation committee.

Soon, the transportation priorities of the younger Shuster merged and aligned with those of A4A.

In 2016, Calio pushed hard for a bill that would restructure the Federal Aviation Administration, effectively giving the airlines control over the nation's air traffic control system. Calio appeared before Shuster's committee, testifying in support of the bill. Two days later, the committee passed it. A week later, Shuster, Rubino, and Calio slipped out of town, escaping to a posh Miami hotel to celebrate their victory. Other Washington denizens, in Miami for a fundraiser, spotted the three lounging poolside and dining together in fancy restaurants.[36] The bill eventually died in Congress.

Shuster steadfastly proclaimed his innocence of any corruption or impropriety. His relationship with Rubino, indeed, did not run afoul of the House Ethics Manual—which is, of course, a poor reflection on the House Ethics Manual. Besides his relationships with Rubino and Calio, Shuster appointed an A4A vice president to serve as staff director for the transportation committee's subcommittee on aviation and hired the husband of a senior A4A vice president as his personal chief of staff.[37]

In 2018, Shuster declared he would not stand for re-election, blaming the "liberal media" for the conflict-of-interest scandal that dogged him.

What are the chances he landed on his feet as a well-paid lobbyist, as father did when he left the chairmanship?

Shockingly, in 2019, he became a lobbyist, joining Squire Patton Boggs, one of Washington's largest firms.

Call this the intergenerational revolving door.

HEY DAD, CAN YOU INSERT AN EARMARK FOR ME?

LOBBYING IS SO LUCRATIVE that it seems anyone related to current or former members of Congress can cash in with a choice influence-peddling gig.

Wives, husbands, brothers, sons, daughters, in-laws, nieces and nephews—all have easy access to members of Congress. It's why special interests court them with oversized salaries.

Chet Lott, son of former Senate majority leader Trent Lott (R-MS), lobbied for BellSouth, which racked up a string of profitable legislative victories while his dad ran the Senate in the 1990s. Chet's prior experience? He ran several pizza franchises and played polo.[38]

Former Senate majority leader Harry Reid (D-NV) has four sons and a son-in-law who have worked as lobbyists. In 2002, Reid helped pass legislation to open "tens of thousands of acres of federal land for private development," which turned out to be highly profitable to his sons' clients.[39]

Reid and Lott weren't the only high-ranking politicians holding office while their children lobbied Congress. Senator Orrin Hatch (R-UT), former Senator John Breaux (D-LA), former House Speaker Dennis Hastert (R-IL), and former Congressman Billy Tauzin (R-LA) all held office while their sons lobbied Congress on sensitive, high-stakes corporate issues. And yes, Breaux, Hastert, and Tauzin all spun through the revolving door as soon as they left office, becoming high-paid Washington lobbyists. In 2016, a federal judge sentenced Hastert to 15 months in prison for fraudulently laundering hush payments to one of four male students he sexually molested as a high school teacher and wrestling coach. Hastert promised to pay $3.5 million for his former student's silence—a sum he could never have afforded on a congressman's or Speaker's salary.

Senator Roy Blunt (R-MO) is another pol who likes to keep it all in the family. Abigail Perlman, Blunt's girlfriend, worked as a lobbyist for the tobacco giant Phillip Morris in 2003. In the waning hours of debate on the measure that would create the Department of Homeland Security, Blunt, then the third-highest ranking GOP House member, quietly inserted a provision that would make millions for his girlfriend's client.[40] Turns out the tobacco giant was not only a generous donor to Blunt's re-election campaigns, but was also the employer of Andrew Blunt, the congressman's son. The provision was pulled before the bill passed.

In 2007, Congress passed some restrictions on family lobbying, but the rules were not consistent in both chambers. For example, the House banned spouses from directly lobbying their husbands and wives, but the Senate did not. As you can guess, the restrictions were full of loopholes and were virtually meaningless.

In 2012, *The Washington Post* conducted a study of congressional campaign disclosure forms since the 2007 lobbying restrictions passed. The newspaper found more than 500 companies had spent about $400 million on Washington lobbying teams that included at least one member who was related to a sitting member of Congress. The newspaper identified 56 family-member lobbyists. Further, 48 of those family members became lobbyists *after* their relatives had been elected to Congress.[41]

Surely there are many more of these curious "all-in-the-family" politician-lobbyist sagas today running through the nation's capital than the *Post* study revealed. Much of this activity is difficult to detect and routinely conducted on the down low.

So, are these people corrupt?

Perhaps.

And do these relationships and interactions corrupt the system?

They don't help.

But what is definitely known is that they create the appearance of corruption. And how can average Americans trust their government when such activity is openly accepted in the halls of Congress?

A *St. Petersburg Times* editorial observed: "This may be the way Washington works (family members lobbying Congress), but it still smells to high heaven. Lobbyists have a place in our democratic system of government, but this 'all in the family' approach is unacceptable. It should be illegal."[42]

Americans should demand action against this shady practice

that occurs in our nation's capital and state governments as well. It's unhealthy for our democracy and should be banned. Our supposed leaders should know better.

Corrective action should include a lifetime ban on lawmakers becoming lobbyists. And all immediate family of sitting lawmakers should be banned from lobbying the legislative and executive branches for the duration of the Congress member's service and at least five years thereafter.

No exceptions.

America does not need a constitutional amendment to accomplish this.

Congress could do it in a day, if it wanted.

PIGS, NOT PATRIOTS

SURE, LOBBYISTS are needed. But it paints a sad portrait of our so-called leaders who are so quick to cash in on their public service to our country.

The Founding Fathers, after all, envisioned a government of *citizen* presidents and legislators who would return to their roots back home and use their status and knowledge to better their communities—not hang around the capital's trough looking for a quick buck and a swanky lifestyle.

8

COST OF UNLIMITED SPENDING

"Elections are more often bought than won." [1]

~LEE HAMILTON (D-IN)

L
EE HAMILTON IS A RARITY in American politics.
For 34 years the Indiana congressman toiled in the fetid
waters of our nation's capital, managing to keep his reputation intact. He rose through the Democratic ranks to chair the House Committee on Foreign Affairs and several other top posts.

Through it all, Hamilton earned high marks for his integrity, intellect, and ability to work with colleagues across the aisle.

When he retired in 1999, his penchant for putting country before politics made him a logical choice to help lead bipartisan national commissions formed to investigate highly sensitive matters, including the 9/11 Commission, the Commission to Investigate Certain Security Issues at Los Alamos, and the Iraq Study Group that President Bush convened to examine America's Iraq War strategy.

Reflecting on his years in Congress, Hamilton said the largest change he observed in the institution was the increasing hunger his colleagues exhibited for campaign cash:

> The money factor has just become overwhelming in American politics. For any large race, it's a very dominant factor. My colleagues talk about money constantly. The conversation today among members of Congress is so frequently on the topic of money—money,

money, money, and the money chase. Gosh, I don't think I ever heard it when I first came here.[2]

CONSEQUENCES OF THE MONEY CHASE

UNLIMITED CAMPAIGN SPENDING is a bottomless pit.

There's always that next dollar to raise and next donor to schmooze. Drop the dollars into the campaign chest and watch them disappear into the abyss. Now get out there again and raise some more.

It all begs the question: Is there too much money in politics?

This inquiry naturally spurs further questions: Do politicians spend too much time raising money? Does the never-ending cycle of fundraising affect a lawmaker's job performance? Does this perpetual fundraising hurt constituents and the nation as a whole?

These are subjective questions that are difficult, if not impossible, to answer with statistical data. So, it would make sense to consult the lawmakers themselves for the answers. After all, they've labored for years at the intersection of money and politics and have pretty much seen it all. Naturally, they would have some of the best anecdotal evidence to address these questions.

U.S. Rep. Steve Israel (D-NY) retired from Congress in 2017. Before stepping down, Israel wrote a *New York Times* piece, saying he was relieved he would no longer have to beg wealthy special interests for money. After winning his seat in 2000, Israel was immediately initiated into the money chase. Wide-eyed and eager to soak in the institution's history, Israel attended several orientation sessions in Washington, hoping to hear and absorb the wisdom of House predecessors like Abraham Lincoln, John Quincy Adams, and Daniel Webster.[3] Instead, he was taught the number one lesson of his new job: how to get re-elected.

He was crushed.

"A fundraising consultant advised me that if I didn't raise at least $10,000 a week, I wouldn't be back," Israel said.[4]

He heeded the advice.

Throughout his career, Israel attended a blur of fancy cocktail parties and PAC fundraisers, which he described as "panhandling with hors d'oeuvres." He sat in a cramped cubicle off Capitol Hill and dialed for dollars for hours on end. "I'd sit next to an assistant who collated 'call sheets' with donors' names, contribution histories, and other useful information. ('How's Sheila? Your wife. Oh, Shelly? Sorry.')"[5] Israel became so adept at attracting money that party leaders elevated him to the Democratic Congressional Campaign Committee chair, a coveted leadership post for the party's best rainmakers. He was soon crisscrossing the country, frantically shaking down wealthy donors to counteract strategic Republican media buys in contested races. Israel reflected on his time as one of the ultimate insiders in our political system, saying, ". . . as the bidding grows higher, (the average American's) voice gets lower. You're simply priced out of the marketplace of ideas. That is unless you are one of the ultra-wealthy."[6]

In 2003, first-term U.S. Rep. Brad Miller (D-NC) snagged a coveted seat on the Financial Services Committee, a powerful panel that oversees the financial industry. It is a highly sought-after assignment, yielding some of the biggest corporate campaign checks written to members. It is known to Washington insiders as the "cash committee." Since 1980, House leaders have added 17 seats to the committee, accommodating members' high demand to serve on it. The panel now boasts 61 members. The increase necessitated the rearrangement of the committee room, with the installation of four tiered rows of member seats.[7] Months after retiring, Miller reflected on the institution's dash for cash. "Freshmen are pushed and pushed and pushed to raise money," Miller said. "It's how they are judged by the leadership and the political establishment in Washington." He added, "It's only natural that it has got to be on your mind that a vote one way or the other is going to affect the ability to raise money."[8]

Many members appointed to the Financial Services Committee have little knowledge of Wall Street and its inner workings.

In 2013, freshman U.S. Rep. Andy Barr (R-KY) won appointment to the committee even though he had no business experience, no business degree, and little if any knowledge of financial markets. Yet within six months, Barr pulled down as much campaign cash—nearly all of it from big banks and insurance giants—than even his party's leaders. In April 2013, Barr invited bank executives and their lobbyists to his House office, pledging to fight for them to maintain a $500 million industry tax break.[9] He also filed legislation blocking government regulators seeking to prevent banks from issuing predatory mortgages to low-income customers unlikely to meet repayment schedules.[10] In fact, Barr seemingly worked overtime for every financial sector special interest who wrote him a big check.

It's not surprising that Republicans and Democrats alike on the so-called cash committee joined together, helping Wall Street bankers roll back provisions of the Wall Street Reform and Consumer Protection Act, also known as Dodd-Frank. After all, bankers' Super PACs are among Washington's most generous.

For politicians, raising campaign cash from special interests is not only degrading, it's time-consuming. A member of Congress usually spends 80 percent or more of his or her time in office raising campaign funds.

Senator Evan Bayh (D-IN) decided in 2010 to retire rather than run around the country one more time begging the rich for money. "It's miserable," Bayh said of the experience. In a *Washington Post* interview, Bayh recounted:

> It is not uncommon to have a fundraiser for breakfast, for lunch, and for dinner, and if you have spare time in between, you go to an office off Capitol Hill, and you dial for dollars. Then the weekend rolls around, and you get on a plane and travel the countryside with a tin cup in your hand. And it gets worse each cycle. . . . You want to be engaged in an honorable line of work, but (citizens) look at us like we're worse than used-car salesmen. . . . When candidates for public office are spending 90 percent of their time raising money, that's

time they're not spending with constituents or with public policy experts." [11]

Senator Alan Simpson (R-WY), the cagey, three-term former member of the upper house, wrote a 2006 column decrying the time politicians waste chasing campaign dollars:

> When we were spending so much time raising money, we simply could not devote quality time to thoughtful decisions and debate. It lowered the substance of our work. I liked to feel that I was always doing the best job possible—but I also know well that if I had spent less time fundraising, I could have spent more time learning the ropes about vital legislation. Given the inflated and excessive cost of campaigns, many of us couldn't raise the full chunk for the campaign in our own states. So off we would go to New York, Illinois, Texas, or California for our fundraisers. Even if you might think fundraising to be a fine use of a legislator's time, it's pretty hard to see how raising a bundle 2,000 miles from home actually helps your constituents too much. Don't read me wrong. It's not that I think all fundraising is bad. I've had to raise hundreds of thousands of dollars in my political career. The important ability to persuade the voters to provide you with financial assistance is a sure sign that a candidate has their support. But it shouldn't be the only sign, and it shouldn't take up so much time. [12]

When Senator Wendell H. Ford (D-KY) decided against a 1998 re-election run for a fifth term, the outspoken assistant minority leader didn't hold back his distaste for the increasing role of money in politics:

> The job of being a U.S. senator today has unfortunately become a job of raising money to be re-elected instead of a job of doing the people's business. . . . I do not relish, in fact, I detest the idea of having to raise $5 million for a job that pays $133,000 a year. Because of the political money chase, Washington, D.C., is fast becoming the center of our lives, not our people back home. Democracy as we know it will be lost if we continue to allow government

to become one bought by the highest bidder, for the highest bidder. Candidates will simply become bit players and pawns in a campaign managed and manipulated by paid consultants and hired guns.[13]

Senator Ernest Hollings (D-SC) in 1999 submitted a Congressional Record entry supporting Senate Joint Resolution 6, a constitutional amendment proposal requiring campaign spending limits for federal candidates. In the entry, he bemoaned the increasing importance of campaign money, its effect on his colleagues, and the toll it was taking on political decorum:

> I remember Senator Richard Russell used to say, 'They give you a six-year term in this U.S. Senate: two years to be a statesman, the next two years to be a politician, and the last two years to be a demagogue.' Regrettably, we are no longer afforded even two years as a statesman. We proceed straight to demagoguery after an election because of the imperatives of raising money.[14]

In 2011, as House Tea Party leader Michele Bachmann (R-MN) rose in the presidential polls, she told *Newsmax* magazine:

> I think . . . because of the corrupt paradigm that has become Washington, D.C. . . . votes continually are bought rather than representatives voting the will of their constituents . . . . That's the voice that's been missing at the table in Washington, D.C.—the people's voice has been missing. The lobbyists have been here. [15]

And then, there was Senator Robert C. Byrd (D-WV). During the 1997 Senate debate on campaign finance reform, Byrd ambled up to the microphone in the near empty chamber and shouted to those who would listen: "Money! It is money! Money! Money! Not ideas, nor principles, but money that reigns supreme in American politics." [16]

And who knew better than Byrd?

Elected in 1958, he served more years in the Senate than anyone in history.[17] Through more than 50 years in the chamber, he saw it all. And he earmarked it all. In 1999, Citizens Against Government Waste, a fiscal watchdog group, dubbed Byrd the "King of Pork" after he topped $1 billion in pet projects that he siphoned from the federal budget to his state. The senator's response? "They call me 'The Pork King.' They don't know how much I enjoy it."[18]

With an ingrained habit of overspending, either via the budget or their re-election campaigns, do today's politicians have an inkling of what it would cost to run a campaign on a reasonable budget that would sufficiently allow them to get their messages out to voters?

Probably not.

Unlimited spending drives the system. There is no incentive for candidates to limit fundraising and run cost-efficient campaigns. And with wealthy donors extracting promises and favors from candidates needing money, money is expected in return. The result is a bloated, out-of-control budget with deficits accumulating year after year, no matter which party controls Congress.

So, is there too much money in politics?

Judging from the anecdotal evidence from those who are closest to the issue, the answer is "yes."

To revive our ailing democracy, average Americans need to rise up and establish long overdue boundaries for our political system. This is imperative since our elected lawmakers are trapped in unlimited spending's vicious cycle and are incapable of leading themselves and us out of this morass.

THE CRITICS WEIGH IN

NEWT GINGRICH, FORMER U.S. HOUSE SPEAKER and 2012 Republican presidential candidate loves to compare the amount corporations spend to advertise their products to the amount political candidates spend to advertise themselves.

It's a corollary argument to critics' claim that more and not less money should be spent on political campaigns. This philosophy can be traced back to the 1990s Republican Revolution when the party took control of Congress after 40 years in the wilderness. On his Newt.org website, Gingrich asserted:

> Let's also be honest about what it costs to communicate in America. Three antacids: Pepcid AC, Tagamet and Zantac spend $300 million a year (to advertise). So the concept of what you should put in your stomach if you need an antacid, we spend $300 million a year . . . . By contrast, in 1992, a major political party spent $100 million . . . Congressional spending for all the congressional seats was $600 million.[19]

Gingrich's argument seems reasonable at first. But who's the "we" of whom Gingrich speaks—"*we* spend $300 million per year (on antacid advertising)?" It's certainly not the American public. It's the pharmaceutical companies. Frankly, a consumer doesn't need to be bombarded with $300 million of antacid commercials to know which brand to buy after eating too many cheeseburgers. And we all know how misleading such ads are: "Our antacid is the leading antacid in the country; Tests have shown our antacid stops stomach upset faster than all others; Four out of five doctors prescribe our antacid for their own families." These ads basically provide you with little or no real information—just a lot of flashy packaging, platitudes, and distorted facts about competitors—just like . . .

The point Gingrich and company miss is that the free market is different than democracy in a number of ways that a comparison between the two, particularly in this case, is neither fair nor accurate.

Voters do not need to be inundated with political ads to make informed choices. More substance in our elections could be obtained using far less money. Candidates don't need to be sold to us like a bottle of pop. If Johnson & Johnson and Merck & Co.

want to spend $300 million to sell their antacids, then fine—even if there are companies that produce far better medicines but have far fewer resources with which to advertise. This country does not bind the free market to tenets of equality, integrity, and impartiality. But it does with democracy. This country can brook inferior antacids, but not inferior leaders. And America is in serious need of good leadership. We can no longer afford a system that rewards inferior candidates simply because they are wealthy or have amassed the most campaign dollars with which to advertise themselves.

Gingrich's argument is a completely random comparison that does nothing to undercut average Americans' contention that there is too much money in American politics.

Perhaps Senator John McCain (R-AZ) put it best when Senator Mitch McConnell (R-KY) used the Gingrich argument in a campaign finance debate, but used yogurt instead of antacids. McConnell stated that Americans spend more on yogurt than on elections, thus concluding that candidates should be spending more on their campaigns. McCain parried: while "there is no crisis of confidence in yogurt, there certainly is about the present system of campaign finance." He added, "If yogurt spent all its money attacking ice cream and ice cream spent all its money attacking yogurt, we wouldn't eat either one of them."[20]

NEGATIVE POLITICAL ADS

CAMPAIGN REFORM CRITICS argue that negative ads are generally good for the political system because they transmit valuable information to voters. Such ads are also self-regulating, they argue, because a candidate running excessively negative ads can irritate the public and actually lose votes.

A skeptic would disagree.

First, negative ads obviously transmit information, but whether such information is valuable is highly debatable. Look no further than your television come election time. Negative ads are far more likely to be exaggerations or distortions of an opponent's character or record than about vigorous comparisons of policy proposals. Of course, there will always be negative political ads. But with a reasonable cap on spending, candidates wouldn't be able to bombard voters with endless torrents of distorted, trashy ads that drag down the quality of public discourse.

Second, opponents are correct in their assertion that negative ads can turn off voters, but they rarely do. In today's high-tech, sound-bite world, the designing of such slick, negative ads has risen to an art form, albeit a sad one. Most writers and producers know how far to push the envelope. And only the most egregious ads provoke outrage and backlash from voters and the media. As the 2016 election showed, the limit of what has historically been acceptable behavior by political candidates has been pushed out even further. It is anyone's guess just how coarse and juvenile attack ads will become.

Even Gingrich, a black belt in attack politics, admitted that the negativity level in American political campaigns is harmful. Reflecting on the type of nation his grandchildren will inherit, Gingrich stated on *Meet The Press*, " . . . the negativity has gotten to the point, whether it was right or wrong in '94, it has now gotten to the point where it's pathological. I mean, where you have consultants who, who don't know how to write a positive commercial. That's bad for the country. Maybe good for their candidate, it's bad for the country."[21]

PRESSURE TO CHEAT

WITH FISTFULLS OF CAMPAIGN DOLLARS and no cap on spending, well-funded candidates heading into an election's final stretch cannot resist flooding the airwaves with negative attack ads.

This unlimited spending stokes the arms race for campaign cash ever higher as opponents scramble to counterpunch with their own cheap shots in the contest's waning moments. Distortion displaces clarity. Candidates go for the jugular, trying to land that one knockout blow before Election Day. Issues become secondary.

Some candidates in high profile races have mutually agreed to abide by *voluntary* spending limits, acknowledging the corrupting forces of unfettered spending and the public's distaste of its effects. Part of the deal usually involves forgoing attack ads. But in a tight race, pressure mounts to break the cap and regain the precious, all-important money advantage. And the ammunition that extra money buys is almost always TV attack ads.

A good example is the 1996 Massachusetts U.S. Senate race between incumbent Democrat John Kerry and Republican Governor William Weld. The two wealthy blue bloods agreed to a voluntary spending limit for each campaign: $5 million for advertising and $500,000 in personal funds.[22] They agreed on seven debates, including one featuring an open, "Lincoln-Douglas"-style format. And they agreed to meet up after the race in a local pub— the loser to buy the winner a beer. The national media widely hailed the arrangement.

At first, the reviews were exceptional as the upper-crust, Boston Brahmin, Ivy League-educated candidates delved into the issues and were respectful of one another. The public benefited as the debates amply showcased the candidates and how they would represent the state and help shape the nation's future.

In one debate, Weld was asked by the moderator how he would reform the financing of political campaigns in America. The governor responded: "I think the way to get the undue influence of money out of political campaigns is to limit the spending in any given race. And the closest we can come, given the Supreme Court limitations on the amount that a person can spend on their own campaign, is to say 'we're going to offer free television. And if you accept it, then you have to agree to abide by this, that and the other conditions.'"

But when the race tightened in October, the agreed-upon

spending cap went by the boards as the two desperate camps argued over the agreement's technicalities. Kerry was the first to break the pact. Soon, the dam split wide open and negative TV ads deluged the airwaves.

The "Brahmin Brawl" was on.

Kerry began running negative TV ads using the technique of morphing his opponent's face into an unpopular politician, in this case morphing Weld into Senator Jesse Helms (R-NC).

Weld's ads tied Kerry to former Massachusetts Governor Michael Dukakis (D-MA), Kerry's old boss, painting Kerry as a tired, tax-and-spend liberal.

Issues? Gone.

Honor? Gone.

Integrity? Gone.

Level playing field? A fond memory.

Courtesy of Jeff Danziger

Kerry pulled out the come-from-behind victory after dumping $1.7 million of his own money into the campaign in the final weeks—much of it on negative TV ads.[23] He ended up spending nearly $9 million to Weld's $6.6 million.[24]

So while such agreements to voluntarily limit spending are to be applauded, they rarely work when exposed to the extreme pressure of a tight race. Such scenarios are also doomed to fail absent a nonpartisan referee empowered to make judgements on whether certain spending violates the rules.

WHAT DO VOTERS THINK?

CAMPAIGN REFORM FOES CLAIM candidates need every last penny to be competitive and adequately get their messages out to voters.

Are they right?

Well, have you ever heard anybody *not* involved in campaigns, be it a friend, neighbor, or acquaintance complain during an election cycle that there were too few candidate lawn signs around town? Or too few political ads on television, radio, print, or online? Or too few texts sent to their cell phone seeking donations? Or too few slick, glossy campaign brochures clogging their mailbox? Or too few people calling them at home, pressuring them to make a campaign contribution?

With a spending cap in place, would the public's ability to sufficiently learn about the candidates and their views be impaired? Would voters be victimized by viewing only 99 TV attack ads instead of 100?; or 449 bumper stickers slapped on cars and telephone poles instead of 500?; or 1,499 lawn signs plastered around town instead of 1,500?; or 2,999 political tracts papered on car windshields instead of 3,000?

Surely, there are spending boundaries that can be adjusted to allow all candidates to sufficiently get their messages out to the voters.

Spending limits will curb the excess money that is almost always used for negative advertising.

It will free politicians from the tin cup beg-a-thons they must endure under the current system to keep their jobs.

It will free them from the yoke of indentured servitude to wealthy special interests who pay for their political careers.

And it will free up their time to do what they're supposed to be doing: meeting with and listening to their constituents and researching, learning, and analyzing complex legislation they must vote on in the best interests of the country.

9

BUCKLEY V. VALEO: Part I
Need for a Constitutional Amendment

"Quite frankly, I had some strong reservations . . . . But we got together in a spirit of cooperation, a willingness to work together, to give a little and take a little, and the net result is legislation that I think the American people want. It is legislation for the times.."[1]

~ GERALD FORD, 38th U.S. president, at the Federal Election Campaign Act Amendments of 1974 signing ceremony.

CAMPAIGN SPENDING LIMITS is part of America's history. It is not "reinventing the wheel."

Campaign spending limits was once the law of the land as far back as 1911, with the passage of the Publicity Act Amendments. The 1911 law set spending limits at $5,000 for U.S. House candidates and $10,000 for U.S. Senate candidates.[2] A number of campaign expenditures, however, were excluded from the caps, including: travel, food, stationery, postage, telephone and telegraph services, campaign leaflets and other printed material for distribution. These items today comprise a large bulk of a campaign's expenses. The law, albeit flawed, was a good first step.

In 1921, the Supreme Court killed the Publicity Act's spending limits in its *Newberry v. United States* decision. The Court ruled that Congress lacked authority to institute such limits in state primaries. The Court reversed itself in 1941 in *United States v. Classic.*[3]

Although spending limits and disclosure rules were on the books, they were rarely enforced and largely ignored. No president or Congress created an agency or panel to administer and enforce campaign laws.

By the 1960s, campaign costs began skyrocketing with television's newfound effectiveness to transmit political messages. On September 7, 1964, Lyndon Johnson's presidential campaign ran the first major TV attack ad in American history. The spot was officially entitled "Peace, Little Girl," but was known as "Daisy." NBC ran the ad ran during a break in its Monday night prime time showing of the movie *David and Bathsheba*.

It changed the calculus of political advertising forever.

The ad featured a two-year-old girl in a meadow, randomly counting petals as she plucked them off a daisy. Suddenly, a man's voice booms in and begins the nuclear countdown from 10 to zero. The camera slowly zooms into the girl's right eye, which fills the screen. When the count hits zero, a nuclear bomb is detonated, superimposed within her pupil. Johnson's voice then bellows in with his election pitch as the bomb continues to mushroom.

The attack ad played to the fear of Americans unsettled by Johnson's challenger, Senator Barry Goldwater (R-AZ), who had intimated a willingness to use nuclear weapons to settle foreign policy disputes. Although the Johnson campaign ran the ad only once on national television, the media discussed it endlessly, having a devastating effect on Goldwater's candidacy.

The ascendance of such commercials and their high cost spread anxiety among incumbents—mostly Democrats, then in power. They worried they wouldn't be able to raise the increasingly large amounts of money needed for such ads to help keep their seats. In 1956, federal candidates spent a combined $155 million on their campaigns, with $9.8 million going to television and radio ads. A dozen years later in 1968, total spending nearly doubled to $300 million, with $58.9 million going to television and radio ads—a 500 percent increase over 1956 ad spending.[4]

Along with incumbent fears of defeat, Democratic leaders worried about losing control of Congress. Republicans and Big Business were becoming closer allies, unlocking vast funds to help the conservative cause. The Powell memo, which solidified the Republicans as the party of Big Business, was still a few years away. This confluence pushed the Democrat-controlled Congress to pass the Federal Election Campaign Act of 1971 (FECA), capping the amount of money a federal candidate could spend on political ads (but not on a campaign's overall spending). Senate and House candidates, for example, could choose from the following three options for spending on "communications media":

1. 10 cents multiplied by the number of voters within the jurisdiction the candidate seeks to represent;
2. $50,000;
3. 60 percent of the greater amount of options 1 and 2, with the money spent solely on "broadcast stations." [5]

The 1971 law began building a new foundation for reform.

It would take a shock to America's solar plexus to completely re-examine the role of money in politics and pass a comprehensive campaign finance reform law for the people.

That shock was the mother of all political scandals: Watergate.

WATERGATE AND ITS AFTERMATH
FECA Amendments of 1974

THE WATERGATE SCANDAL stemming from the 1972 presidential election birthed the watershed moment in campaign finance reform history.

Leading up to his re-election effort, President Nixon had been obsessed with securing a large mandate for his second term. He sought out wealthy donors—some of ill repute—to finance a wide-ranging political operation that would secure his victory.

Nixon's scheme began to unravel when police caught a five-man team, secretly hired by the president's campaign operatives, breaking into the Watergate hotel and office complex on June 17, 1972, to bug Democratic Party headquarters. Nixon was anxious to know the Democrats' presidential election strategy.

The Washington Post traced the illicit operation back to Nixon and eventually broke the scandal wide open. It was revealed that Nixon's re-election organization, the Committee to Re-elect the President, or CREEP, committed crimes during and after the 1972 campaign that were fueled with $22 million in illegal campaign contributions. It was never clear whether Nixon personally directed the illegal activity, but he intimated to his team what he wanted. And he was careful to maintain plausible denial if the plans went awry. But Nixon certainly took an active role in the cover-up conspiracy, revealed on the audio taping system he had installed in the Oval Office.

Television brought the scandal into American living rooms when U.S. Senate hearings investigating the scandal were broadcast live. Week after week, Senate Democrats' intense questioning teased out the odious drip of amateurish capers and dirty tricks. It deeply embarrassed the nation and led to Nixon's resignation. And it compelled average Americans to take a sobering look at the lingering loophole in the Constitution that allowed money to pollute the nation's politics.

In the wake of the Watergate break-in and cover-up, citizens understood three things:

1. America's political system was broken and corrupt;
2. unlimited campaign spending was the root cause of the corruption; and
3. serious action and a long-term commitment were needed to fix the system.

These three observations, combined with widespread citizen outrage, spurred 34 states to pass campaign spending limits or enforce those already on the books.[6] In 1974, federal lawmakers followed suit. The Democrat-controlled Congress amended FECA to include campaign spending limits—capping the *entire* amount of money federal candidates could spend in elections.

On October 15, 1974, a Republican president, Gerald Ford, signed the FECA Amendments of 1974 into law. The entire country had clamored for campaign spending limits and achieved it through a bipartisan effort.

Provisions of the new law included:

- *Presidential campaigns:* limited a candidate's spending to $10 million for the primary election and $20 million for the general election. (These caps were pegged to the consumer price index and adjusted at the beginning of each calendar year.)

- *U.S. Senate campaigns:* capped a candidate's spending using two methods, with the method totaling the higher cap applied. The first method required flat-rate spending limits of $100,000 in the primary and $150,000 in the general election. The second method was a formula: "8 cents multiplied by the voting-age population of the state" in a primary election and "12 cents multiplied by the voting-age population of the state" in a general election.[1]

- *U.S. House campaigns:* limited a candidate's spending using one of two methods. The first method applied to nearly every candidate—limits of $70,000 in the primary and $70,000 in the general election. The second method applied to candidates in states with only one congressional district, such as Wyoming and Montana. For these candidates, the spending limits method for U.S. Senate candidates was used.

- *National political parties:* maxed spending by Republican and Democratic national parties on any presidential candidate in a general election to "2 cents multiplied by the voting-age population of the United States." Spending was also limited on any U.S. Senate candidate in a general election at "2 cents multiplied by the voting-age population" of the state where the election would be held, and on any U.S. Representative candidate in a general election at $10,000.

- *Independent expenditures:* capped spending by individuals or groups running political ads for a clearly identified candidate at $1,000 for the primary election and $1,000 for the general election in any calendar year. These so-called independent or "outside" groups ran ads to support their favored candidates and could spend unlimited funds if their activities were conducted independently and without any coordination with the candidates they were supporting.

- *Individual contributions:* limited a citizen's donations to federal candidates to $1,000 per election ($1,000 for primary election; $1,000 for general election), and $25,000 in aggregate in any calendar year to the total number of candidates an individual chose to support.

- *Political group contributions:* capped contributions of political action committees (PACs) to federal candidates at $5,000 per election ($5,000 for primary; $5,000 for general election).

- *Self-financed candidate campaigns:* imposed limits on personal or "immediate family" funds or loans that wealthy candidates could use in any calendar year to fund their own campaigns. The caps included: $50,000 per presidential candidate; $35,000 per U.S. Senate candidate; and $25,000 per U.S. House candidate.

- *Federal Election Commission (FEC):* created as an independent government agency to administer and enforce the nation's campaign finance and election laws.

- *Public financing for presidential candidates:* completed a taxpayer funded system to be administered by the FEC for national candidates. Matching funds would be given to candidates who met strict campaign spending and reporting guidelines. The 1974 FECA Amendments completed the system by extending funding provisions to primaries and nominating conventions that were not included in the Revenue Act of 1971 or FECA of 1971, the two laws that created the foundation for the system.

- *Penalties for violating the new law:* established fines up to $25,000 and imprisonment for up to one year for any person found in violation of the FECA Amendments of 1974.[7]

STATE SPENDING LIMITS

MOST OF THE 34 STATES that passed campaign spending limits by 1974 adopted formulas using the total population or the number of voters in the previous election.

Wyoming, for example, set campaign spending limits at 75 cents per vote cast for the same office in the previous election.[8] So if 200,000 votes were cast in the gubernatorial election, each candidate in the next gubernatorial election would be limited to spending $150,000 (200,000 times $0.75).

Some states focused on capping a specific component of campaign expenditures. North Carolina, for example, restricted spending on media ads to 10 cents per voter. Other states set spending limits for only high-profile races. Florida, for example, capped gubernatorial candidates' spending at $250,000 for the primary and $350,000 for the general election, while candidates in other races were free to spend unlimited funds.[9]

Seventeen states also set limits for donations given directly to candidates. All but two of these states used donation caps in tandem with spending limits to determine a sufficient candidate spending amount. The other two states, Nebraska and Oklahoma, capped individual donations at $1,000 and $5,000, respectively, yet neither passed campaign spending limits.[10] Many of these 17 states set a range of donation limits from $1,000 to $5,000, foreshadowing the federal limits passed in 1974. Some states like Kansas capped individual donations only for its gubernatorial election—$2,500 for both primary and general elections.[11]

BUCKLEY v. VALEO

CONGRESS DESIGNED THE 1974 FECA AMENDMENTS to be a comprehensive campaign finance law that would "get money out of politics" once and for all.

The law sought to end the arms race for unlimited campaign spending, granting independence to politicians to impartially carry out the will and consensus of the citizenry. And it sought to give equal voice to average Americans and restore "We the People" as the rightful owners of America's democracy.

With the spotlight dimming on Watergate, citizens were mollified that their wishes for change had been granted. Americans looked forward to the law's implementation in the 1976 election.

But while the vast majority of Americans were rejoicing at the passage of the FECA Amendments, opposing forces were mobilizing.

On January 2, 1975, nearly three months after President Ford signed the FECA Amendments, a coalition representing the polar, ideological fringes of American politics filed a lawsuit, *Buckley v. Valeo*, in U.S. District Court for the District of Columbia to kill the law. The group claimed campaign spending limits violated the First Amendment—a citizen's right to free speech.

The plaintiffs included: Senator James Lane Buckley (Conservative Party-NY), the lawsuit's lead petitioner; former Senator Eugene McCarthy (D-MN), a liberal stalwart and presidential candidate in 1968, 1972, and 1976; Committee for a Constitutional Presidency-McCarthy '76, American Conservative Union, Conservative Party of New York, Republican Party of Mississippi, Libertarian Party, Conservative Victory Fund, American Civil Liberties Union (ACLU) of New York; and *Human Events*, an American conservative magazine.[12]

The defendants included: the Federal Election Commission (FEC); Francis R. Valeo, U.S. Senate secretary and FEC ex-officio member; U.S. House of Representatives clerk, also an ex-officio FEC member; U.S. attorney general, and the U.S. comptroller general.[13]

The Buckley-McCarthy coalition drew support from moneyed special interests, realizing that caps on campaign spending would strip their ability to influence and manipulate elections, laws, and politicians.

Buckley v. Valeo soon reached the U.S. Court of Appeals. The judges rejected the case, ruling that campaign spending limits served to protect the "clear and compelling interest" of the nation's citizens, preserving the integrity of the election process.[14]

Unbowed, the plaintiffs quickly appealed to the U.S. Supreme Court—and won. On January 30, 1976, over a year after the nation's new anti-corruption measure passed into law, it's cornerstone provision—campaign spending limits—was killed before it could be given a chance to work. And so were the spending cap laws that 34 states had passed.

Few were satisfied with the Court's decision. The ruling was a mix of tortured logic and naïveté, setting off a raging debate that continues today.

Instead of an up-or-down vote, the Court issued a *per curiam* decision—an opinion issued collectively by all nine justices. The ruling split hairs by calling campaign spending limits a "substantial" restraint on the "quality and diversity of political speech," while deeming campaign donation limits a "marginal" restriction on the "contributor's ability to engage in free communication."[15]

To clarify, the justices struck down *spending* limits as a violation of First Amendment rights, but allowed *donation* limits to stand.

The Court's primary reason for nullifying campaign spending limits was its insistence that *any* restriction on the amount a candidate desired to spend to get his or her views out to the public—in light of the rising cost of television and other mass media advertising—violated the candidate's First Amendment right to free speech:

> . . . virtually every means of communicating ideas in today's mass society requires the expenditure of money. The distribution of the humblest handbill or leaflet entails printing, paper, and circulation costs. Speeches and rallies generally necessitate hiring a hall and publicizing the event. The electorate's increasing dependence on television, radio, and other mass media for news and information has made these expensive modes of communication indispensable instruments of effective political speech.[16]

But the Court saw no free speech violation in limiting the money campaign donors may give to candidates:

> To the extent that large contributions are given to secure a political quid pro quo from current and potential office holders, the integrity of our system of representative democracy is undermined. Although the scope of such pernicious practices can never be reliably ascertained, the deeply disturbing examples surfacing after the 1972 election demonstrate that the problem is not an illusory one.[17]

To further buttress its case allowing donation limits, the Court highlighted the importance of the *perception* of corruption and its effect on public confidence in the political system:

> Of almost equal concern as the danger of actual *quid pro quo* arrangements is the impact of the appearance of corruption stemming from public awareness of the opportunities for abuse inherent in a regime of large individual financial contributions.[18]

To understand the Court's view on corruption, one must understand the following distinction between regulated and unregulated donations:

- *Regulated donations* are given by a donor directly to a candidate's campaign fund or a political action committee (PAC). They are the only kinds of donations that are capped by the federal government and still exist today.

- *Unregulated donations* are given by a donor to independent groups working to elect the candidate the donor supports. It is illegal for these independent groups to communicate or coordinate strategy with the candidate and candidate's campaign staff. It's a law rarely enforced and frequently flaunted. Thus, it easily allows a wealthy donor to indirectly donate unlimited sums to elect the desired candidate.

This distinction is why candidates seek favor from wealthy special interests. Regulated, direct donations are capped at around $5,000 to candidates and $10,000 for PACs, whereas unregulated donations can be in the millions.

In its *Buckley* ruling, the Supreme Court believed that *inherent* corruption and the *perception* of corruption exist when individuals and groups give large donations *directly* to politicians. But it failed to see these same corruptions when politicians beg wealthy interests for large donations funneled *indirectly* to independent groups supporting their campaigns.

This raises the following questions:

How could this 1976 Court—and the current Supreme Court, which firmly supports *Buckley*—not acknowledge the inherent and appearance of corruption that are created when our so-called leaders prostrate themselves before wealthy elites to preserve their political careers and stay in power?

How could they not acknowledge the inherent or appearance of corruption when the Invisible Empire invites ambitious politicians to posh political retreats around the country to extract tacit favors in exchange for large contributions?

How could they not acknowledge the inherent or appearance of corruption when politicians beg for money from wealthy donors whose interests these politicians must sit in judgment of once elected?

How could they not acknowledge the inherent or appearance of corruption when a wealthy special interest spends millions of dollars on independent expenditure ads supporting their desired candidate or issue?

How could they not acknowledge the inherent or appearance of corruption when candidates can easily learn, be appreciative of, and be indebted to their wealthy "independent expenditure" benefactors?

And how could this 1976 Court and the current Supreme Court not acknowledge the inherent and appearance of corruption when candidates amass unlimited cash, often leading them to spend surplus funds on questionable campaign activities? After all, it was a $22 million pot of surplus money collected from various shady sources that allowed the Nixon campaign to break into the opposing party's headquarters to steal documents, wiretap the phones of perceived enemies, break into businesses to steal personal information with which to smear political opponents, and so on.

No *inherent* or *appearance* of corruption?

It is, by far, the weakest point buttressing the *Buckley* ruling.

The justices in 1976 were negligent for not recognizing and acknowledging the intrinsic corrupting nature of unlimited campaign spending. And it was the height of naïveté that they could not foresee how easy it would be for wealthy special interests and power brokers to circumvent the donation limits left in place. Their gross oversight led to the proliferation of such ruses as 527 groups, bundling, nonprofit political groups, politicians' charities, and various independent expenditure groups.

And why did the Court leave intact the nation's presidential public financing law that capped a presidential candidate's spending as a condition of receiving public funding? Sure, public financing is a voluntary system, but wasn't the Court acknowledging that *some* spending boundary existed for candidates to sufficiently get their messages out to voters?

The *Buckley* Court's interpretation of free speech is the one roadblock denying average Americans the best and most effective method of getting money out of politics.

It is the singular reason that the money incentive remains intact today, and political corruption continues unabated with no end in sight. The Court overruled the wishes of the president, Congress, and the will and consensus of the American people.

In sum, the Court left only one path to reverse the *Buckley* ruling and *permanently* restore campaign spending limits to American citizens: a constitutional amendment.

We could wait, of course, for the Court's composition to change to a pro-reform majority and overturn *Buckley*. But when will that happen? And if the Court's philosophy does change, what will prevent it from changing back to an anti-reform majority when one of its aging justices either retires or passes away?

Only with a constitutional amendment can we permanently address this problem. We need to begin a new era in America—long delayed—of a better government that is, in fact and spirit, worthy of a great democracy.

So why didn't the nation snap to attention and pass a campaign spending limits amendment after the 1976 *Buckley* ruling?

In a word, power.

The extremists and wealthy special interests fought like lions to protect their political and economic power by successfully dividing the citizenry and raising doubts about campaign spending limits. They warned that spending limits would take away citizens' free speech rights and put the nation on a path to communism or worse. The extremists were abetted by the public's exhaustion over the Watergate scandal—an embarrassing, ugly, and drawn-out affair. Further, the nation was in the heat of a presidential race. Most Americans during this period were eager to move on. They wanted closure. They wanted a fresh start.

In hindsight, it was arguably the biggest missed opportunity in history to right the ship of American democracy.

10

BUCKLEY V. VALEO: Part II
Name Recognition & Free Speech

S ENATOR JAMES LANE BUCKLEY fought back tears on the evening
of November 2, 1976, giving his concession speech to about
400 subdued supporters in New York City's Waldorf-Asto-
ria Hotel.[1]

Buckley, a Conservative Party member and older brother of
right-wing firebrand William F. Buckley, had just lost his U.S.
Senate seat to challenger Daniel Patrick Moynihan, a Democrat.

Earlier that year, Buckley, as lead petitioner, won his U.S. Supreme Court case, *Buckley v. Valeo*, that killed campaign spending
limits.

Buckley opposed the FECA Amendments during Senate debate, claiming campaign spending limits would violate a candidate's right to free speech. A challenger, he asserted, needs to
spend more money to increase his or her name recognition to be
competitive against an incumbent. In fact, Buckley proposed an
amendment to the bill, allowing a challenger to spend 30 percent
more than any spending cap set for incumbents.[2] The amendment
failed.

Buckley's subsequent actions, however, belied his words in
the Senate chamber. In his 1976 re-election effort, Buckley, now
with spending limits in his rear-view mirror, shelled out more
than $1.5 million—the second highest spending total in U.S. Sen-
ate races that year.[3] Moynihan's campaign, in comparison, lagged

far behind in donations, with staffers often deferring their pay to keep the campaign afloat. Much of Buckley's contributions came from out-of-state donors.[4] Awash in cash, he saturated television, radio, and print with negative attack ads assailing Moynihan.

JAMES LANE BUCKLEY

In the end, incumbency and name recognition held little value for Buckley. Moynihan trounced him handily by 600,000 votes, 55 to 45 percent. Unfortunately for Buckley, the Watergate scandal's lingering stench undercut his and other conservative campaigns. In any other year, Buckley likely would have kept his seat.

So was Buckley a First Amendment patriot concerned about a challenger's right to spend in unlimited amounts to be competitive or just another incumbent addicted to special interest money as a near guarantee of re-election?

Or could he have deceived himself that he was the former, when in reality he was the latter?

Buckley, now in his 90s, still believes the permeation of money throughout the political system is not the root cause of corruption. In a 2010 speech at the Quinnipiac University School of Law in Hamden, Connecticut, Buckley asserted:

> This source of corruption, alas, is inherent in the democratic system, and it can only be controlled, if at all, by finding ways to encourage legislators to subordinate ambition to principle.[5]

Right.

Just like he did in 1976 when his political career was at stake. His ambition was challenged, so he stockpiled money to protect it. He panicked. He grabbed. He spent. In the end, he subordinated principle to ambition—just like most politicians.

Bottom line: Buckley's reasoning on unlimited spending is as naïve and confused as the Supreme Court decision that bears his name.

NAME RECOGNITION REDUX

NAME RECOGNITION ISN'T EVERYTHING in politics, although critics of campaign spending limits believe otherwise.

Sure, there are rare elections in which a candidate has outsized name recognition. The 2016 presidential election comes readily to mind. But Donald Trump, a celebrity businessman and reality television star, stood out from a crowded field by tapping into an anti-politician "authenticity" that the Republican base and many swing voters craved at the time. Name recognition alone did not win him the election. Jeb Bush and Hillary Clinton outspent Trump, but Trump had the more persuasive message.

But that's a rare case.

In most every race on all government levels—federal, state, and local—the candidate with the most money almost always wins. Campaign spending limits seeks to eliminate this money advantage.

The paradox in the name recognition argument is that critics view spending limits as disadvantageous to *challengers*, whom they say need more money to create name recognition among voters.

Supporters, on the other hand, view spending limits as disadvantageous to *incumbents*, who would have far less money to spend, thus creating a more level playing field among candidates.

The Supreme Court, in fact, leaned on the critics' view of name recognition to buttress its key argument in *Buckley v. Valeo*.

The Court decided that challengers needed every penny possible to afford the rising cost of television and radio ads to cultivate name recognition and get their messages out. Otherwise, their First Amendment right to free speech would be violated:

> Moreover, the equalization of permissible campaign expenditures might serve not to equalize the opportunities of all candidates, but to handicap a candidate who lacked substantial name recognition or exposure of his views before the start of the campaign.[6]

Anti-reformers, including the Court, are correct about one thing: It is true that challengers would be hurt if spending caps were set too low. If a Senate campaign's total spending, for example, were limited to $1,000, it would certainly prevent a challenger from developing name recognition and reaching voters. The challenger's free speech right would indeed be violated. Gary Jacobson, famed campaign finance expert and author, agrees with this point. Jacobson, who is highly regarded by anti-reformers and considered the "dean of campaign finance statistics" in the United States, supports the concept of campaign spending limits as long as the caps are set high enough for challengers to adequately achieve name recognition and communicate with voters.[7]

So critics' cynical reliance on name recognition as the reason to ban campaign spending limits is a ruse.

The name recognition argument can be illuminated by considering what the average U.S. Senate incumbent and challenger spent on their campaigns in 2016, a presidential election year, and comparing the dynamic had there been spending limits in place.

Senate incumbents in 2016 raised an average of $12,232,828 for their respective campaigns. Challengers raised an average of $1,467,696.[8] That's nearly a 9-1 incumbent spending advantage.

But what if a spending limit had been set at say, $3 million for Senate races? In this scenario, an incumbent senator would have $9.2 million *less* to spend, while challengers would have $1.5 million *more* to spend, assuming challengers could raise the extra amount—evening all candidates at $3 million. And challengers likely would be able to raise the extra funds, since potential donors are more apt to give to a challenger they deem more competitive in funding. Many donors have a diminished interest in funding a challenger being outspent 9-1, perceiving them as a lost cause. (A check-off box on income tax returns could also backfill some funding for challengers.)

It's pretty obvious looking at these numbers that the name-recognition argument collapses. Sure, a challenger must initially spend to whip up name recognition. But with $1.5 million more in his or her campaign account, a challenger could buy a ton more name recognition. Couple that with the incumbent's vastly reduced war chest that otherwise would have been used to burnish his or her record, launch endless attack ads on opponents, and communicate an air of inevitable victory, and you've got a much more competitive race.

Finally, let's look at the critics' incumbent-protection argument from another perspective. If campaign spending limits curtails challengers' name recognition efforts and is so beneficial to incumbents, then why hasn't there been an incumbent *stampede* to pass a constitutional amendment in Congress to attain this great advantage? After all, this is a body chock full of some of the most self-serving, self-promoting, and self-aggrandizing human beings on the planet. And one of the highest priorities in their lives—if not the highest—is getting re-elected. In virtually every congressional term since the *Buckley* ruling there has been at least one bill filed seeking a constitutional amendment for campaign spending limits.

They are all dead on arrival.

Campaign spending limits would indeed kick a lot of incumbents to the curb. Incumbents know this. Spending limits would encourage more challengers and make nearly every re-election competitive instead of an incumbent cakewalk.

So the critics' argument that campaign spending limits would be a great advantage to *incumbents* is demonstrably false. It's designed to confuse the public. The last thing incumbents want is to strengthen potential challengers. The height of their cynicism is that incumbents know voters dislike "career politicians." So these incumbents often act as though they, too, are outraged at any policy that would supposedly harm challengers while helping incumbents remain in power. It's why they've worked so hard to brand spending limits as a violation of challengers' free speech rights.

And many voters believe them.

How do they get away with it?

Well, many people are so hateful and distrustful of incumbent career politicians that they'll listen to anyone who spouts off against incumbent career politicians—even if it's an incumbent career politician.

QUANTITY v. QUALITY OF EXPRESSION

IF MONEY IS FREEDOM OF SPEECH, then those with the most money can buy the largest quantity of political expression. And those with the largest quantity of political expression almost always win elections.

But wouldn't that suggest we end up choosing candidates of quantity rather than quality? Aren't we supposed to elect leaders of the highest *quality* to guide our nation? So why did the *Buckley* Court focus on the quantity of expression they claimed spending caps would limit? And why did they fail to reflect on the quality of expression that would result?

Let's look at quantity first.

The *Buckley* Court buttressed its reasoning against spending limits by quoting the landmark 1964 *New York Times v. Sullivan* decision:

> Thus, we consider this case against the background of a profound national commitment to the principle that debate on public issues should be uninhibited, robust, and wide-open . . .[9]

Using that as a springboard, the *Buckley* justices added:

> A restriction on the amount of money a person or group can spend
> on political communication during a campaign necessarily reduces
> the quantity of expression by restricting the number of issues dis-
> cussed, the depth of their exploration, and the size of the audience
> reached.[10]

Most would agree that political debate in America should be
"uninhibited, robust, and wide-open." But we live in a society.
This means we can't do everything we want because it would infringe on the rights of our fellow citizens. It's why laws and legal
systems were created.

There are some citizens who would like to walk into a city
council meeting with a bullhorn and shout over everyone else in
an uninhibited, robust, and wide-open manner. In this case, only
one person would be heard and not the entire community. If this
person shouted for the entire two hours of the meeting, wouldn't
the *quantity* of expression be the same as if 25 or 30 members of
the audience and several council members each got a chance to
speak during those same two hours? Keeping with the *Buckley*
Court's reasoning, the person with the bullhorn could cover
many topics, discuss them in detail, and reach a large audience as
well, if the meeting were broadcast on streaming video, which is
commonplace.

But which "quantity of expression" would provide citizens
with the best information, viewpoints, and alternatives: one loud-
mouth with a bullhorn or the elected board and 25 to 30 citizens
sharing a microphone? Which quantity of expression would best
allow citizens to participate in creating the city's vision and planning its future? Which quantity of expression would best bond
citizens together and instill confidence in their government? And
which quantity of expression would best reflect the will and consensus of the community?

Applying this concept to elections, would debate on public

issues be more uninhibited, robust, and wide-open if only one candidate had a bullhorn— in other words, a large campaign war chest filled with free speech dollars to drown out and overwhelm competitors—or if all candidates could afford to compete, sharing the microphone to voice their viewpoints and ideas with voters?

Further, debate is *not* uninhibited, robust, and wide-open when incumbents and wealthy candidates wave their money belts in the air like truncheons to scare away less wealthy competitors —one of the most basic tactics employed on *all* levels of politics—federal, state, and local.

Debate is suppressed.

Citizen participation is discouraged and democracy inhibited.

Quantity of expression, surely, is only half of the equation.

Now, let's turn to *quality* of political expression, which the Supreme Court failed to consider in its ruling against campaign spending limits.

For background, let's first visit a Supreme Court case, *Randall v. Sorrell,* that challenged the *Buckley* ruling, but failed. In 1997, Vermont instituted a campaign spending limits law in defiance of the Supreme Court's ban. The Vermont law restricted campaign spending during two-year election cycles to $300,000 for gubernatorial candidates, $4,000 for state senate candidates and $2,000 for state representative candidates.[11] On June 26, 2006, the Supreme Court ruled 6-3 against the Vermont law, thus allowing the 1976 *Buckley v. Valeo* ruling to stand.

Justice Stephen Breyer, in writing the *Randall* majority opinion, quoted a *Buckley* ruling passage to emphasize that *any* restriction on the quantity of political expression would violate a candidate's First Amendment right to free speech:

> Indeed, the freedom to engage in unlimited political expression subject to a ceiling on expenditures is like being free to drive an automobile as far and as often as one desires on a single tank of gasoline.'[12]

Breyer misses the point.

First, elections are not open-ended affairs that stop when all candidates run out of breath talking about themselves, as a car running out of gas. Elections are comparisons—sizing up the candidates—within a finite period. A political *race* is formally conducted within an election cycle that has a beginning and an end in which citizens compare the candidates to see which would be the most intelligent, honest, creative, resourceful, and effective representative. Voters don't care which candidate speaks the loudest or the longest. That's of little help in choosing the best leader.

Second, how can voters adequately compare candidates when one contender has the resources to engage in unlimited "quantity of expression" and the others do not? To illustrate using Breyer's analogy, let's say there are five drivers competing in a 100-mile car race. The cars all get roughly the same number of miles per gallon. But only Car 1 is filled with enough gas to make it to the finish line, while the other four only have enough gas to make it just over half way. Holding all other variables constant, who is the best driver? Is it the driver whose car had enough gas to cross the finish line? The logical way to make the comparison would be to analyze how each driver performed up to the 50-mile mark—the half-way point when each car had enough gas to compete. If the driver of Car 3 led all others by 10 miles at the half-way point, wouldn't he or she generally be the best driver?

Of course, the question remains whether the amount of gas and the race's 50 miles are sufficient to judge each driver's performance. Or in campaign finance terms—whether a capped spending amount would be sufficient for candidates to adequately and fairly get their messages out to voters during the course of the campaign. The answer is yes. There is obviously an appropriate mix of donations and spending that would work for candidates to communicate with voters. And, as stated earlier, independent, nonpartisan citizens panels would be fully capable of setting such parameters and administering spending limits.

If you're skeptical that spending and donation limits can be calculated to allow candidates to sufficiently reach voters, look no further than public financing of campaigns. This *voluntary* system, instituted on the presidential level and in a handful of states, cities, and local jurisdictions, requires candidates to abide by strict spending and donation limits as a condition of receiving public money to help fund their campaigns. These candidates rarely, if ever, have complained that the public funds they received were insufficient to get their messages out to voters—unless the race included wealthy, self-funded candidates or those with big war chests who eschew public funding.

Third, when candidates are elected, they are rarely allotted unlimited political expression. They do not have an unlimited quantity of time to speak to colleagues on the House or Senate floor—except for a Senate filibuster. In Congress, with 434 colleagues in the House or 99 in the Senate, members have a relatively *limited* time to express themselves in their chamber and committee rooms. Indeed, the most effective politicians are those who can make their point in the most convincing way using the fewest words in the shortest time.

Quality over quantity.

Long-winded, wordy windbags who take eons to get to the point—if ever—are the bane of fellow politicians and are frequently tuned out by their colleagues when they take the microphone. They are usually the most ineffective of representatives and less apt to persuade their colleagues on important issues.

So why shouldn't we impose spending caps to show voters how talented and persuasive candidates can be with a set amount of funds to spend in a set timeframe? To bring this point into sharper focus, Justice John Paul Stevens, in his *Randall* dissenting opinion, responded to Breyer's car analogy by asserting:

> Just as a driver need not use a Hummer to reach her destination, so a candidate need not flood the airways with ceaseless sound bites of trivial information in order to provide voters with reasons to support her.[13]

With our Supreme Court placing more value on quantity than quality, is it any wonder why so many elections on all levels of government are often dominated by the wealthiest in the community?

Is it any wonder why our elections are so negative, loaded with trivial, shallow slogans and little substance?

And is it any wonder why we have so many leaders of such low quality?

IS BUCKLEY OBSOLETE?

IF THE *BUCKLEY* SUPREME COURT JUSTICES in 1976 could have peered into the future and seen a future president of the United States directly and instantly communicating political messages to millions of people worldwide—for free—on a Twitter account, would they still have killed campaign spending limits?

If they could have seen candidates setting up websites, apps, and complex algorithms to efficiently send customized donor appeals directly to voters' smart phones, collecting millions via credit cards and PayPal—all at a fraction of what those activities would cost using TV, radio, and staff time—would they still have killed campaign spending limits?

In other words, has the advent of the Internet changed the campaign finance calculus to the point of making the 1976 *Buckley v. Valeo* ruling obsolete?

It is an entirely appropriate question to raise, since the crux of the *Buckley* ruling cited the rising cost of television and other mass media advertising as the primary reason campaign spending limits would violate free speech. Restricting spending, they said, would substantially restrict a candidate's ability to communicate:

> The electorate's increasing dependence on television, radio and other mass media for news and information has made these expensive modes of communication indispensable instruments of effective political speech.[14]

But today, there is no "increasing dependence on television, radio, and other mass media (newspapers and magazines)." There's an increasing dependence on digital, web-based communication—something the justices did not foresee. Candidates today have a broad menu of digital options to reach more people than ever before to solicit donations and votes.

Missed the candidate's announcement speech? No problem. Just dial it up on the candidate's website or YouTube channel.

Want to find the latest info about the candidate or where his or her next rally will be? Easy. Just check out the candidate's daily e-newsletter blast on your mobile device.

Want to attend the candidate's rally or town hall meeting, but it's too far away? No sweat. Just watch the event's live stream on Facebook.

Campaigns today are working overtime, hiring more computer geeks than ever to drain every last dollar out of the public to finance campaigns and secure votes.

It has become an unnecessary orgy of digital excess and invasion of privacy.

Microtargeting has become one of the more common web-based fundraising techniques used by politicians. Candidates hire firms to gather consumers' intimate digital data to better target campaign appeals for political donations. Corporations have been microtargeting for years, advertising directly to selected groups of consumers more likely to buy their products and services, instead of paying for expensive ad buys distributed to the general public.

Here's how it works:

First, political microtargeters gather as much information as possible on voters. This entails buying lists of names from different data-gathering companies, culling information about us from voting lists, Internet searches, social media websites, magazine subscriptions, real estate and other public records. The nuggets they seek include: age, gender, race, income, home values, preferred car models, assorted financial data, hobbies, club

memberships, party affiliation, voting frequency, charitable donations, lifestyle preferences, prescription drugs, groceries, websites visited on our desktop, the kind of music we listen to, the
kind of coffee we drink, and just about anything else that has an
electronic data trail.

Second, this information is fed into computer modeling software and crunched.

Lastly, voters are grouped into "target clusters," which could
be a refinement of 10, 50, 100 or thousands of marketing segments. Political ads and solicitations are then customized per clus-
ter and sent out to voters' computers, laptops, tablets, smart
phones, and other devices.

Microtargeting rose to prominence in the 2004 presidential
election. Alex Gage, a political microtargeting pioneer, was credited by many as the strategist who won the key state of Ohio for
George W. Bush, pushing him to victory. During the campaign,
Gage grouped voters into such segments as: "Flag and Family Republicans" and "Tax and Terrorism Moderates." [15]

Alex Lundry, research director for TargetPoint, Gage's firm,
explained how microtargeting worked in the 2004 campaign:
"For example, a group of 'Flag and Family Republicans' might receive literature on a flag-burning amendment from its sponsor,
while 'Tax and Terrorism Moderates' get an automated call from
Rudy Giuliani talking about the War on Terror, even if they lived
right next door to each other." [16]

Lundry also described microtargeting as a "search and rescue"
mission that has the power and precision to identify and reach a
single voter. This person, for example, may be a blue-collar independent voter who "drives a truck, owns a gun, has three kids,
and is very angry about illegal immigration," but who lives in an
overwhelmingly Democratic district. [17] Such voters have traditionally been bypassed by campaigns as too expensive to ferret
out. Lundry added, "And as technology continues to progress, the
speed, efficiency and cost effectiveness of microtargeting will improve . . . ." [18] Lundry's observation foretold the increasing

"efficiency and cost effectiveness" that incumbents and other candidates enjoy today with their excess campaign funds.

The rise of social media has led to a further microtargeting refinement. In 2013, Facebook released its new tool, Custom Managed Audiences, tailored for politicians soliciting donations and votes.[19] The tool allows campaigns to upload a voter list to Facebook, which then works with third party companies that manage databases. The third party matches the names on the list to Facebook member profiles. Campaigns can then track and translate data on a Facebook member's profile, particularly any political posts, party affiliation, and whether the member is a registered voter. Then, without a member's know-ledge or approval, a political ad or solicitation magically appears in their feed or somewhere else on their screen.[20] In 2014, Facebook upgraded the tool, making it affordable for many smaller state and local political campaigns.

Tech companies are also refining apps that zero in on mobile users. They can send political ads to smart phones in a defined area at a specific time, like when people gather in large numbers at a campaign rally, college campus, concert, NASCAR race, football game, or parade.[21]

Microtargeting produces potential donor lists that are extremely valuable to today's politicians. When a candidate receives an endorsement from another politician, it usually means the candidate is being given access to the politician's goldmine—that is, his or her personal voter list the candidate can now use to prospect for new donors.

Perhaps the zenith in current creepiness is digital billboards designed with embedded cameras in them. These cameras record and interpret the facial expressions and eye movements of people reading the billboard. The data is then fed through an algorithm that interprets emotional reactions to different parts of the billboard's message. The feedback is used to tweak the billboard's message for maximum impact and effectiveness.[22]

What does the future hold?

An easy prediction is that ever more invasive technology, fueled by unlimited campaign spending, will continually erode our privacy, eating at our wallets and pocketbooks. Citizens' private lives will be probed further for personal data. Candidates will need more money from donors, of course, to buy the latest technology, chasing their tails trying to gain any advantage possible to win an election.

If campaign spending limits were enacted, however, there would be an incentive to use the cheapest, most effective technologies available—and less invasive, too. If a future president can Tweet at 3 a.m. at no cost and hold the world's ear with his message, then there are surely innovative ways to cut down traditional costs of campaigning to communicate political messages to voters.

The Supreme Court's *Buckley* decision would have been different if the web had vaulted to such communication heights years earlier.

Times change.

Buckley v. Valeo is obsolete.

A campaign spending limits amendment is the one path to the future that will provide a modern political foundation on which to build a better government.

It's time to press the refresh button on our political system and create a better, stronger democracy for the new millennium.

11

THE ART OF CIRCUMVENTION
What Hath Buckley Wrought?

ALAN MOLLOHAN had a great idea.

The Democratic congressman from West Virginia decided to create the Robert H. Mollohan Family Charitable Foundation in 2000 in honor of his late father. Mollohan claimed he founded the charity to provide scholarships to constituents. What could be better than to help the futures of the young men and women in his district?

In September 2005, the foundation held its annual golf tournament. It did not publicly announce the event's sponsors, but a picture on its website revealed one of the underwriters: Cassidy & Associates, Washington's third largest lobbying firm.[1] In fact, the tournament's winning team included Martin Russo, a former congressman and Cassidy's chief executive officer.

Keep in mind these charities are lightly regulated. They can receive tax-deductible donations from influence peddlers and operate outside of campaign finance laws. They aren't required to disclose donors' identities. The scam is that while donations given directly to a candidate are capped by federal law, donations to a politician's charity are largely unregulated and can be given in unlimited amounts. Such charities are convenient fronts, providing special interests a back door to curry influence with lawmakers. Either above board or with the wink of an eye, the lobbyist has achieved his or her aim—to perform a favor in the form of cash or gifts for an appreciative politician in a position to further the interests of the lobbyist's clients. Mollohan, from his perch as a high-ranking member of the House Appropriations Committee, was in a position to help a lot of people, including himself.

The charity scheme had been such a bonanza for politicians that House leaders broadened it in a 2003 ethics package passed so quietly the House Committee on Ethics was caught unaware. The so-called "charity rule" loosened guidelines, allowing members to accept free travel, meals, lodging, vacations, and other goodies from any IRS-certified charity as long as the freebies were part of a specific event sponsored by that charity.[2] It was yet another loophole politicians stretched a bit wider to catch a few more special interest dollars in their nets.

It should be no surprise that a component of super lobbyist Jack Abramoff's shell game of influence included a hefty number of charities set up to funnel money and gifts to politicians. Today, lobbying firms have "philanthropy practices" that concentrate on connecting their clients with policymakers' charities.

These charities also create jobs for the politicians' family members and friends to oversee the operations.

And what better way to illustrate the charity scam than to tell the tale of Congressman Mollohan, otherwise known at the time as *Vice Chairman Mollohan of the House Committee on Ethics*! After Mollohan's golf tournament caught the eye of the media, curious about the charity's donors, Mollohan quietly stepped down from his ethics committee post.

Politicians' charities are just one of the many tricks used to circumvent campaign finance laws. With such weak regulations and slack enforcement in America's political system, it's incredibly easy to funnel money through back channels to feed the hunger of unlimited campaign spending, and perhaps, assist a lawmaker striving for a fancier lifestyle. Congressman Mollohan proved to be a circumvention master.

In the early 1990s, Mollohan had another great idea. Working in tandem with his upper chamber counterpart, Senator Robert

Byrd (D-WV), Mollohan, using the leverage of his House Appropriations Committee seat, earmarked so much budget pork for his district that his constituents had trouble handling all the dollars flooding in. So he took the unusual step of setting up five nonprofit groups back home to manage the $250 million in federal bacon.[3]

Coincidentally, as Mollohan placed friends and a former aide in control of the nonprofits, his personal wealth soared. From 2000 to 2004, his assets grew from $565,000 to nearly $6.3 million.[4] Mollohan's real estate business, in particular, was suspiciously booming.

In 2005, Dale R. McBride, a childhood friend of Mollohan's who headed one of the nonprofits, partnered with the congressman to buy a $2 million beachfront parcel in Bald Head Island, South Carolina. The pair also purchased a 300-acre West Virginia farm for $900,000.[5] McBride, a top donor to Mollohan's campaigns, was also a director of the Robert H. Mollohan Family Charitable Foundation. Many of Mollohan's business associates and nonprofit employees, in fact, were heavy donors to his re-election campaigns.

In early 2006, Mollohan's apparent conflict of interest caught the attention of the U.S. Department of Justice, which began investigating whether Mollohan illegally profited from his cross-pollination of government and business dealings. But that didn't stop Mollohan from easily winning re-election that November. He won with 60 percent of the vote, outspending his Republican opponent by more than 2 to 1: $1.6 million to $766,000. It was the first time in 24 years he was seriously challenged. Mollohan had "inherited" his congressional seat from his father, a former longtime West Virginia congressman.

With the Democrats taking control of Congress in 2007 and preaching clean government, you would think party leaders would have relegated Mollohan to the back bench.

Not a chance.

Mollohan was handsomely rewarded even though the Justice

Department probe hung over his head. Speaker Nancy Pelosi (D-CA) appointed him chairman of the House Appropriation's Subcommittee on Commerce, Justice, Science, and Related Agencies, which, by coincidence, oversees the Justice Department budget. Under pressure, Mollohan eventually recused himself from deliberations on the department's funding.

In February 2007, Citizens Against Government Waste, a nonpartisan watchdog group, named Mollohan "Porker of the Year." Mollohan beat out his 434 House colleagues and all 100 senators for the title by abusing his position to funnel questionable funds to his district, and perhaps to himself.[6]

In 2010, voters finally had enough and booted Mollohan out of office. He lost his seat in the Democratic primary to a state legislator, Senator Mike Oliverio. The senator assailed Mollohan during the campaign for his long history of ethics transgressions, calling him "one of the most corrupt congressmen."[7]

In 2011, Mollohan became a Washington, D.C., lobbyist. He has a successful practice and is making more money than ever. Mollohan's career trajectory was all too predictable.

BACKDOOR INFLUENCE PEDDLING

ABSENT THE FOUNDATION OF CAMPAIGN SPENDING LIMITS, the Supreme Court, Congress, Internal Revenue Service (IRS), and Federal Election Commission (FEC), have collectively bungled and undermined campaign finance reform through the years, creating loopholes for wealthy interests to buy our elections, laws, and politicians.

There are so many ways corporations, unions, political groups, and wealthy individuals can flush money through backdoor channels to get their influence peddling dollars to their desired politicians. The more well-oiled of these circumvention vehicles include: independent expenditure groups, PACs, Super PACs, 527s, political nonprofits, charities, bundling, inaugurals, party nominating conventions, presidential libraries, and more.

Historically, wealthy interests' donations mostly flow to the circumvention scheme that accepts unlimited contributions while providing the best shield for donors' identities.

In the 1940s, weak federal enforcement of campaign finance laws led to the creation of "independent expenditure groups," a scheme that remains popular today.

The Supreme Court gave its blessing to these groups, ruling that since they act independently of the candidates they support, there is no corruption. But these "independent" groups are often run by former staff members, friends, or family members of the candidates. They effectively skirt federal laws that regulate donations made directly to candidates' campaigns. These independent groups, for example, have taken on many of the tasks traditional campaign operations have conducted, including political advertisements, phone banking, polling, get-out-the-vote drives, etc. Wealthy donors can donate to these groups in unlimited amounts, and the groups can spend in unlimited amounts. The one drawback is that the donors' identities must be made public.

In the late 1970s, the FEC weakened the Federal Election Campaign Act by allowing political parties to use contributions collected on the state level, creating so-called "soft money." Wealthy donors could now give large amounts to state parties, which then funneled the dollars back to the federal parties, circumventing federal rules limiting contributions to federal candidates' campaigns. Many states had no requirement to reveal donors' identities. Further, many states allowed corporations and unions to donate their general funds, which found their way to federal candidates, circumventing federal rules.

In 2002, the Bipartisan Campaign Reform Act, also known as McCain-Feingold, banned federal parties and candidates from raising and spending soft money. It shocked wealthy interests, who needed a new circumvention scheme, and fast. Fortunately for them, through FEC and IRS blundering, political groups that organized under section 527 of the IRS Code were treated as tax-

exempt organizations, and a gap in the law allowed 527s to operate outside of FEC regulation. Big money soon deluged 527 coffers. At first, 527 groups could conceal their donors' identities,
but Congress eventually required disclosure.

In 2010, the Supreme Court ruling in *Citizens United v. Federal
Election Commission* blew up the nation's 63-year-old ban on corporate and union donating and spending, opening the way for the
creation of today's Super PAC. Wealthy donors could now use
company funds in unlimited amounts to directly influence elections, although they were banned from donating directly to candidates' campaigns. Super PACs quickly became the circumvention scheme of choice, even though federal law required the disclosure of donors' identities.

The *Citizens United* ruling also opened the door for the political
nonprofit, the most popular circumvention scheme today. These
"social welfare" groups are organized under the Internal Revenue
Code 501(c)(4) and are tax exempt. Under the Code, their mission is to "further the common good and the general welfare of
the people of the community." Such activities may include, for
example, raising money to help feed starving children, providing
medical care to low-income people, assisting young people seeking affordable housing, and any number of social welfare endeavors. The rule is that no more than 50 percent of the nonprofit's
activities may be political in nature.

The IRS rarely enforces it.

While a nonprofit must report to the IRS the donation
amounts it receives and the identities of those giving more than
$5,000, the names are hidden from the public. These anonymous
donations are called *dark money*, because the public doesn't know
where the money came from. In July 2018, at the urging of
wealthy conservative donors, President Trump made these contributions a little darker by eliminating the requirement that those
donating over $5,000 reveal their names to the IRS.

Political nonprofits provide cover for both corporations and
politicians. A corporation may donate dark money to a nonprofit

that is supporting a controversial politician or issue, inoculating itself against a potential consumer backlash. And a politician's nonprofit, operating independently from the candidate, of course, may receive dark money donated by a controversial corporation without fear of a voter backlash.

To illustrate, the Target department store chain in 2010 donated $150,000 to MN Forward, a business-backed PAC seeking to install Republican candidate Tom Emmer as Minnesota's governor.[8] Emmer had fought against gay rights legislation while serving in the state legislature. As a PAC, MN Forward had to disclose its donors. Target, based in Minnesota, faced a consumer and investor backlash across the country. Three management firms and institutional investors, including the New York City Employee Retirement System, angry over Emmer's gay rights opposition, threatened to pull their investments in Target. They urged the company to overhaul its political donation policy. The standoff garnered national headlines, leading Target Corp. CEO Greg Steinhafel to acquiesce and issue a public apology for supporting Emmer. If the $150,000 had been given to a political nonprofit, Target could have avoided any controversy. It is why the donor class values dark money in American politics.

In early 2014, the IRS proposed new rules requiring nonprofits to expand their social welfare activities beyond 50 percent. The proposed change caused an uproar across the political spectrum by those on the left and right who had come to rely on nonprofits as huge campaign cash cows. The political heat forced the tax agency to back down. The IRS is still licking its wounds from a scandal several years earlier when it singled out and scrutinized a handful of nonprofits tied to the Tea Party. The agency's nonprofit enforcement has been paralyzed ever since. In the 2016 election cycle, the IRS failed to enforce the 50 percent rule. "It's anything goes for the next couple of years," Paul Streckfus, a former IRS examiner of nonprofit groups, said of the agency's hands-off approach. "The whole system has really collapsed."[9]

The six-member Federal Election Commission (FEC), with its

dysfunctional design of three Republicans and three Democrats, remains gridlocked on taking action against scofflaw nonprofits as well. The Democratic members want to revoke nonprofits' tax-exempt status and regulate them as political committees. But the three Republicans have blocked any such measure.

There is no resolution in sight.

WHAT HATH BUCKLEY WROUGHT?

THE SUPREME COURT'S 1976 *Buckley v. Valeo* ruling birthed the sheer absurdity that exists today in the circumvention funding game.

In deciding the case, the Court admitted it had scant campaign finance expertise, yet plowed ahead nevertheless, issuing guidelines that were naïve and easily circumvented.

The Court's first step in *Buckley* was to separate political ads into two categories:

1. **Express advocacy**: ads that directly call for the support or defeat of a clearly identified candidate.

2. **Issue advocacy**: ads that address political issues that do not call for the support or defeat of a clearly identified candidate.

The Court decided that express advocacy ads would be regulated, that is, anyone running such ads would be limited in how much they could donate to independent groups producing the ads. Issue advocacy ads, since they did not seek to support or defeat a particular candidate, were deemed outside the bounds of regulators and had no donation limits.

Here's where it gets silly.

The Court defined express advocacy as political ads that use the following words and phrases, dubbed by pundits as the "magic words":

- vote for
- elect

- support
- cast your ballot for
- (name of candidate) for Congress
- vote against
- defeat
- reject [10]

As you might imagine, it took politicos, special interests, influence peddlers, and campaign managers about a nanosecond to navigate around this guideline. All they had to do was change a few words to make their "regulated" express advocacy ads into "unregulated" issue advocacy ads.

For example:

Express advocacy: Congresswoman Smith voted for a tax increase that resulted in the worst economy in U.S. history. *Vote against* Congresswoman Smith.

Issue advocacy: Congresswoman Smith voted for a tax increase that resulted in the worst economic downturn in U.S. history. Don't let Congresswoman Smith get away with killing American jobs and wrecking our economy.

What's the difference between the two ads?

The express advocacy ad used the magic words "vote against," so the donation amounts accepted by the group running the ad would be capped. The issue advocacy ad used none of the magic words, so the donations could be collected and spent in unlimited amounts.

A good example of the magic words loophole can be found in the 2000 presidential race. The Democratic Party ran an ad supporting Vice President Al Gore that concluded with the lines: "Eight Nobel Prize winners in economics warn: George W. Bush's plans exhaust the surplus and do not add up. Is that the economic change you want?" [11] The Democratic Party maintained the ad used only issue advocacy. After all, no magic words were used, right? Yet is there any doubt about whom the ad directs citizens to vote for? A little snipping of words here, some circumvention there, and—shazam!—billionaires, power brokers, and special interests were free to plow tens of millions of dollars into funding political ads to elect their candidates of choice.

By 2013, the Supreme Court had expanded the definition of express advocacy to include communications that are the "functional equivalent" of express advocacy. It's a bit more stringent, but still a regulatory fig leaf.

The definitions of express and issue advocacy, and the magic words, still play a part in administering what is left of America's campaign finance laws.

POLITICAL ACTION COMMITTEES

TO UNDERSTAND SUPER PACS TODAY, it would be prudent to learn about their origin.

In 1907, Congress banned corporations from contributing directly to candidates' federal campaigns. In 1943, it banned unions from doing the same.

It didn't take unions long, however, to devise a legal circumvention of the ban. While the law prohibited unions from using their treasury money (members' dues) for campaign donations, it permitted them to set up political groups to collect voluntary donations from union members and their families to contribute to candidates. This type of group became known as a political action committee (PAC).

In 1943, the Congress of Industrial Organizations (CIO), one of the largest unions of the day, set up the first PAC (CIO-PAC) to collect voluntary donations from members and funnel them to Democratic candidates. The CIO-PAC had an immediate effect, raising $1.4 million to influence the 1944 election.[12] The Republicans cried foul, claiming the Roosevelt administration was bought and paid for by the CIO.

Corporations joined the PAC game in the early 1960s to counter the rising influence of union PACs. Barred from donating company money directly to candidates, they solicited voluntary donations from their stockholders, managers, employees, and family members. In 1961, the American Medical Association (AMA) founded one of the first business PACs—the American Medical Political Action Committee (AMPAC)—still one of the biggest and most influential PACs today.[13] Over the years, corporate PACs grew steadily in number and strength.

Although most PAC donations are capped at $10,000 to any candidate during an election cycle, there are many PACs within a particular economic or labor sector. When combined, they pack an enormous punch for influencing elections and issues.

Super PACs, in comparison, are banned from giving money directly to candidates. But they can spend corporate money in unlimited amounts as long as those activities are not coordinated with the candidate they seek to elect.

LEADERSHIP PACs

POLITICIANS, NEVER HESITANT TO EXPLOIT a good loophole, hopped aboard the PAC train as well.

In the 1980s, Senate and House leaders set up their own "leadership PACs" to raise money for their colleagues in tight races. Individuals and other PACs can contribute up to $5,000 to each leadership PAC.

At first, only a few of the most powerful senior members established leadership PACs. Naturally, lobbyists and their special interest clients generously contributed to these new money magnets.

But instead of benevolently assisting colleagues in tight races, many senior leaders used their PAC money as a billy club to keep rank-and-file members in line, threatening to withhold precious campaign dollars if they didn't vote with leadership.

These leadership PACs have proven to be such an effective backdoor fundraising tool that their numbers have surged dramatically. In the early 1990s, only a small group of Senate and House members wishing to climb the political ladder into leadership established PACs. Today, not only do the vast majority of members have leadership PACs, but even freshmen have them, immediately racking up chits by spreading around campaign cash. In the 2014 election cycle, there were over 507 leadership PACs that donated a total of $51 million to candidates.[14]

There's really not much difference between these politicians and lobbyists—using money to get what they want in government. Is it any wonder Congress has been unable to clamp down on influence peddling?

Leadership PACs were originally banned from funneling cash back to the politicians who created and controlled them. But that soon changed. In yet another example of how unlimited spending corrupts lawmakers and why politicians cannot be trusted to police themselves, Congress pushed through rule changes that allowed members to use their leadership PACs to pay their own overhead costs like travel, consulting, and polling. Indeed, the rules governing leadership PACs today are so loose that many politicians use them to pay personal and entertainment expenses and hire spouses, sweethearts, friends, and relatives for political consulting and other jobs. Politicians also use the cash to dole out gifts like iPads, cufflinks, bracelets, etc. to family members, friends, and supporters.

Much of this goes on right under the noses of average Americans. It seems the politicians like it that way and are loathe to surrender such perks.

Rep. Joel Hefley (R-CO), who railed against this fundraising practice, noted: "My impression is that a lot of people use leadership PACs as a slush fund."[15] Hefley, who left office in January 2007, introduced a bill, H.R. 5839, in his last session of Congress to ban leadership PACs.

Not one of his 434 House colleagues signed on as a co-sponsor to support the bill.

INCUMBENT ROLLOVER ACCOUNTS

UNLIMITED SPENDING CREATES another little-known perk for incumbents: rollover accounts.

These accounts hold campaign funds that can be "rolled over" to the next race. Ever wonder why an unopposed incumbent still fundraises during an election? The incumbent knows that the more money he or she stockpiles, the more likely they will scare off potential challengers.

Rollover accounts are also used to: fund a future run for higher office; climb the House or Senate leadership ladder by donating to incumbent colleagues in close re-election races; and give oneself a golden handshake when ousted from office or retiring.

The rules governing rollover accounts are predictably loose. The funds are often used for parties, dinners, and other entertainment events that have a tenuous connection to political issues.

State politicians are also enamored of rollover accounts. If an incumbent decides to use the account as a springboard to a higher office or better paying job, for example, they get to keep the money, no matter the consequence to the public.

In December 2015, California Assembly Member Henry Perea left office before his term ended to grab a lucrative gig with the nation's largest drug lobbying firm, Pharmaceutical Research and Manufacturers of America, also known as Big Pharma. By leaving abruptly, Perea, a Democrat representing California's 31st District, left Fresno County taxpayers holding the bag. County officials estimated it would cost $500,000 to hold a special election to fill Perea's seat.[16] Fresno is mostly farm country. They don't have an abundance of wealthy taxpayers pumping up their revenue stream. Why is this California politician interesting? Well, when Perea ditched Fresno citizens for his six-figure lobbying job, leaving them with a $500,000 budget hole, he absconded with his campaign account balance of $800,000.[17] A Republican lawmaker, also representing a part of Fresno County, quickly filed a bill requiring lawmakers leaving abruptly to use their rollover accounts to pay for special elections that fill their seats. It's sad that such a bill is even necessary.

In 1989, President George H. W. Bush called for the elimination of incumbent rollover accounts. He also urged that any excess campaign funds be used to pay down the national debt, fund the major political parties, or refund the contributors. It failed. It is a reform that is long overdue.

BUNDLING

CONFUSING, isn't it?

How come federal law caps political donations given directly to a candidate at $5,400 (2018 donation ceiling) in an election cycle, yet we continually read about wealthy individuals handing millions of dollars directly to high-profile candidates?

What gives?

Do America's laws not apply to the wealthy?

Well, since campaign finance laws banned individuals from giving unlimited contributions *directly* to candidates, wealthy special interests and power brokers needed a circumvention tool to regain their political access and clout. It led to the design of a clever little gimmick known as bundling.

While federal law caps individual donations to candidates, there is no law against a person soliciting their friends, collecting $5,400 from each of them and presenting these donations in a "bundle" to the candidate. It should not come as a shock that bundling is practiced almost exclusively by extremely wealthy people, tapping their wealthy friends for donations. Lobbyists are also active bundlers, mining their networks of special interest clients seeking favors.

Candidates always reward their biggest bundlers, because they are extremely valuable to a campaign.

President Bush in 2004, for example, bestowed elite status to bundlers who rounded up at least $200,000 from their friends. These bundlers were dubbed "Rangers." Those who bundled at least $100,000 were "Pioneers."

Candidates usually host a big party for their best bundlers to thank them for their rainmaking abilities and collect their bundles. So, if a candidate like Bush invites his Rangers and Pioneers for a big blowout bash at a posh Houston hotel, he can easily cart off $3 million or more in one night.

During the 2008 election, Hillary Clinton's bundlers who collected at least $100,000 were branded "Hillraisers" by the campaign. Barack Obama's campaign boasted nearly 50 bundlers who attained membership in his "Big Changers Club" by gathering at least $500,000 apiece for the future president. Since regulations are weak, reporting is spotty. The Obama campaign reported the bundlers in "ranges" with the highest range being $500,000 and above. It's possible that one bundler could have raised $10 million or more. We may never know.

Donald Trump refused to name his 2016 bundlers. While Trump largely self-funded his primary race, he raked in hundreds of millions of dollars for the general election.

Many pundits predict bundling will continue to be the fundraising backbone of presidential and congressional campaigns for years to come.

And what do bundlers like Bush's Rangers, Hillary's Hillraisers, and Obama's Big Changers get for their efforts?

A whole lot of access—and more.

Scratch a U.S. ambassador to a European or other highly desirable foreign post, and you'll likely uncover a wealthy presidential bundler.

Bush held barbecues at his Crawford, Texas, ranch for his biggest bundlers. They got much more than chicken wings, ribs, and potato salad from their host. According to Craig McDonald of the nonprofit group Texans for Public Justice, Bush's bundlers sought preferential treatment concerning federal regulations affecting their business interests as well as appointments to top government and diplomatic posts. In fact, more than 60 of Bush's 241 Pioneers in 2000 were rewarded with top appointed administration posts.[18] It is pretty much the same in every White House.

In 2003, *USA Today* researched and profiled the demographics of Bush's Rangers and Pioneers. They found these presidential benefactors to be elite fundraisers who "span the world of finance, real estate, industry, and politics. The common denominator: each is wealthy and has access to others with fortunes. With few exceptions, they are white, male, and over 50."[19]

Not exactly representative of "We the People."

Many of those in Obama's Big Changers Club were appointed to plum, lucrative posts, such as foreign ambassadorships and high-ranking jobs in federal departments, commissions, and public corporations.

In September 2012, two Pennsylvania State University professors, Johannes W. Fedderke and Dennis C. Jett, released a study that found a direct link between the amount of political donations individuals gave to Obama and the foreign diplomatic assignments they received. The study, "*What Price the Court of St. James? Political Influences on Ambassadorial Postings of the United States of America*," traced political donations made to Obama through 2011. The study also examined the rewarding of diplomatic posts since the 1950s Eisenhower administration. It found roughly 30 percent of ambassador postings have been consistently granted to non-career diplomats—in other words, big donors, elites, and the president's close chums. And nearly all the plum, non-dangerous assignments—like Great Britain, the combined post of France and Monaco, and others in Western Europe—went to these non-career diplomats.

During the 2008 election, Obama promised he would end the tradition of crony appointments to ambassador posts. But that sentiment evaporated after Obama's campaign raised about $1 billion to successfully capture the White House. Obama's payback to his rich benefactors increased the 30 percent tradition of non-career ambassador postings to 40 percent.[20]

The professors found that to compete for the highly-coveted France-Monaco post, an individual donor giving to a nonprofit or other unregulated group supporting Obama needed to pony up about $6.2 million, while a bundler needed to rustle up about $4.4 million. And as for the Court of St. James (Great Britain), the most prestigious post of all, the jockeying came down to Anna Wintour, editor of Vogue magazine, and Matthew Barzun, a dot-com millionaire and chairman of Obama's fundraising operation. Neither was exactly steeped in British history, letters, and diplomacy. Barzun won out. He had brought more coin to the president.

Obama, like past presidents, was unfortunately trapped in a dysfunctional system ruled by money. It does nothing to debunk Americans' belief that our government is bought and paid for.

INAUGURALS

MOST CITIZENS VIEW presidential and gubernatorial inaugurals as historic events marking the beginning of new political eras.

The celebrations embrace the country's or state's tradition and uplift citizens' morale with the promise of a fresh start.

But behind the bunting, big crowds, marching bands, and lofty speeches, inaugurals are more often a politician's payback to financial supporters—an opportunity for special interests, power brokers, wealthy donors, and fellow politicians to party and bask in their coming fortunes for backing a winner.

The big money, of course, is in presidential inaugurals. There are no spending or donation limits for these spectacles. And nearly all the major donors have a financial interest in issues to be decided—in whole or in part—by the president and the executive branch's regulatory agencies.

George W. Bush's inaugural committee raised over $40 million for his 2005 celebration.[21] According to *The Associated Press*, the list of inaugural underwriters each donating $250,000 included: "AT&T; Bank of America; Bristol-Myers Squibb; United Parcel Service; San Diego Chargers owner Alex Spanos; American Financial Group of Cincinnati and one of its top executives, Carl H. Lindner; New Energy Corp. of South Bend, Ind.; Thomas Stephenson, a partner in Sequoia Capital in Atherton, Calif.; and Maryland-based Strongbow Technologies Corporation."[22] Included among $100,000 donors were: "Pepsi-Cola Co.; Tyson Foods; Goldman Sachs Group; California Farm Bureau Federation; Titus Electrical Contracting of Austin, Texas; Hunting Engineering Co. of Bridgeton, Mo.; Intervest Construction of Daytona Beach, Fla.; and Computer Associates International of Islandia, N.Y."[23]

President-elect Obama capped donations for his 2009 inauguration at $50,000. But how many average Americans have that kind of cash lying around? Obama's inaugural committee still raised about $45 million.[24] Although Obama refused to accept donations from Big Business, Big Labor, registered lobbyists, and PACs—the big players within those industries and groups were well represented.

In 2013, Obama discarded the caps on corporate donations and raised $79 million for his inauguration. He was largely aided by his Super PAC, Priorities USA Action, which raked in individual contributions as large as $2 million.

President Trump's inauguration broke all spending records, topping out at a weighty $107 million. Although Trump sold himself to voters as an outsider impervious to special interests, the usual suspects larded up his inauguration fund with millions of special interest dollars. The Invisible Empire's caesars of America's coal, oil, gas, pharmaceuticals, and financial industries generously gave Trump money—and wish lists for pet projects, legislation, deregulation, and tax breaks. They also helped the president stock his cabinet with some of their executives. Further troubling was the revelation of a lobbyist illegally laundering $50,000 in foreign money to buy four inauguration tickets for a Ukrainian businessman. The high number of foreign business moguls, particularly from Russia, attending the inauguration piqued the interest of the Federal Bureau of Investigation.

So is all this presidential inauguration spending necessary for America?

Most would agree that acknowledgement of a new political era deserves some pomp for such a grand nation. But spending $107 million for special interests to party into the night with administration officials is unnecessary and unseemly.

When it comes to inaugurals and similar events, average Americans must understand that wealthy interests aren't participating for patriotic reasons.

They are not giving.

They are buying.

POLITICAL CONVENTIONS

PARTY NOMINATING CONVENTIONS are similar to inaugurals.

The charade is that the convention is supposedly held for the delegates attending the event and average Americans watching on television. But just like Congress, party leaders run the show and the rank-and file are mostly props. The convention halls are replete with lovely red-white-and-blue balloons, crisp American flags, catchy political signs with catchy slogans, campaign buttons, and, of course, the old, loud, weird guy dressed up in a dirty, frayed Uncle Sam costume—walking on stilts and reciting passages from the Declaration of Independence.

But who's footing the bill for the festivities?

You guessed it—the usual corporate and special interest suspects. The real action at these shindigs is not on the stage. Conventions are crawling with influence peddlers flitting in and out of luxury boxes taking in the festivities and buttonholing influential lawmakers to offer campaign contributions and discuss legislation.

The party is for the important pols and the influence peddlers. The joke is on average Americans.

CURBING THE CIRCUMVENTION CIRCUS

SO WOULD CAMPAIGN SPENDING AND DONATION LIMITS eliminate or at least blunt all these circumvention scams?

Yes.

First, campaign spending and donation caps should be applied to any individual or group supporting political activities. It would kill the money incentive instantly. Candidates would no longer need to raise exorbitant sums, so they would no longer need to entice their best money gophers to hit up their rich friends for millions in exchange for chummy barbecues and diplomatic posts. Organizers of inaugurals, conventions, and other similar affairs would need to reach out to average Americans to fund these events and not rely on wealthy special interests.

Second, if individual contribution limits were set at $600 instead of $5,400, bundlers would have to rustle up about 335 donors instead of just 37 to hand Bush, Obama, or Trump a bouquet of 200,000 kisses. Also, the lower donation limit would bring many more average Americans within reach to equally participate in supporting their candidates of choice and eliminate the gross inequity of special access for the wealthy few.

Third, a constitutional amendment for campaign spending limits must include a provision granting citizens the right to ban or regulate all current and future circumvention schemes.

So, what hath *Buckley* wrought?

A loophole of a political system that only special interests, power brokers, and lobbyists could love.

12

CITIZENS UNITED & SUPER PACs

In order to achieve the widest possible distribution of political power, financial contributions to political campaigns should be made by individuals and individuals alone. I see no reason for labor unions—or corporations—to participate in politics. Both were created for economic purposes and their activities should be restricted accordingly." [1]

~ SENATOR BARRY GOLDWATER (R-AZ),
conservative icon and 1964 presidential nominee

DONALD TRUMP SCRUNCHED his puffy eyes, pink eyebags, and orange pancaked face at his interviewer, Sean Hannity, as the *Fox News* host peppered the candidate with questions.

It was August 6, 2015, and the first Republican 2016 presidential debate had concluded minutes earlier.

Hannity needled Trump about the real estate magnate's donations to Hillary Clinton's political campaigns in years past. Trump said he donated because he wanted something in return, insinuating he could get whatever he wanted by donating to politicians. Then, the following exchange occurred:

SH: But it is a truth, though. People donate for the purpose of buying influence. Maybe the only difference is you're honest about it.

DT: When I see the candidates . . . raising $50 million, $40 million, $30 million—from friends of mine, $100 million. Those peo-

ple are not, like, charities, you understand. You know, they
want. These are total tough cookies. I know many of them. I
probably know most of them. And when they give millions
and millions of dollars, they're not doing it, you know, for the
good of the American Cancer Society. They're doing it for
themselves.

To most Americans, Trump spoke a truth few would contest.
Yet this widely held observation on political corruption somehow
eludes the Supreme Court's conservative justices.

Despite all the history, scandals, investigations, studies, and
data—as well as the experience of working smack in the middle
of Washington, D.C.—Chief Justice of the United States John
Roberts and Associate Justices Anthony Kennedy, Clarence
Thomas, Samuel Alito, and Antonin Scalia inexplicably failed to
acknowledge—or admit—how American politics really works.
These five justices constituted the majority in the *Citizens United
v. Federal Election Commission* decision that green-lighted corporations and unions to use their profits, general funds, and any other
money available to buy our elections, laws, and politicians.

They obviously knew their decision would unleash a tidal wave
of billions of influence-peddling dollars into our politics.

Yet they saw no problem; no inherent flaw in the system.

The justices' simplistic view of money's corrupting influence
in politics, as marbled throughout Kennedy's *Citizens United* majority opinion, is virtually limited to outright bribery, or *quid pro
quo*. It would seem that corruption only occurs when a politician
is caught accepting a bag of money from a special interest in exchange for a favor—and perhaps, with it all caught on video, Ab-
scam-style. Then, and only then, these justices would admit to
the presence of corruption.

The justices may have forgotten that it was not a *quid pro quo*
that unearthed Watergate, the scandal fueled by $22 million in
illegal contributions. It was uncovered by a low-paid security
guard working in the Watergate complex, noticing masking tape

the burglars left on a door lock.

And there was no quid pro quo that blew open the Abramoff scandal, uncovering a staggering web of corruption in Washington. It was a super lobbyist who couldn't keep his mouth shut, bragging around town about the politicians he bought off and the clients he scammed.

And the justices may have forgotten that there aren't many *quid pro quos* that reveal most of the thousands of political scandals big and small throughout all layers of government.

Justice Kennedy wrote in *Citizens United* that wealthy interests donating large sums to politicians merely seek "ingratiation and access," which does not cause corruption.[2]

Chief Justice Roberts, in his *McCutcheon v. FEC* majority opinion four years later, expounded on Kennedy's assertion:

> (Ingratiation and access) embody a central feature of democracy—
> that constituents support candidates who share their beliefs and in-
> terests, and candidates who are elected can be expected to be re-
> sponsive to those concerns. Any regulation must instead target what
> we have called '*quid pro quo*' corruption or its appearance. That Latin
> phrase captures the notion of a direct exchange of an official act for
> money. The hallmark of corruption is the financial *quid pro quo*: dol-
> lars for political favors.[3]

It is astonishing that Kennedy, Roberts, and their conservative colleagues view political corruption in such stark terms.

Black and white.

No gray areas.

If there were ever an issue that is brimming with gray areas, it's campaign finance.

When deciding *Citizens United* and the half dozen other cases that trampled campaign finance laws, all of these justices required a provable *quid pro quo* before corruption could be ascertained.

But is there a provable *quid pro quo* when wealthy special interests foot the bill for the political careers of elected politicians, who beg them for money?

Is there a provable *quid pro quo* in the power of indebtedness wealthy backers have over the politicians they finance?

Is there a provable *quid pro quo* when big donors socialize, vacation, and sometimes enter into business ventures with their favored politicians?

Is there a provable *quid pro quo* when lobbying firms hire and pay healthy salaries to a politician's wife, children, relatives, or friends even though they have little to no political experience?

Is there a provable *quid pro quo* when wealthy special interests intimate lucrative job offerings to politicians after they've ended their public service?

Is there a provable *quid pro quo* when the wealthy interests' lobbyists socialize with their clients' favored politicians, sometimes managing or fundraising for their political campaigns, or providing lists of high-roller donors for more cash?

Is there a provable *quid pro quo* when wealthy backers' lobbyists write legislation that is then given to their clients' indebted politician "friends" to submit to Congress and state legislatures?

Is there a provable *quid pro quo* when these bills pass into law, enriching these special interests while eroding the disposable incomes of average Americans and our quality of life?

Is there a provable *quid pro quo* in the many favors that, in Trump's words, "you know, they want," are doled out for their investments in our political system?

As recounted in Chapter 2 of this book, all of the above activities would not be tolerated in our judicial system: the defendant donating money to the judge's campaign, the judge begging the defendant for campaign donations, the defendant writing swaths of the judge's decision, the defendant acting as the judge's campaign fundraiser or treasurer, the defendant palling around with the judge and jury—all while the case is ongoing.

These activities would be viewed as corruption in any courtroom, although there is no *quid pro quo*, as defined by the Supreme Court's conservative justices.

Before Roberts, Kennedy, and their conservative brethren rendered such far-reaching decisions as *Citizens United* and *McCutcheon*, they should have checked with those who have actually toiled in Washington's trenches, instead of keeping their own counsel and viewing political money in the abstract.

There is, indeed, an indebtedness that occurs when money changes hands in politics. You may not see it or capture it on video, but it's inherent in virtually every transaction, whether the participants want to admit it or not.

The following are excerpts of written comments by a former political professional who could have assisted the justices during their "fact-finding" phases of these critical, influential campaign finance cases:

> Each time a lobbyist or special interest makes a political contribution to a public servant, a debt is created. Lobbyists are very adept at collecting these debts. Unfortunately, the true debtor on these obligations is the American people. In a very real way, congressmen who take contributions from lobbyists and special interests are selling our nation to repay their debts of gratitude. . . . During the years I was lobbying, I purveyed millions of my own and clients' dollars to congressmen, especially at such decisive moments. I never contemplated that these payments were really just bribes, but they were. Like most dissembling Washington hacks, I viewed these payments as legitimate political contributions, expressions of my admiration of and fealty to the venerable statesmen I needed to influence. . . . Congressmen accept donations and solemnly recite their oath of office: 'My vote is not for sale for a mere contribution.' They are wrong.[4]

The author?

Jack Abramoff.

Abramoff offered more insight into Washington realpolitik in a *60 Minutes* interview with Lesley Stahl that aired on November 6, 2011.

The following are excerpts:

LS: How many congressional offices did you actually own?

JA: We probably had very strong influence in 100 offices at the time.

LS: Was buying favors from lawmakers easy?

JA: I think people are under the impression that the corruption only involves somebody handing over a check and getting a favor. And that's not the case. The corruption, the bribery ... because ultimately that's what it is. That's what the whole system is.

LS: The whole system's bribery?

JA: In my view. I'm talking about giving a gift to somebody who makes a decision on behalf of the public. At the end of the day, that's really what bribery is. But it is done every day and it is still being done. The truth is there were very few members who I could even name or could think of who didn't at some level participate in that.

LS: I really think what you were doing was—was subverting the essence of our system.

JA: Yes. Absolutely right. But our system is flawed and has to be fixed. Human beings populate our system. Human beings are weak.

LS: And you preyed on that?

JA: I did. I was one of many who did. And I'm ashamed of that fact.

LS: Could you do the same thing today? I'm asking you whether you think the system's been cleaned up?

JA: No, the system hasn't been cleaned up at all.

LS: At all?

JA: There is an arrogance on the part of lobbyists, and certainly there was on the part of me and my team, that no matter what they come up (with) we, we're smarter than they are, and we'll overcome it. We'll just find another way through.

It seems the corrupting influence of money in politics is utterly obvious to virtually everyone in the United States (and the rest of the world), except to the five humans who had the power to decide *Citizens United*, *McCutcheon*, and other recent campaign finance cases.

To Justice Kennedy and his conservative colleagues, more money injected into our politics simply means more voices are heard and more information is disseminated to voters. To them, more money means more democracy.

Justice Scalia, in his *Citizens United* concurring opinion, wrote:

> Indeed, to exclude or impede corporate speech is to muzzle the principal agents of the modern free economy. We should celebrate rather than condemn the addition of this speech to the public debate.[5]

Yet Scalia's view runs counter to Ayn Rand's conservative-libertarian philosophy of complete "separation of state and economics"; and conservative icon Barry Goldwater's assertion that "financial contributions to political campaigns should be made by individuals and individuals alone"; and a chorus of other right-wingers, including the Koch brothers, who rant against crony capitalism. Further, corporate managers also have their citizens' ballot vote, or free speech, so they are, in effect, double-dipping.

As far back as 1910, President Theodore Roosevelt (R), in a speech in Osawatomie, Kansas, clearly saw the harmful effect of corporate money that the modern day Supreme Court blindly ignores:

> It is necessary that laws should be passed to prohibit the use of corporate funds directly or indirectly for political purposes; it is still more necessary that such laws should be thoroughly enforced. Corporate expenditures for political purposes, and especially such expenditures by public service corporations, have supplied one of the principal sources of corruption in our political affairs.[6]

Abramoff, reflecting on the justices' naïveté in deciding campaign finance cases, observed, "I do think there is a disconnect. And I understand it because none of them have been in the political process."[7]

THE ROAD TO CITIZENS UNITED

IN 2002, PUBLIC DISGUST OVER THE ENRON SCANDAL, replete with the energy giant's large, shady political donations to relax industry regulations, gave Congress the kick in the rear needed to finally pass McCain-Feingold, a landmark campaign finance reform bill. As expected, excessive lobbying by anti-reformers dramatically watered it down.

The law was, nevertheless, a blow to wealthy special interests. It took away powerful weapons in their influence-peddling arsenal.

McCain-Feingold banned the Republican National Committee (RNC), Democratic National Committee (DNC), congressional campaign committees, and other national party groups from collecting unregulated soft money donations through party state machinery. While hard money is a capped, regulated donation given directly to a candidate or PAC, soft money is an unregulated donation given in unlimited amounts to a national party group for party-building activities. But over time, party leaders began funneling soft money to support specific candidates, thus circumventing the cap on hard money given directly to candidates. Until 2002, parties were using soft money to buy TV and radio ads supporting their favored candidates, sans the "magic words," of course. They were functioning much like independent expenditure groups, which McCain-Feingold also sought to regulate. The law banned these independent groups from running political ads called "electioneering communications" that mentioned a clearly identified federal candidate (express advocacy) via broadcast, cable, or satellite communication within 30 days before a primary and 60 days before a general election that reached 50,000 or more people. The provision discouraged some independent groups, like 527s, from lobbing unsubstantiated, scurrilous claims close to Election Day about a candidate they opposed, leaving the candidate with little time to adequately respond.

This electioneering provision greatly upset a certain conservative political nonprofit by the name of Citizens United.

In January 2008, Citizens United released a 90-minute documentary it had produced entitled, *Hillary: The Movie*. It resembled an extended political advertisement attacking then-Senator Hillary Clinton (D-NY), the frontrunner for the Democratic presidential nomination at the time. Citizens United denied the movie constituted express advocacy and was therefore not an electioneering communication. It also sought to make the movie available by video-on-demand, allowing people to see the movie when they pleased. This meant that viewers could watch the movie within the 30-day period before several presidential primaries, violating McCain-Feingold's electioneering provision. Citizens United denied any violation, saying video-on-demand only allowed one household at a unique time to view the movie. Fearing the FEC would find the movie and ads for the movie in violation of McCain-Feingold, Citizens United sought declarative and injunctive relief. It filed a lawsuit, *Citizens United v. Federal Election Commission*, that eventually reached the Supreme Court.

On January 21, 2010, the Court issued a 5-4 decision dismissing the nonprofit's arguments. It declared the movie and its ads were indeed express advocacy and the video-on-demand's system of 34.5 million subscribers meant the movie could easily be seen by 50,000 or more viewers at any time.

But the Court didn't stop there.

Before the case had been settled, the five conservative justices, Anthony Kennedy, John Roberts, Antonin Scalia, Samuel Alito, and Clarence Thomas, asked Citizens United's attorneys to submit briefs that supported lifting the ban on corporate and union money in federal elections. This went far beyond the scope of the case. The Court then unexpectedly pivoted and put the ban issue center stage—and eviscerated 63 years of federal law, the Taft-Hartley Act of 1947, and a landmark 1990 Supreme Court case, *Austin v. Michigan Chamber of Commerce*. The Court's action granted carte blanche to corporations and unions wishing to use their billions of dollars in general treasury funds to influence American politics.

It's rare for the Supreme Court to overturn one of its own rulings. Worse, the *Citizens United* plaintiffs had absolutely no intention of challenging *Austin* or other settled law. It only sought to advertise and air its movie by challenging a McCain-Feingold electioneering provision.

Campaign reformers denounced the "activist" conservative majority for venturing afield of the lawsuit's parameters. The Court, in essence, created law from the bench—usurping the power of Congress.

What compelled the Court to take such drastic action?

It is unsure, but the Koch brothers' fingerprints were all over *Citizens United*. Campaign finance reform tops their hate list. The brothers have fought for 40 years to preserve their privilege of buying what they want out of government. The Supreme Court, to them, was just another institution to co-opt, helping to further their political goals. During the *Citizens United* hearing, the Koch-founded Cato Institute, among six other Koch-funded think tanks and lobbying groups, pummeled the Supreme Court with position papers and amicus briefs to influence the outcome in their favor. Theodore Olsen, *Citizens United*'s lead counsel, is a Cato Institute member and attorney for Koch Industries. After the Court's ruling, it was revealed that Justices Scalia and Thomas had been guests at lavish retreats hosted by the Koch brothers.[8] The justices did not recuse themselves from the case.

The McCain-Feingold law struck at wealthy special interests buying America's elections, laws, and politicians.

The Invisible Empire struck back.

BUCKLEY, NOT CITIZENS UNITED

MANY WHO ARE UPSET TODAY about big money dominating our nation's politics see the 2010 *Citizens United* ruling as the ultimate bogeyman responsible for our political system's ills.

It is not.

The culprit responsible for today's political malaise is the 1976 *Buckley v. Valeo* ruling.

Nevertheless, groups have sprung up around the country agitating for a constitutional amendment to overturn *Citizens United*. They insist the amendment is the solution to cleansing our political system. Many of them believe *Citizens United* banned campaign spending limits, equated corporations as people, created Super PACs singlehandedly, and opened the floodgates for so-called "dark money" from undisclosed donors to infect and overwhelm our country's elections.

None of this is true.

First, *Citizens United* is the most important campaign finance ruling of the twenty-first century. But overturning it by amendment would not come close to curbing political corruption. In essence, this thinking presupposes that America's political system pre-2010 functioned just fine—no corruption, no wealthy special interests buying politicians, no independent groups fueled with billionaire cash running television ads supporting or smearing candidates and distorting issues, no Invisible Empire. The political system's ills obviously began much earlier than 2010 and run much deeper.

Second, the *Citizens United* ruling has *nothing* to do with campaign spending limits. It was the Court's 1976 *Buckley* ruling that banned limits, including spending caps on independent expenditure groups. Yet, nearly every amendment bill filed in Congress to overturn *Citizens United* includes a provision to re-institute campaign spending limits. And none of these bills require independent, nonpartisan citizens panels to administer and enforce the law. So we're not solving *anything* by overturning *Citizens United* and keeping Congress—an institution utterly incapable of policing itself—in charge of a system in which it has a deep, vested interest.

Third, *Citizens United* equated corporations as people in one respect—free speech rights. In writing the majority opinion,

Justice Anthony Kennedy leaned on a 1978 case, *First National Bank v. Bellotti*, to support this claim:

> Corporations and other associations, like individuals, contribute to the discussion, debate, and the dissemination of information and ideas that the First Amendment seeks to foster. The Court has thus rejected the argument that political speech of corporations or other associations should be treated differently under the First Amendment simply because such associations are not 'natural persons.' [9]

This was the Court's intellectual underpinning to lift the 63-year-old ban on corporations and unions using their treasury funds in unlimited amounts to run independent political ads. But the ruling did not create "corporate personhood," which actually evolved over a period of time through a string of Supreme Court rulings.

Groups like movetoamend.org seeking to overturn *Citizens United* by amendment want to topple such auxiliary corporate personhood rights as:

- denying government inspection of a corporate property without a warrant or prior permission;
- denying a jurisdiction from assessing higher taxes on corporate chain stores or other "outside" enterprises that may be a threat to local businesses.

The campaign spending limits amendment proposed in this book specifically focuses on cleaning up the nation's political system and will achieve this by applying spending and donation limits to *all* individuals and *all* entities and groups seeking political influence, including corporations and unions. The amendment need not stray into policing corporate behavior anywhere outside the political arena to achieve its purpose.

Fourth, *Citizens United* was indeed a key ruling in creating Super PACs, but it's only in part. While it opened the floodgates of corporate and union treasuries to deluge the political system with billions of more dollars, it did not address whether these new funds could be used for express advocacy—that is, supporting or opposing a clearly identified candidate. That question was settled in March 2010, just months after the *Citizens United* ruling. SpeechNow.org, a political nonprofit, had requested a Federal Election Commission (FEC) advisory opinion asking if it could run express advocacy ads without having to file as a PAC and obey PAC donation and spending limits. The FEC could muster only two commissioners and not the required quorum of four to issue an advisory opinion. So, SpeechNow.org sued. On March 26, 2010, the U.S. District Court of Appeals for the District of Columbia Circuit, heavily influenced by the *Citizens United* decision, ruled in *SpeechNow.org v. FEC* that there is no corruption or appearance of corruption in allowing such a group to run express advocacy ads. This ruling, together with *Citizens United*, created the Super PAC—basically, a PAC on steroids that not only could run express advocacy ads, but could do so muscled with billions in unlimited amounts from corporate and union treasuries. Super PACs, however, still cannot give money directly to candidates as can regular PACs.

Lastly, while Super PACs opened the floodgates of corporate and union spending, we must remember that, pre-*Citizens United*, wealthy individuals like the Koch brothers, Foster Friess, Bob Perry, George Soros, and other ideological billionaires have always been able to donate unlimited sums to independent expenditure groups. For special interests, the one drawback is that Super PACs must disclose donor names and the amounts given.

SUPER PAC NONSENSE

JUSTICE KENNEDY WROTE in *Citizens United* that independent groups (like today's Super PACs) may be of "little assistance" to a candidate they seek to elect, since they are legally banned from coordinating their activities with the candidate's campaign.

Kennedy and his majority saw no such problems with these independent groups because, along with the collusion ban, they were barred from giving money directly to candidates. Justice Kennedy used the following *Buckley v. Valeo* passage to support this point:

> Unlike contributions, such independent expenditures may well provide little assistance to the candidate's campaign, and indeed may prove counterproductive. The absence of prearrangement and coordination of an expenditure with the candidate or his agent not only undermines the value of the expenditure to the candidate, but also alleviates the danger that expenditures will be given as a *quid pro quo* for improper commitments from the candidate.[10]

It is hard to imagine that Justice Kennedy—or any Supreme Court justice, for that matter—could be so gullible.

How could Kennedy see no "danger" of *quid pro quo* when money is passed *indirectly* from special interests to their desired candidates through groups like Super PACs?

Did he think candidates are so stupid and clueless they don't know or care where the money came from and what strings are attached?

Did he believe wealthy donors would not care about informing the candidates of who gave them the money and what was expected in return?

Did he believe a candidate's Super PAC would be set up and run by nonpartisan, professional administrators and not the candidate's family members, personal friends, or former campaign staffers?

Did he not grasp that Super PACs would be established as parallel campaign organizations designed to circumvent federal contribution limits?

To illustrate this nonsense, Republican presidential candidate Mitt Romney in July 2011 gave a campaign speech to a roomful of his loyal, wealthy supporters at a fancy New York City restaurant overlooking Central Park. The organizers did not bill the event as an official Romney fundraiser. The supporters were invited to the dinner by a political group, Restore Our Future, a Super PAC founded and operated by former Romney campaign aides.[11] As soon as Romney gave his speech and left the restaurant, the former staffers worked the room for Super PAC donations to support Romney's campaign. This ruse is legal because the Super PAC was supposedly acting independently of the Romney campaign.

And, like the national party soft money scheme, candidates have offloaded a number of critical campaign tasks to their Super PACs, like running expensive television, radio, and digital advertisements; organizing grassroots, door-to-door efforts in support of the candidate; and running data collection, voter registration, and opposition research. This, too, is a legal circumvention of the Court's myopic campaign finance rulings.

The Super PAC charade clearly shows the foolishness that has been foisted on Americans by an out-of-touch, naïve Supreme Court dabbling in an issue of grave importance to the nation's democracy. The issue of campaign finance should be yanked away from them and placed before the people in amendment form.

One big corrective measure is all it will take.

CITIZENS UNITED LEGACY

THE "WISDOM" OF THE *Citizens United* ruling also introduced Sheldon Adelson to America.

Adelson, a billionaire Las Vegas casino mogul, single-handedly resuscitated Newt Gingrich's flagging 2012 presidential campaign by dumping $10 million into the former Speaker's Super PAC, Winning Our Future, during the South Carolina primary. Adelson's casino cash financed some of the ugliest negative attack ads ever produced. Gingrich pulled out the surprise victory over frontrunner Mitt Romney.

One person.

One person purchased a primary victory for their preferred candidate and virtually negated public participation and the power of citizens' votes.

With Adelson's millions and Gingrich's and Romney's Super PACs leading the way, the Florida primary that followed was the most negative campaign on record, according to the Campaign Media Analysis Group (CMAG), which tracks political ads. From January 23-29, 2012, the two campaigns and their supporting Super PACs ran a total of 11,586 political ads on television. Of that total, 10,633, or 92 percent, were negative. In fact, of the 4,969 television ads aired by Romney's Super PAC, 100 percent of them were negative, according to CMAG.[12]

In late spring 2012, Adelson dropped $10 million into the Super PAC of Mitt Romney, the last Republican presidential candidate standing. By the time the general election ended, the casino billionaire's total contributions rose to $150 million.[13] All told, Adelson funded nearly 12 percent of Romney's total spending of $1.2 billion on the presidential race.[14]

When Senator John McCain (R-AZ) heard how much Adelson spent on the 2012 election and the access and influence the casino mogul gained, the Arizona senator laid the blame for America's sorry state of politics at the feet of the Supreme Court and its *Citizens United* ruling. "The worst decision by the Supreme Court in the twenty-first century," McCain lamented. "Uninformed, arrogant, naïve."[15]

And what did Adelson want? Freedom, of course! Just like the Koch brothers. Adelson pushed his politician friends to ban online gambling in the United States. Why? Because it horned in on his Las Vegas casino business.

Adelson and the Koch brothers talk a good game of unfettered free markets—until those same free markets produce competition that could cost them a ton of money. Then they give their libertarian philosophy a mulligan. Adelson needed government to stop online gambling from eating into his casino profits. The Kochs needed government to stop wind and solar company tax credits from endangering the brothers' fossil fuel profits.

In 2015, two presidential candidates, Sens. Lindsey Graham (R-SC) and Marco Rubio (R-FL) carried Adelson's water by filing the second iteration of the Restoration of America's Wire Act that would effectively ban online gambling. Graham and Rubio duked it out trying to please Adelson to access his Super PAC money and 2016 presidential endorsement.

Quid pro quo, anyone?

Adelson's Super PAC cash also allows him to interject himself into foreign policy. He is a major backer of Israel's right-wing Likud Party and its leader, Prime Minister Benjamin Netanyahu. Adelson owns *Israel Hayom*, a major daily newspaper in Israel. He gives the newspaper away for free, allowing him to spread his divisive, warmongering views far and wide among the Israeli population.[16] When Netanyahu addressed the U.S. Congress in March 2015, Adelson sat conspicuously in the visitor's gallery as Netanyahu's guest. Adelson has so much freedom of speech he can shape Israeli foreign policy with his propaganda bandbox, while using campaign donations domestically to shape U.S. foreign policy.

In 2015, Adelson secretly purchased *The Las Vegas Review-Journal*, the largest newspaper in Nevada, a pivotal electoral state in presidential elections.[17] His identity was revealed only after dogged efforts of the newspaper's top reporters. The *Review-Journal* had been a thorn in Adelson's side, running stories critical of his politics and casino dealings.

And where is the power of average Americans to counteract wealthy special interests like the Koch brothers and Sheldon Adelson, who have a global reach in business, politics, and media? Well, it's disappearing by every dollar these plutocrats toss into our sick political system.

Today, the dream of wealthy, elite special interests is nearly complete. Political power in America is being concentrated in even fewer wealthy hands.

The citizen's one ballot vote since the Supreme Court's 1976 *Buckley v. Valeo* ruling continues to shrink, losing more of its value and power than ever before.

And the Supreme Court is as clueless and out-of-touch on campaign finance as ever.

We live in a country where our Supreme Court blithely assumes citizens are not bothered by the cesspool of political money that pollutes America today. It is stunning to read this excerpt of Justice Kennedy's *Citizens United* opinion, with emphasis on the last sentence:

> . . . we now conclude that independent expenditures, including those made by corporations, do not give rise to corruption or the appearance of corruption. . . . The fact that speakers may have influence over or access to elected officials does not mean that those officials are corrupt. . . . The appearance of influence or access, furthermore, will not cause the electorate to lose faith in our democracy.

Seems Justice Kennedy is a tad late on that one. The ship of Americans' faith in our money-soaked democracy has sailed.

About 45 years ago.

On the U.S.S. Buckley.

13

THE DO-NOTHING REPUBLICANS
Free Speechers or Freeloaders?

"In America, money does not equal speech. More money does not entitle one to more speech. The powerful are not entitled to a greater voice in politics than average people. Everyone has an equal say in our government; that's why our Declaration of Independence starts with 'We the People.'" [1]

~ SENATOR MITCH McCONNELL (R-KY), 1998 Senate campaign finance reform debate. (Note: The *Constitution* begins with "We the People")

AH YES, the Do-Nothings.

They are the hardcore, hardline anti-reformers. The proud contrarians.

If conventional wisdom says the sky is blue, they say it's green. If conventional wisdom says campaign spending limits curbs political corruption, they say it causes it. They dwell in the Bizarro World of American politics. They can't be reached by logic, reason, telephone, Morse code, or any other form of communication.

The Do-Nothings are preventing any meaningful campaign finance reform from becoming law. They think our current political system works just fine. And it does—for them.

Just who are these people, anyway?

Are they free speech defenders, envisioning themselves

cloaked in Founding Fathers' powdered wigs and knickers, saving America from evil reformers shredding the Constitution? Or are they cynics, freeloading on a rotten system that perpetually enriches them and their wealthy friends at the expense of average Americans? Or perhaps they are a confused blend of the two?

The Do-Nothings, if pressed, will admit there's *some* corruption in the system, but it's not a big deal. It's simply a byproduct of conducting the people's business in a free market society. In other words, don't hold your breath waiting for this crew to lead the charge against political corruption.

The Republican Party is the party of the Do-Nothings—and of Big Business. The U.S. Chamber of Commerce is the top lobbying spender in America, funneling nearly every cent to Republican candidates, issues, and causes.[2] The Republican Party today is completely addicted to Big Business's largesse. Such treasure is the ultimate aphrodisiac that can bend an entire party's thinking to its will.

The Democrats, of course, have tried to keep pace in the money sweepstakes. They've fallen in love with Big Business, too. But Big Business just wants to be friends. They know Democrats don't drink the free market, trickle-down Kool-Aid like the Republicans. They're not soul mates. It's why Democrats often lag in the political money game. So it's no surprise that Republicans would rather die than give up their reservoirs of campaign money—their most potent political advantage.

HOW TO SUCCEED IN POLITICS WITHOUT REALLY TRYING

SO HOW WOULD THE DO-NOTHINGS KEEP wealthy special interests from buying what they want in politics?

How would the Do-Nothings keep them from corrupting the government, making laws for their own profit, blundering the nation into unnecessary wars, killing consumer and environmental protections, diluting the voting power of average Americans, selling the country out to foreigners, running up the nation's debt with budget carve-outs and tax cuts to the wealthy, exporting American jobs to Asia and elsewhere, and ruining our nation's reputation among the fellowship of nations?

Do nothing, of course!

It makes so much sense.

And it's so easy to do.

The Do-Nothings claim that any attempt to reign in the reckless behavior of moneyed interests is pointless—even dangerous. The Do-Nothings' Grand Solution is to lift all money limits and let the good times roll, but require candidates to disclose who is giving and getting money. But full disclosure is a moving target with today's Do-Nothings. They maintain that names of donors should be disclosed to the public, yet they have been fighting the Internal Revenue Service and the Federal Election Commission to keep their donors anonymous and their "dark money" flowing into Republican coffers.

Here's a quick rundown of the Do-Nothings' major tenets:

- Campaign finance laws do not curb corruption, they cause it.
- Campaign spending limits protects incumbents from competition and hurts challengers trying to establish name recognition.
- Wealthy donors do not corrupt politicians—they simply give their money to candidates who share their political beliefs.
- Politicians do not give their wealthy donors any more access or special treatment than they would to the poorest of their constituents.
- More campaign money—not less—is needed for the good of democracy.
- More lobbying means more and better information is given to elected and appointed officials tasked with making political decisions.
- The free market should reign supreme so that campaign money will rightly flow to deserving candidates who work the hardest to

collect it.

- Wealthy candidates do not buy public office—they are simply proven leaders whose success stories appeal to voters.
- Politicians, contrary to media accounts, make impartial decisions, unswayed by campaign donations, free meals, free vacations, promises of lucrative jobs (usually lobbying) for themselves or relatives, or any other exchange of value.
- Disclosure of donor names and the amounts they contribute are the only information necessary for citizens to make their own judgments about whether or not a candidate is tainted by special interest money.
- Citizens should have the freedom to spend any amount of money they want on elections.

BARRY BONDS FOR CONGRESS?

BRADLEY A. SMITH, LAW SCHOOL PROFESSOR and conservative election lawyer, is perhaps the nation's leading voice opposed to campaign finance laws. He is the perennial hired gun congressional Republicans trot out to squelch proposed campaign finance laws that gather a little too much traction.

According to Smith's faculty bio on Capital University Law School's website, he has been called "the most sought-after witness" when Congress considers campaign finance issues. Smith is a classic Do-Nothing contrarian. He firmly believes that campaign laws designed to curb the outsized influence of America's wealthy donor class are folly, pointless, and harmful for America.

On February 27, 1997, the Do-Nothings in Congress summoned Smith to Capitol Hill to torpedo the McCain-Feingold bill, which was gaining steam.

The following is an excerpt from Smith's testimony before the House Judiciary Subcommittee on the Constitution:

The stated goals of the 1974 FECA (Federal Election Campaign Act) Amendments were to lower the cost of campaigning, reduce

the influence of so-called 'special interests,' open up the political system to change, and 'restore confidence in government.' So what has actually happened in the 20 years since the 1974 Amendments took effect? Well, campaign spending has increased by more than 350 percent; PAC contributions have increased by more than 800 percent; House
incumbents, who had previously outspent challengers by approximately 1.5 to 1, now outspend challengers by nearly 4 to 1; incumbent re-election rates have risen to record high levels, spurring the demand for term limits; and public confidence in government has fallen to record lows. Clearly, the 1974 FECA Amendments have been a dismal failure.[3]

Let's review.

First, Smith's opening sentence accurately describes what the 1974 FECA Amendments *would* have accomplished had the law, which included campaign spending limits, been fully implemented.

Second, he cites evidence that the 1974 FECA law was a dismal failure by pointing out that "campaign spending has increased more than 350 percent" during the 20 years since it passed. But he cynically fails to mention that the Supreme Court struck down campaign spending limits, the law's cornerstone. Spending caps were never implemented, so of course spending increased during those 20 years.

Third, he states PAC contributions have "increased by more than 800 percent," yet he testified against an early version of the McCain-Feingold bill that included a PAC ban.[4] Smith and fellow Do-Nothings denounced the ban as an unconstitutional abridgement of free speech. Excessive lobbying led to the provision being stripped from the bill.

Fourth, Smith cites the increasing ratio of incumbent spending to challenger spending: 1.5 to 1 rising to 4 to 1. This book has already shown examples of how spending limits would eliminate this unfair incumbent money advantage.

Fifth, Smith states that "incumbent re-election rates have risen to record high levels," intimating that the 1974 Amendments law was to blame for the drop in the public's confidence in government, which he states had "fallen to record lows." Let's look again at the U.S. House incumbent re-election chart on the next page.

A quick glance shows Smith's contention is false. Overall, incumbent re-election rates pretty much stayed the same from 1974 to 1997, the period Smith is referencing. They did not rise at all. They actually fell a bit from 1976 to 1982. And as far as blaming the 1974 Amendments for low public confidence in government, that's just nonsense.

You've got to admire the professor for the size of his shovel.

U.S. House Re-Election Rates: 1964-2014

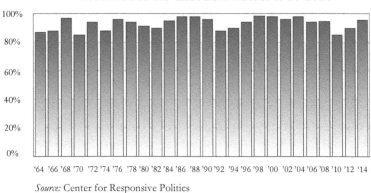

Source: Center for Responsive Politics

If you distill the main arguments of Smith and his fellow contrarians, you get this:

Since past legislative efforts to reign in wealthy special interests from exerting undue influence on elections have been weak and have created unintentional loopholes that are easily exploited to circumvent these laws, it is clear that all efforts to root out corruption by regulating campaign money are doomed to failure and should be stopped. The real solution is deregulation and full disclosure, so we know who is getting the money and how they are using it.

But that's like saying:

Since past efforts to contain steroid use in professional baseball have been weak and have created unintentional loopholes for those using the latest technology to develop newer drugs that can escape detection, it is clear that all efforts to root out this corruption by regulating steroids are doomed to failure and should be stopped. The real solution is deregulation of these drugs and full disclosure of who is giving and receiving steroids and how they are being administered.

So would deregulating performance-enhancing drugs for baseball players and letting the fans know who is on the juice, where they got it, and how it's being used restore integrity to the game? Or would it make more sense to design better rules to stamp out steroid use so everyone is competing on a level playing field, and fans could better judge who the exceptional players truly are and whether their heroics are the product of natural talent and honest, hard work?

Let's use another example:

Microsoft is constantly trying to stay one step ahead of hackers who attack computers using Windows software by infecting them with computer viruses. Microsoft fights back by designing new "patches" to the network, but hackers eventually find ways around the patch. Microsoft's efforts are doomed to failure and should be stopped.

So, just because determined hackers will always find a way to exploit the system, or get around the latest patch—like the way donors and influence peddlers get around the latest campaign finance rules—should Microsoft stop trying to protect everyone's computer? Or should it just give up and let these thieves infect the entire system and have their way with us?

LINCOLN AND THE DO-NOTHINGS

WHEN THE LIBERTARIAN MAGAZINE *REASON* asked Professor Smith what the ideal campaign finance system would look like, he replied: "The ideal system is the system we had that elected

Abraham Lincoln . . . which is no regulation."⁵

Perhaps we should address Smith's Do-Nothing response by taking a stroll back through history to Lincoln's time when elections were unregulated and the political free market reigned. Remember, in such an atmosphere, which the Do-Nothings heartily embrace, everything is up for sale to the highest bidder. So, it would logically mean that votes could be bought and sold like shares of a company.

Sound farfetched?

Well, it was once an accepted practice in American politics. Throughout most of the 1800s, New York City's Tammany Hall political machine openly bought votes to elect its Democratic candidates. The average price of a vote was about $5. The price for those who figured out how to vote more than once—a "repeat voter"—reportedly rose to $30. In the 1844 election, officials reported that *135 percent* of eligible New Yorkers had turned out to vote.⁶

Of course today, if the Do-Nothing political system were in place, votes could fetch much more than $30. Citizens could auction off their votes on eBay or craigslist for a tidy sum. They could join with friends, neighbors, or even whole towns and sell blocks of their bundled votes on the latest voter-selling app. That way, wealthy candidates could just go online and purchase a public office. Then they wouldn't be bothered with lowering themselves, interacting with average Americans and listening to their concerns. This freewheeling, free market system would be so much more efficient, squeezing out all the waste.

The Do-Nothings would have liked the 1800s. Votes were bought and sold like bottles of whiskey.

Similar to current times, if a candidate wasn't wealthy back then, the only real path into public office was sidling up to the big boys.

Can you picture Abraham Lincoln groveling for campaign donations, calling on Northern company fat cats who got rich off government war contracts during his first administration? Can you imagine him sucking up to those war profiteers—begging them to bankroll his flagging 1864 re election campaign?[7] And can you imagine Lincoln in cahoots with extortionists who helped fuel his victory?

Well, it happened.

Lincoln had no choice. There were no meaningful campaign finance laws, no public financing of campaigns, and no government agencies policing campaign shenanigans. Like today, but even more so, the candidate with the most money (almost) always won. Fortunately, Lincoln wasn't caught in a Mathew Brady daguerreotype on bended knee begging for donations from business tycoons. We wouldn't have viewed our beloved president the same way.

Lincoln Republicans were so intent on maintaining their precious money advantage that they enlisted the help of Simon Cameron, a political power broker from Pennsylvania.

SIMON CAMERON
(1799-1889)

Cameron's political machine openly purchased votes and bullied government workers by threatening to take away their jobs if they didn't give 2 percent of their pay to the Republican Party.[8]

Cameron had been a huge boon to Republican coffers over the years. He parlayed his corruption into a U.S. Senate seat in 1857.

He lost the Republican presidential nomination to Lincoln in 1860, but landed on his feet as he swung a deal with the new president to be his secretary of war.[9] It didn't last long, as allegations of corruption and mismanagement dogged him. Cameron resigned, but it didn't matter. Republican leaders kept rewarding his ability to bring coin to the party. They supported Cameron's later Senate campaigns and appointed him to several high-profile jobs, including Minister of Russia, for which Cameron was pitifully unqualified.

Cameron was so corrupt, he achieved eternal notoriety for his utterance:

An honest politician is one who when he's bought, stays bought.[10]

Today's wealthy interests would wholeheartedly agree.

So if you want to bring back the *real* Wild West to the U.S. political system, the Do-Nothings are your guys.

REPUBLICAN WRECKING BALL

THE STORY OF POLITICAL CORRUPTION today, in large part, is the story of the Republican Party. Since the 1976 *Buckley* decision, Republicans have lodged lawsuit after lawsuit, chipping away at any and all campaign reforms designed to curb money's influence in America's political system.

James Bopp Jr., Republican National Committee vice chairman and election lawyer who filed the original *Citizens United* complaint, summed up the Republicans' strategy: "We had a 10-year plan to take all this down," Bopp said after the Supreme Court's 2010 *Citizens United* ruling. "And if we do it right, I think we can pretty well dismantle the entire regulatory regime that is called campaign finance law."[11]

Bopp's 10-year timeline seems accurate in retrospect.

In 2002, after the McCain-Feingold bill passed, Senator Mitch

McConnell (R-KY) immediately filed a lawsuit, *McConnnell v. Federal Election Commission*, challenging the new reform law. In December 2003, the Supreme Court ruled against *McConnell*, although it struck down some minor sections of the law. Reformers were jubilant, with such a far-reaching law surviving a rigorous court challenge.

But the celebration was short-lived.

President George W. Bush, who reluctantly signed McCain-Feingold into law, appointed conservative judges John Roberts in 2005 and Samuel Alito in 2006 to the Supreme Court. These two anti-reform justices quickly formed a solid voting block with conservative justices Clarence Thomas and Antonin Scalia. The reconstituted Court, with Justice Anthony Kennedy positioned as the conservative swing vote, soon displayed its distaste for campaign reform laws. In quick succession, the Court ruled in favor of a slew of Republican-led, anti-reform lawsuits that set a course for the future:

- 2006 — *Randall v. Sorrell*: Republican lawyer Bopp argued against Vermont's 1997 campaign reform law. The ruling crushed Vermont's direct challenge to the 1976 *Buckley v. Valeo* ban on campaign spending limits.

- 2007 — *Wisconsin Right To Life, Inc. v. Federal Election Commission*: Wisconsin Right To Life, a conservative nonprofit, anti-abortion group, convinced the Court to strike down the McCain-Feingold provision that banned independent groups from airing issue advocacy ads within 30 days of a primary election and 60 days of a general election. The group had sought to run issue advocacy ads within the 30-day blackout period before the 2004 Wisconsin federal primary.

- 2008 — *Davis v. Federal Election Commission*: Jack Davis, a wealthy Republican businessman from upstate New York, sued to kill McCain-Feingold's "millionaire's amendment." This provision allowed federal candidates of modest means running against wealthy, self-financed candidates to receive triple the $2,300 donation limit. The provision sought to make less wealthy candidates more competitive. Davis had spent millions of his own dollars, failing four times to capture New York's 26th District House seat. On his second try in 2006, Davis, a longtime Republican who switched his affiliation to Democrat, declared he would spend more than $350,000 of his own money on his campaign, which would have triggered the millionaire's amendment. Davis sued. The Court ruled that McCain-Feingold violated Davis's constitutional right to free speech. Davis lost the election anyway. On his fourth failed attempt in 2011, he switched his affiliation again, this time to Tea Party. Nearly all the money he spent on his campaigns came from his own pocket.[12]

- 2010—*Citizens United v. Federal Election Commission*: Citizens United, a conservative nonprofit, represented by Koch Industries lawyer Theodore Olsen, contested provisions of the McCain-Feingold law concerning the timing of express advocacy ads close to Election Day. They lost that argument. But the Court pivoted to another argument not included in the lawsuit, to overturn a 63-year-old ban on corporations and unions using their treasury funds in unlimited amounts to influence political campaigns. This decision eventually led to the creation of Super PACs.

- 2011—*Arizona Free Enterprise Club, et al. v. Bennett* and *McComish v. Bennett* (two cases the Supreme Court combined into one): A libertarian advocacy group, Arizona Free Enterprise Club, and conservative Arizona state senator, John McComish, each brought a case to kill the provision of Arizona's 1998 public financing law that provided additional, escalating funds to candidates who opted into the public financing system (and agreed to spending and donation limits) to keep them competitive with wealthy candidates who refused public financing and attendant spending limits. The Court's conservative majority found that the provision violated wealthy candidates' First Amendment rights to free speech.

- 2012—*American Tradition Partnership, et al v. Steve Bullock, Attorney General of Montana*: American Tradition Partnership, a conservative advocacy group, challenged a Montana state law that banned corporations from making campaign contributions to political committees or groups that engaged in express advocacy. The law challenged the 2010 *Citizens United* ruling that allowed corporations to give money directly from their treasuries for political purposes. The Court sided with the plaintiff and against the state of Montana, without even hearing oral arguments. It reiterated the key point it made in its *Citizens United* ruling: "political speech does not lose First Amendment protection simply because its source is a corporation." [13]

- 2014—*Shaun McCutcheon, et. al. v. Federal Election Commission*: Wealthy Alabama businessman and Republican National Committee (RNC) member Shaun McCutcheon teamed with RNC leaders to overturn the Federal Election Campaign Act Amendments of 1974 provision that limited an individual's aggregate contributions.

- 2014—*Republican National Committee v. Federal Election Commission*: The RNC, hot on the heels of its *McCutcheon* victory, filed a new lawsuit together with the Republican Party of Louisiana seeking to overturn the McCain-Feingold "soft money" ban. The RNC wanted to return to the days when political parties could collect unlimited amounts of money and seed it to candidates and independent expenditure groups. In other words, the national party wanted to regain its seat at the adult's table as an election kingmaker. A lower federal court dismissed the case, but the plaintiffs may likely seek an audience with the Supreme Court at some future date.

- 2016—*Evenwel v. Abbott*: A conservative Texas voter, Sue Evenwel, aided by a conservative advocacy group, sought a revision to the state senate's redistricting map that would give more political voice to white rural voters at the expense of non-white urban voters. In a challenge to the one citizen, one vote precept, Evenwel wanted only registered voters to be counted instead of all citizens in determining the size and boundaries of state senate districts. In April 2016, the Supreme Court ruled against Evenwel.

Thanks to the Republicans' dismantling of campaign finance laws, the rate of money spent on elections today has eclipsed the galloping rate of health care costs and private college tuition. [14] And the inflationary pace will only accelerate in future years as more money is injected into the system, spurring higher campaign costs and squeezing out more potential candidates who cannot afford the higher prices to run.

GEORGE WILL MAKES THE CASE
FOR CAMPAIGN SPENDING LIMITS

CAMPAIGN SPENDING LIMITS would abridge free speech, but protect it as well.

The purpose of limiting free speech is to ensure everyone is equally heard, as in the "one citizen, one vote" democratic principle. But is abridging the First Amendment wrong in the pursuit of equality and curbing corruption?

Let's ask George Will, conservative commentator and one of the nation's foremost critics of campaign spending limits.

In June 2006, Will penned a scathing "epitaph" in *The Washington Post* for Vermont's campaign spending limits law after the Supreme Court killed it by refusing to overturn *Buckley v. Valeo*. "Campaign finance reform is what it pretends to combat: corruption," Will fumed. "The Supreme Court should have said something like that when it struck down, as unconstitutional abridgements of free speech, Vermont's severe limits on contributions to and spending by campaigns." [15] Basically, Will is stating that any abridgement of free speech that seeks to achieve equality and combat corruption is sacrilegious, scurrilous—and, well, corrupt.

Harsh words.

But let's visit 1996 as Will strenuously defends the Phoenix Preparatory Academy in its legal fight to uphold its school uniform policy. The Arizona private school instituted the policy to combat gang violence, sliding attendance, and poor test scores—in a sense, corruption. Two of the 1,174 students enrolled objected to the policy and sued the school, claiming their First Amendment rights were being abridged.

In his *Newsweek* column, Will sided *against* the two students.

He depicted their lawyer as having the "Southwest's most serious case of a civil liberties fetish."[16] In classic hyperbole, Will then mocked the lawyer's defense of the students' rights by saying "(the lawyer) decided the school uniform policy was the thin end of the wedge of fascism, or at least a rape of the First Amendment—clothes as speech . . . "[17]

And what was Will's rationale that the First Amendment rights of these two students, who refused to wear school uniforms, were *not* being abridged?

Well, it was because the academy allowed each student to wear a button on their school uniform on which they could make any statement they wanted (within reason). In other words, their freedom of speech was being abridged or *limited*, but equal with all other students. "Students are allowed to wear buttons bearing political, religious and other messages," Will wrote. So the two students "cannot claim to be utterly oppressed."[18]

But isn't that the same argument in support of campaign spending limits?

By limiting spending, you are limiting First Amendment rights, just like the school was limiting the rights of students by not allowing them to fully express themselves with their choice of attire. Further, the one button students were allowed to wear gave each classmate an equal opportunity to express themselves and have their voices heard. The one button is akin to a capped amount of campaign spending, giving candidates equal opportunity to express themselves and have their messages heard by voters. And with the smaller, equal button space each student was allotted, it forced them to make their messages count. Spending limits, too, would force candidates to focus and hone their messages to make them count, instead of using unlimited spending to slime their opponents with endless attack ads.

To appropriate George Will's reasoning and apply it to campaign spending limits, candidates are allowed to freely express themselves within the limits of a campaign spending cap, so candidates "cannot claim to be utterly oppressed."

DISCLOSURE AS PANACEA

THE DO-NOTHINGS ARE MOST CONTENT to curl up in the warm lap of "disclosure" as the remedy for all campaign finance ills.

Somehow, they believe, revealing the names of donors (sometimes) and their donation amounts will thoroughly cleanse America's political system of its rot.

They are not alone.

Many moderate Democratic and Republican politicians, when asked how they would instill honesty, impartiality, and integrity into American politics, blandly reply: "Sunshine is the best disinfectant."

But America has passed dozens of campaign disclosure laws since the Publicity Act of 1910 with little effect in relation to the overall corruption problem.

Today, there are hundreds of wealthy contributors and political groups that pop up every election season seeking to influence the political process. They hide behind a blur of shell entities with trite, interchangeable names like: Americans For A Better Future, Freedom Fighters for Democracy, Justice For All Americans, etc. Many of these groups don't even have a membership. They're run by shadowy, partisan operatives with little or no accountability. It is virtually impossible to keep track of all this.

Supreme Court justice Anthony Kennedy and other "sunshiners" believe the Internet is the solution to healing America's sick, corrupt system. Kennedy wrote in his 2010 *Citizens United* majority opinion that the Internet will allow "prompt disclosure of expenditures." He claimed that with this new technology, "citizens can see whether elected officials are 'in the pocket' of so-called moneyed interests." In Kennedy's mind, this makes perfect sense. But the problem with being holed up in wood-paneled chambers and living in the rarified air of the Washington, D.C., elite for too long is that you tend to lose touch with the general population.

An unhealthy number of Americans are, unfortunately, politically illiterate. The Annenburg Public Policy Center at the University of Pennsylvania conducted a 2017 study that showed only 26 percent of Americans can name all three branches of government. Thirty-seven percent could not name a right guaranteed by the First Amendment.

And as for Kennedy's belief that Americans can ferret out compromised, corrupt political candidates, a May 2013 Gallup poll revealed that only 35 percent of respondents could name their U.S. representative in Congress.[19] A 2015 poll by Fusion TV, a cable and satellite television station geared to millennials, showed only 23 percent of respondents aged 18-34 could name one of their state's U.S. senators.

Apparently, the proponents of disclosure laws as panacea somehow expect average Americans, many of whom have no idea how the country works or who their elected representatives are, to have the skills and time needed to:

- research all the candidates for office, their work profiles, benefactors, funders, and friends;
- sift through all the shadowy shell groups to see who runs them, who funds them, and what their agendas are;
- spend countless hours poring over thousands of Excel spreadsheets, tracing millions in contributions; and
- decipher which politicians are "in the pocket" of special interests.

Really?

These "sunshiners" need to get out more.

The public, of course, could rely on the media to expose the identities of big money donors and how much and to whom they contribute. But ironically, many citizens and many of the same Do-Nothing politicians promoting "disclosure as panacea" are the same ones denouncing the "fake media" as partisan and untrustworthy.

Let's face it, the empty slogan of "sunshine is the best disinfectant" is just another excuse for doing nothing.

And it works—just not for average Americans.

THE PUBLIC'S AIRWAVES

WHAT A great idea!

Require television stations to give free or discounted air-time so candidates wouldn't have to raise huge sums of campaign cash to get their messages out. After all, the public owns the airwaves. It's so simple, right?

Wrong.

The Do-Nothings would not approve. To them, it would be an egregious government takeover of private industry.

Yes, the public owns the airwaves, but the Federal Communications Commission (FCC) gives the nation's broadcasting corporations free licenses to use the airwaves—and the corporations, with the support of the Do-Nothings, refuse to give any free or discounted airtime back to the public for political ads.

In 1934, broadcasters convinced Congress that the industry deserved free operating licenses because it provided programming, such as news and public service announcements, which served the public interest. The issue was revisited in the mid-1990s when the broadcasters approached the FCC seeking free licenses for the new high-definition digital TV spectrum. Broadcasters' plea for free licenses prompted a blistering response from former Senator Bob Dole (R-KS), the 1996 Republican presidential nominee. Dole claimed the new spectrum, which the public owned as well, was worth $12 billion to $70 billion if auctioned off to broadcasters. The FCC estimated the price at $37 billion. Dole wrote in a March 27, 1997, *New York Times* opinion piece:

> The broadcasters insist that they need these airwaves—on which they will duplicate their programming in digital—to make the transition to high-definition television. O.K., but why not pay a fair price? Since 1993, wireless phone and direct-broadcast satellite companies have paid for airwaves to upgrade or offer new services. Just last year, the government auctioned off licenses for the lower-quality spectrum, raising a whopping $20 billion. We don't give away trees to newspaper publishers. Why should we give away

more airwaves to broadcasters? The airwaves are a natural resource. They do not belong to the broadcasters, phone companies, or any other industry. They belong to the American people.

Dole's plea fell on deaf Do-Nothing ears. The issue hasn't been seriously explored since.

Advanced democracies around the world with campaign spending cap laws routinely grant candidates free air-time, greatly reducing the cost to get messages out to voters. Free air-time should be a part of America's campaign spending limits system, too.

14

The Benefits of Campaign Spending Limits

STEVE POIZNER WAS CLEARLY RATTLED, snapping his head in a strange herky-jerky motion as he addressed a campaign gathering supporting his 2010 California gubernatorial bid.

He railed against the reckless, unlimited campaign spending of his Republican primary opponent, billionaire Meg Whitman, former CEO of the online giant eBay. Whitman, a political novice who never bothered to vote most of her life, was leading in the polls by a hefty margin. Poizner, California's insurance commissioner, was outraged that Whitman had no government experience yet stood to vault ahead of him into one of the most important governor seats in the country, just by virtue of her money.

"When people really sit down to fill out their ballots or go into the election booth," Poizner told supporters, "I think they're going to be disturbed by the fact she hasn't voted for 28 years straight, and then all of a sudden she spends $90 million, four times more than anyone's ever spent ever in the history of Republican primaries in gubernatorial politics . . . That amount of spending is going to really backfire on her."[1]

It didn't.

Whitman trounced Poizner 64 to 27 percent to win the nomination.

Poizner thought the campaign system was corrupt, and that he had gotten a raw deal. After all, Poizner, a Silicon Valley billion-aire himself, spent far less to buy *his* political career. He couldn't possibly compete in the gubernatorial primary with the paltry $30 million of his own fortune he spent on the race.

As for Whitman, she soldiered on to November, spending a total of $177 million to try and capture the seat, including a whopping $144 million of her own money.[2] She'd have likely rolled into the governor's chair, too, had she not run smack into a brick wall, otherwise known as the Brown political dynasty. Jerry Brown, a former California governor, state attorney gen-eral, and presidential contender, whose father had been a storied California governor, beat her handily in the general election. Brown spent $36 million to secure the victory.[3]

Spending the most money in a campaign is a *near* guarantee of political victory in American politics, as the Whitman saga shows. Brown was an outlier—the only Democrat who had the pedigree to overcome her huge money advantage. What were the odds she would face a former governor in his 70s, coming out of the wood-work, who would run for an office he held nearly 30 years prior? If he hadn't thrown his hat in the ring, there simply was no one else who could have stopped her.

The point is that if Whitman were of modest wealth, she'd have been roped off from competing. She certainly wouldn't have been perceived as a legitimate candidate. In fact, she likely would have been denied a microphone to participate in the candidate de-bates. And she would have been treated like the seven other "no-body" Republican gubernatorial candidates in the race, who each garnered 2 percent or less of the vote. The media would have ig-nored her, and she would have been considered a crank, standing outside the debate hall—as some low-profile candidates do—with duct tape over her mouth and a scrawled sign that read "Let Me Debate!"

But no, she purchased a "legitimate" candidacy. Worse, she likely stole the space that might have been occupied by more wor-thy and talented citizens who couldn't afford to buy their way into the game. It's one of the reasons why America has a dearth of learned, trustworthy politicians representing us. The problem is, of course, the Constitution's loophole that allows wealthy people to buy more democracy than others. It's been a glaring symptom of poor democratic health, growing every election cycle, as it takes ever higher sums to participate.

Will Rogers, famed humorist, writer, and social commentator, once observed: "Politics has got so expensive that it takes lots of money to even get beat with nowadays."[4]

WILL ROGERS

If effective spending limits were enacted, voters would have a better and deeper candidate pool than the usual "lesser of two evils" choice we drearily see . . . every . . . single . . . election. There would be a lot more average Americans who could afford to throw their hats in the ring and have a decent chance of winning without sidling up to party power brokers and slickening up with special interest money.

But what about Bernie Sanders, the Vermont senator and 2016 democratic presidential candidate, and a few others who have garnered political success by only accepting small donations?

There will always will be, rare, low-donation candidates who manage to squeak through the machinery with a viable candidacy.

But this kind of candidacy is not the rule. It is the exception. If campaign spending limits were instituted, it would become the rule. As long as money remains the mother's milk of politics, these low-donation candidacies will remain outliers.

LIST OF BENEFITS

A CAMPAIGN SPENDING LIMITS CONSTITUTIONAL AMENDMENT will accomplish the following changes in American politics if spending and donation limits are implemented fairly and effectively:

- *Restore the power of each American's vote*: By overturning *Buckley* and stripping the ability of wealthy special interests to buy America's elections, laws, and politicians with their "free speech" dollar votes, political power will be redistributed to average Americans, the rightful owners of our democracy. The ideal of one citizen, one vote will be restored.

- *End the money incentive and arms race*: Instituting this most critical element of political reform will move the focus of campaigns away from money and toward issues, where it belongs. Victors will no longer be determined by who raises the most money, but whose leadership and ideas resonate best with voters.

- *End politicians' dependence on special interests*: Setting low campaign donation limits will cut the umbilical cord between candidates and wealthy interests. A limit of $600 (adjusted periodically for inflation), for example, will be set for *all* donors, including individuals, political groups, unions, and businesses. This action, coupled with a ban on bundling and other circumvention schemes, will grant our elected leaders the independence they need to make impartial decisions that are in the best interests of all Americans.

- *Increase competition and voter choice*: Lowering the cost of mounting a credible campaign will tear down the barriers to competition for elected office in all levels of government. It will encourage talented citizens regardless of income level and occupation to run, creating a deeper candidate pool for voters who are routinely stuck with a choice of the lesser of two evils.

- *Stop wealthy candidates from purchasing public office*: Spending limits would not only block wealthy people from using their personal fortunes to buy their way into public office, but would also curb their appointments to cushy diplomatic posts or high-level administration jobs for which they are not qualified.

- *Increase voter turnout*: Citizen participation is absolutely essential to maintaining a vibrant democracy. For decades, many average Americans have shown their disgust at our political system by tuning out and refusing to vote. Curbing money's influence in politics will quell the cynicism of many who believe the political system is rigged against them. By creating a more equitable and fair system that is open to all voices, more citizens will engage in politics. With more citizens voting and participating in the process, a truer picture of the will and consensus of the country will emerge. And with more voters engaged, elections will no longer be distorted by the outsized voting power of the extreme right and left, whose adherents religiously turn out at the polls.

- *Encourage candidates to be more accessible*: Encouraging candidates to reach out to a broader donor base instead of a handful of wealthy people to fill campaign coffers will energize our democracy. Candidates will have more time to meet voters, debate opponents, and develop legislative solutions to problems. Restricting spending will hinder wealthy candidates and powerful incumbents from hiding behind their money, employing the old strategy of ignoring poorly-funded challengers who often call for public debates and open discussion of the issues.

- *End the saturation of negative campaign ads*: Clipping the spending wings of over-financed candidates and independent groups will sharply curtail the deluge of negative ads that pollute and pulse through the airwaves, distorting the candidates and issues every election cycle. There are currently many citizens well-qualified for public office, but they refuse to run.

They are intimidated by the wealthy candidate's ability to fund opposition research that digs up "dirt" on an opponent. Everything is fair game for opposition researchers, no matter how invasive. The material is then distorted, twisted, and spun into negative attack ads, embarrassing the opponent, and perhaps their family members and friends. With spending caps in place, candidates will be forced to use their limited funds more judiciously, which means burnishing their own credentials and character instead of denigrating another's.

- *Force candidates to demonstrate budgeting skills*: Forcing a candidate to manage his or her campaign budget with finite resources—a talent that takes skill, wisdom, creativity, and resourcefulness—will be an eye-opening experience for voters. After all, budgeting is arguably the primary duty and responsibility of an elected official. Without spending limits, voters cannot get a good read on budgeting skills if a wealthy candidate solves their campaign revenue problems by simply reaching into his or her pocket for a few million dollars with little regard for the campaign's total cost. There is an utter disconnect in our political system that rewards a candidate who spends like a drunken sailor to get elected, while promising voters a fiscally-responsible, budget-cutting platform once in office. When the system sends the message that unlimited spending equals success, there shouldn't be any mystery why this country is so mired in debt. We ask government to do more with less. Why shouldn't we ask this of candidates as well?

- *Curb big government and bloated federal and state budgets*: Lobbyists generously donate large sums to campaigns and Super PACs of lawmakers, enticing them to insert budget pork like earmarks and carve-outs into federal and state budgets. It encourages big government, not efficient government. The results are endless deficits and mounting debt from spending America does not need, such as: bridges to nowhere, privately-contracted Navy supply ports that gouge taxpayers, contractor-supplied military hardware the military doesn't need or even want, private contractor gouging of military personnel for food, laundry, and other services. It's the same corruption as the 1980s military procurement scandal that revealed contractor gouging for such items as: hammers ($435 each), toilet seats ($600 each), and coffee pots ($7,000 each). Then there are the taxpayer-funded studies. A recent crop compiled by Senator Tom Coburn (R-OK) included: $856,000 to study the time it would take to teach mountain lions to ride a treadmill, $307,524 to study the swirl from sea monkeys swimming in the water, $202,000 to study whether Wikipedia is sexist, and $171,000 to study the gambling habits of monkeys.[5]

- *End party "ownership" of public offices*: Capping spending and donation limits will diminish the influence of political parties and increase the influence of average Americans. The major parties will no longer have the incentive to amass huge sums with which to play kingmaker, particularly on state and local levels. It will end the power grab of Republican and Democratic party bosses across America who hand-pick nominees based on service to the party or pedigree while often forcing more talented and capable people to "wait their turn." The major parties do not own political offices, although many of their leaders think they do. This shift in power to average Americans will allow more voices to be heard, creating a more robust pool of candidates. Parties should stick to party-building and other support activities.

- *Diminish outside domestic influences in elections*: Capping spending and donations will curb the influence of wealthy out-of-state donors seeking to manipulate federal, state and local elections that are often pivotal to retaining or wresting control of Congress, a state legislature, or a governorship. Wealthy interlopers also work to unseat and silence outspoken, high-profile politicians in another state whose views they find irritating. It is common sense that the citizens of a state or local jurisdiction should pick their own leaders—not wealthy elites who live hundreds or thousands of miles away.

- *Diminish foreign influences in elections and protect national security*: Many large U.S. corporations today are multinational and can give unlimited donations to candidates' Super PACs and other political groups. These companies, which may be partly owned by foreign investors, routinely borrow money from foreign banks and conduct business with foreign governments. With many international dollars exchanging hands, their allegiances are likely to become entangled and muddled. With the expansion of unregulated dark money in campaigns, in which donors may legally remain anonymous, political donations can be impossible to trace. Spending caps would help quash the potential of foreign meddling in U.S. elections.

- *Diminish the power of incumbent "rollover" accounts*: Spending limits will discourage the incumbents' practice of stockpiling unspent donations from past campaigns (or raising donations when unopposed) to discourage competitors, fund a future run for higher office, climb the House or Senate leadership ladder by donating to incumbent colleagues in close re-election races, or give oneself a golden handshake when ousted from office or retiring voluntarily.

- *Foster ballot initiative fairness*: Spending caps will curb in-state and out-of-state corporate interests from virtually dictating policy to local citizens. Corporate spending on ballot initiatives has been rising in recent years, dwarfing the spending of local groups. In 2014, corporate entities spent $272 million on the top 50 ballot initiatives across the country. That is 75 percent of total spending compared to 25 percent for mostly local, independent groups.[6] With such a large spending advantage, these corporate groups won 96 percent of the time, according to the Center for Public Integrity, a nonpartisan, Washington, D.C., think tank.

IMPORTANCE OF DONATION LIMITS

UP TO THIS POINT, THIS BOOK HAS FOCUSED mainly on campaign expenditures. Let's turn our attention now to campaign donations, a critical part of the campaign reform equation.

Although the 1976 Supreme Court allowed *contribution* limits to stand, the feeble rules left in place have been eviscerated over the years, making it easy for wealthy interests to circumvent the laws, funneling their money to their desired candidates.

Contribution limits, if properly designed and enforced, would work in tandem with spending limits to even political power and access for all Americans and curb today's back-door circumvention schemes.

If all contributions from donors seeking political influence were capped at $600 per U.S. House election, for example, it would flatten wealthy interests' outsized influence.

Let's use our $600 U.S. House donation limit to illustrate the importance of setting appropriate political contribution caps. And let's set a spending ceiling of $300,000, instead of the $1.5 million incumbents routinely spend to retain their seats.

Many average Americans can afford to donate up to $600 to one or more candidates. The cap would also mean that Super PACs, phony political nonprofit groups, billionaires, corporatists, and all others would be limited to donating no more than $600 per each candidate or political group, per election. This means that a candidate could reach his or her $300,000 spending ceiling with only 500 of their district voters contributing the $600 maximum. To put this in perspective, the U.S. Census Bureau in 2010 apportioned approximately 710,767 citizens per congressional district. So even if the contribution ceiling were set as low as $50, a candidate would need only 6,000 of those 710,767 citizens to donate up to the limit to reach the $300,000 spending ceiling. And we haven't factored in donations from PACs, checkoff donations on tax returns, and other sources.

Setting low donation limits will clearly sever politicians' dependence on wealthy special interests and political power brokers for campaign money. After all, how could a billionaire, PAC, or party boss threaten and manipulate a politician by withholding a $600 contribution?

Even Supreme Court Justice Clarence Thomas, a fervent campaign reform foe, stated that low donation limits would likely never provoke a *quid pro quo* with politicians. In *Randall v. Sorrell,* the 2006 case that killed Vermont's 1997 campaign spending cap law, which included a $200 contribution limit for campaign donors, Thomas wrote:

> Indeed, it is almost impossible to imagine that any legislator would ever find his scruples overcome by a $201 donation." [7]

RESERVING A RIGHT

THE AMENDMENT PROPOSED IN THIS BOOK will not force Congress, the states, or local jurisdictions to adopt spending limits or take any action at all.

It will simply reserve a right for citizens—a tool for the bettering of democracy.

If the Constitution is amended, Congress, the state legislatures, and local elected bodies will have the power to enact legislation allowing campaign spending and donation limits for elections.

The most important provision that any spending cap law must include is authorizing independent, nonpartisan citizens panels to set spending and contribution limits and administer the law. It is the only reasonable method to protect these laws from partisan manipulation. Special interest elites, party power brokers, and ambitious politicians will not give up their power, their fortunes, and their bloated livelihoods without a bitter struggle. They will bring all they have to bear on undermining and overturning laws enacting spending and donation limits.

It is an absolute certainty.

15

The FEC & Independent, Nonpartisan Citizens Panels

"The public does not trust a system where we (Congress) set our own rules, we're our own advisers, we're our own investigators, we're our own prosecutors, we're our own judges, and we're our own jurors." [1]

~SENATOR SUSAN COLLINS (R-ME), urging the creation of a nonpartisan oversight agency for Congress

FOR 27 YEARS, SENATOR BOB PACKWOOD (R-OR) enjoyed cornering young, unsuspecting 20-something female staffers in Capitol Hill elevators, his inner office, or other isolated areas and thrusting his tongue down their throats while groping them.

By the time he finished his career in Congress, the 61-year-old senator, husband, and father faced 41 charges of sexual harassment.

But Packwood wasn't worried.

Congress had exempted itself from the sexual harassment law it had passed for the rest of the nation. He eventually resigned his seat in 1995 when the media's drumbeat for his political demise would not abate.

After Packwood's departure, Congress quickly passed the 1995 Congressional Accountability Act, revoking Congress's exemption from a slew of labor, civil rights, and other measures, including sexual harassment, it had passed in prior sessions. But it continued to quietly exempt itself from other regulations, such as:

- investigatory subpoenas to obtain information for safety and health probes;
- posting of workers' rights in offices;
- protection for whistleblowers against retaliation;
- employee training on workplace rights and legal remedies;
- record keeping requirements for workplace injuries and illnesses;
- Freedom of Information Act;
- Americans With Disabilities Act requirements for sidewalks and restrooms.[2]

Congress also has a history of passing, then gutting reforms after its members are caught in violation. Under the cover of a midnight session when few members are present or a late Friday afternoon when members are preparing to return home to their districts, an amendment can quietly slip through with a furtive wink from leadership.

A recent example is Congress's insider trading scandal.

For years, members of Congress had been receiving confidential information during hearings and meetings on stocks, bonds, hedge funds, and other investments, then using that information to make millions in the financial markets. Domestic doyenne Martha Stewart, you may remember, spent time in the clink for the same ethical lapse. But Congress had exempted itself from insider trading laws.

A 2012 *Washington Post* analysis revealed that 131 sitting members of Congress or their family members bought and sold as much as $218 million in stocks and bonds of 323 companies from 2007 to 2010.[3] Further, all the companies had submitted legislation beneficial to their bottom lines that these 131 members had sat in judgment of, either in their assigned committees or full House votes.

According to the *Post*:

- *Senator Tom Coburn* (R-OK) reported buying $25,000 in bonds in a genetic technology company around the time he released a hold on legislation the firm supported;
- *Rep. Ed Whitfield* (R-KY) sold between $50,000 and $100,000 in General Electric stock shortly before a Republican filibuster killed legislation the company claimed was crucial to its profitability;
- *The family of Rep. Michael McCaul* (R-TX) bought securities between $286,000 and $690,000 in a high-tech company interested in a bill—highly profitable to the company—under his committee's jurisdiction.[4]

Faced again with a burgeoning scandal, Congress grudgingly passed the Stop Trading On Congressional Knowledge Act. President Obama signed it into law on April 4, 2012, at a media-soaked ceremony attended by both Republicans and Democrats.

A year later, Obama quietly signed a bill that gutted important provisions of the law, including the availability of disclosure forms that often contain evidence of insider trading. True to form, the stealth legislation began its passage with then-House Majority Leader Eric Cantor (R-VA) gaveling the bill through on the House floor on a sleepy Friday afternoon. Most members had already left for the weekend. With few in the chamber who even knew what the bill was, there was no debate. It took Cantor all of 30 seconds to sneak it through.[5] The administration announced the new law in a one sentence email.[6]

Gaveling through bills under the noses of congressional members and state legislators is standard operating procedure in this country. It's yet another reason why Americans distrust government. Indeed, the frequent inappropriate behavior and number of tawdry scandals that pour out of Congress and state legislatures every year is a testament to lawmakers' inability to police themselves.

ADMINISTERING SPENDING LIMITS

IN VIRTUALLY EVERY CONGRESSIONAL SESSION, members submit bills calling for a campaign spending limits constitutional amendment. All these measures concern federal elections and place Congress in charge of administering the law.

Big mistake.

If a campaign spending limits law is not independently and impartially administered, political partisans will simply manipulate, pervert, or water it down, rendering it useless. It's why the spending cap laws America passed in 1911, 1971 and 1974 were doomed to fail, even without the Supreme Court's assistance.

Politicians on all levels simply cannot be trusted to oversee the setting of such limits that would have a direct impact on their own political careers and on which party will control the legislative branch. Giving lawmakers control of spending limits would be just another opportunity, like redistricting, to warp and corrupt the democratic process for their own gain.

It is a blatant conflict of interest and a prescription for failure.

Political parties seek power, not fairness. It's a major reason why Congress is in frequent gridlock, with rigid ideological factions refusing to compromise and pass legislation for the good of the country. To party leaders, making their opponents look bad is key to winning control of the House or Senate.

To them, gamesmanship is more important than statesmanship.

To them, winning power is more important than moving the nation forward.

Congress and state legislatures are institutions in severe need of oversight. These elected bodies appoint ethics committees and oversight panels that fail time and again to corral the excesses of money, power, and ego. It's why these bodies must be stripped of administering and enforcing campaign finance and spending cap laws. And it's why independent, nonpartisan citizens panels are essential to perform this duty to protect the people's interests.

FEDERAL ELECTION COMMISSION

THE 1974 FECA AMENDMENTS, aside from instituting campaign spending limits, created the Federal Election Commission (FEC), the first-ever U.S. government agency solely dedicated to administering and enforcing campaign finance laws.

The FEC was supposed to be an independent entity—above the fray of partisan politics. But Congress appointed itself as the agency's overseer. Worse, the FEC's deeply flawed design allowed Congress and other partisans to undermine its independence and effectiveness at nearly every turn.

The FEC is composed of six voting members. The 1974 FECA gave power to the House, Senate, and president to each appoint two commission members. The Supreme Court ruled in *Buckley v. Valeo* that this appointment method violated the separation of powers, as Congress appointed four of the six commission members, while the president appointed only two. In response, Congress amended FECA in 1976, authorizing the president to appoint all six members from nominees recommended by Congress. The Senate retained its authority to confirm the appointments. The 1976 law also decreed that no more than three commission members may belong to the same political party—a prescription for gridlock.[8]

It's rare in government to see an important panel composed of an even number of members. Most committees or commissions usually comprise an odd number to avoid potential gridlock. So it's no surprise the FEC suffers frequent stalemates and inaction on the major issues the agency has faced in its 44-year history.

To encourage failure and dysfunction, Congress often jerks the FEC's funding back and forth during yearly budget deliberations. It also meddles in FEC affairs during the confirmation process, holding appointees hostage while Congress negotiates unrelated issues with the president. The agency operates on a $66 million budget and employs 375 staffers. Its design and structure has basically neutered its functioning. Today, the FEC is largely seen as deadwood—a huge stumbling block to effective political reform.

Since 2008, the FEC has deadlocked on more than 200 votes.[9] The three Republican members are far more radical than prior GOP commissioners in their fervor to block any sensible regulation. Four votes are needed to resolve a complaint, render an advisory opinion, or launch an investigation of improper campaign activities. By virtue of denying compromise and doing nothing, the FEC's Republican members are actually making *de facto* policy. If a campaign or political committee comes to the commission seeking direction as to whether an activity is illegal, and the commission gridlocks, it gives the campaign or group a virtual green light to conduct the activity.

One of the most egregious examples of FEC ineptitude is the commission's refusal to address political nonprofit groups in the 2016 election. As noted earlier in this book, these groups are supposed to conduct the majority of their activities benefiting social welfare groups and issues, not on political campaigns. But with the FEC deadlocked (and the IRS failing to regulate dark money), this rule has become a farce, and these nonprofits operate as any other political committee, raising unlimited campaign donations. They have grown into obese cash cows, pumping hundreds of millions of untraced, dark dollars into America's political system.

The FEC is so dysfunctional, law firms representing lobbyists and political power brokers actually market the commission's frequent gridlocks as advertising schemes to drum up business. The following excerpt was taken from the website of Covington & Burling, a high-powered Washington law and lobbying firm, in an article entitled, "The FEC: Where a 'Tie' Can Be (Almost) a 'Win'":

> All but the most risk averse parties should be comfortable treating the failure to obtain an advisory opinion where the vote is 3-3 as a license to go forward with the activity proposed in the advisory opinion request. In this context, a tie is not like kissing your cousin—it's nearly as good as a win for the requestor. If the Commission deadlocks, the requestor can virtually rest assured that the conduct that it placed in issue in the advisory opinion will not be the subject of an enforcement proceeding at the FEC—at least not one that will muster four votes of commissioners to find reason to believe that there has been a violation of the Act.[10]

When past FEC chair Ann Ravel first joined the agency, she fought to "bridge the partisan gap" and set the agency on the path prescribed by law. But the three Republican commissioners quickly spurned her good faith effort. Gridlock continued, greatly frustrating Ravel and her two Democratic colleagues. Before long, the Democrats and Republicans were barely on speaking terms. "The likelihood of the laws being enforced is slim," Ravel said, when she served as FEC chair. "I never want to give up, but I'm not under any illusions. People think the FEC is dysfunctional. It's worse than dysfunctional."[11]

In 2008, Republican FEC Commissioner Donald McGahn began his first term, heralding the commission's current era of extreme gridlock. McGahn, whose candidacy Senator Mitch McConnell (R-KY) championed, had spent a lucrative law career watering down and neutering campaign finance regulations for his Washington clients. McGahn, the two other Republican FEC commissioners, and their respective staff members soon cordoned themselves off from the Democratic commissioners and general FEC staff. They lunched by themselves and plotted strategy together.

McGahn, when asked why he opposed abolishing dark money,

replied: "It's what do you fear more. Do you fear the potential influence that money could buy on policy, which no one has ever proven or is very attenuated?" He added, "I fear the government more than my fellow citizen, so I come down on the side of protecting speech." [12]

That's not exactly impartial behavior befitting an agency designed as an independent referee of campaign finance laws.

In 2017, McGahn left the FEC to work as President Trump's White House Counsel. The president fired him a year later.

Perhaps the incident that perfectly illustrates the contempt Republicans have for the FEC occurred in 2000, when a Republican-designated commissioner seat became vacant. Senators Trent Lott (R-MS) and Mitch McConnell (R-KY) submitted the name of Bradley A. Smith to President Bill Clinton to fill the post. Smith, you may remember, is the Republicans' go-to guy who testifies against any significant campaign finance measure proposed in Congress. Clinton resisted. But the two senators blackmailed the president into nominating Smith by threatening to block his judicial nominees and stall confirmation hearings on Richard Holbrooke, whom Clinton had nominated to serve as U.S. Ambassador to the United Nations. Clinton relented.

In a smug move, Smith had none other than James Lane Buckley, the eponymous plaintiff in *Buckley v. Valeo*, swear him into office. Buckley, then a retired judge, symbolically conducted the ceremony at the headquarters of the Cato Institute, one of the foremost conservative think tanks dedicated to eradicating campaign finance laws.

Campaign finance reforms haven't worked in large part because cynical partisans like McConnell, Lott, Smith, Buckley, and McGahn have undermined them every step of the way. Apparently, they all neglected to read Section 310 (a) (3) of the FECA Amendments of 1974 concerning the five desired qualities of FEC commissioners. To wit: "Members shall be chosen on the basis of their maturity, experience, integrity, impartiality, and good judgment . . ." [13]

If applied not only to Smith, but the gang that nominated him, these guys would be 1 for 5 (experience—and that's tenuous).

INDEPENDENT CITIZENS PANELS

CONGRESS, STATE, AND LOCAL LEGISLATIVE BODIES should never be allowed anywhere near the setting and administering of spending and contribution limits.

The FEC stands as a glaring example of how *not* to administer campaign election law. Congress created the FEC to be an impartial judge, but through a lack of foresight, the agency soon morphed into the partisan, dysfunctional body it is today.

This means the FEC must be razed.

A new body must take its place that is truly independent and protected from the corrupting influences of Congress, money, and partisan politics.

The constitutional amendment proposed in this book *requires* any jurisdiction—federal, state, or local—that passes a spending limits law to appoint an independent, nonpartisan citizens panel to administer and enforce campaign election law.

It may seem an unusual step, but it's the only way spending limits will be effective. If the Founding Fathers had the foresight to require independent, nonpartisan citizens panels to oversee redistricting, for example, it would not be the corrupt, partisan cesspool it has become. Today, redistricting is more often used as a partisan tool to rob average Americans of their political power rather than distribute it fairly and equitably.

We cannot let this happen with campaign spending limits.

Let's examine the nation's redistricting history to get a better idea of why partisan legislative bodies cannot be trusted to police themselves. Redistricting has engendered many scandals and lawsuits that erupt every 10 years when these bodies are tasked with redrawing congressional, state, and local voting district boundaries.

The U.S. Constitution's Article I, Section 4 vests the states with regulating congressional elections. In truth, it is the political party in control of a state house that actually has that power, and with it, the authority to draw political district boundaries. By creatively drawing these boundary lines, the politicians in power often manipulate the lines to corral more voters of the opposing party into fewer districts, resulting in fewer lawmakers of the opposing party being elected. This ensures the power party stays in power. A common power party scheme is to manipulate the boundaries so two or more opposition party incumbents find themselves in the same district, guaranteeing one incumbent will be eliminated. There are many more tricks involving boundary lines that either disburse or condense certain voting populations with the ultimate goal of diluting their political power at the expense of the power party.

"Gerrymandering" entered the American political lexicon in 1812 when Massachusetts Governor Elbridge Gerry (R) signed the state's redistricting map into law. Gerry's Republican Party leaders drew the boundary lines to protect their incumbent legislators against Federalist Party candidates by corralling as many Federalist voters into the fewest districts. The map's contorted boundaries, however, particularly around Boston, were so abnormal—jutting out in strange ways—that they resembled the shape of a salamander. The story goes that a Federalist editor in Boston, upon seeing the new boundary lines for the first time, exclaimed, "Salamander? Call it a Gerrymander."[14]

Fast forward 200 years to 2012, when redistricting lines were last instituted, and you'll find not much has changed. New York, known for having one of the more corrupt state legislatures, erupted in controversy over the redistricting map its state politicians put forth. The map, challenged in court, had a number of voting districts so contorted, they earned derisive sobriquets: The Splattered Bug of the Bronx (34th senate district); The Leftover Lightning Bolt (101st assembly district); The Buffalo Bender (60th senate district); The Lobster Claw (13th senate district); and The

Crocodile (3rd assembly district).[15]

As of 2019, there were lawsuits contesting redistricting maps in 38 of the 50 states (three quarters) based on the 2010 U.S. Census.[16] Most of the plaintiffs accused their partisan state legislatures of grossly manipulating boundary lines to protect incumbents and party power.

There were 37 lawsuits challenging the redistricting maps based on the 2000 U.S. Census.[17]

There is also a bigger prize at stake.

The state legislatures also draw the boundaries of U.S. representative districts. These redistricting lines play a major role in deciding whether Democrats or Republicans will control the House of Representatives over coming decades. There is a tremendous amount of partisan pressure surrounding this process.

Local district boundaries are usually less contentious and partisan than federal and state districts, although moneyed interests in even the smallest jurisdictions may seek to manipulate and corrupt the process to benefit their business interests.

Fortunately, citizens in 13 states have taken redistricting away from the politicians. These citizens understand that in a healthy democracy, politicians do not choose voters—voters choose politicians.

To be effective, independent, nonpartisan citizens panels must reflect the composition of the citizenry—professionally, racially, economically, geographically. In this manner, the administering of redistricting, elections, or other tasks will more accurately reflect the will and consensus of the people and not the ambitions of national parties and their elected politicians to control Congress and the state legislatures.

Partisan politicians and their power broker friends question whether any panel operating in the political arena can be truly independent and nonpartisan. The California Citizens Redistricting Commission (CCRC), in fact, is an outstanding example of how such panels can be chosen and perform their duties in citizens' best interests.

CALIFORNIA SHOWS THE WAY

FOR OVER 10 YEARS, CALIFORNIANS had seen little change in the composition of their 53-member congressional delegation.

Since the implementation of the state legislature's partisan 2002 redistricting map, the incumbents and their parties were so well protected and insulated by district lines that only one race in 255 congressional elections held during that decade resulted in a change of party. The leaders of the Democrat-led legislature also drew the lines for their own state legislative districts, which, of course, resulted in keeping themselves safe from serious challengers.

In 2005, when the trend of high incumbent re-election rates began attracting attention, citizen activists proposed a ballot initiative—Proposition 77—to yank redistricting away from California's state legislature and grant it to a panel of retired judges. The state's U.S. House delegation, led by Democrat Rep. Nancy Pelosi, panicked at the thought of losing control of their respective congressional boundary lines. They successfully petitioned the FEC for a special loophole allowing them to pour money into the election to defeat the measure.[18] Proposition 77 was defeated, but largely because citizens wanted a panel more representative of the citizenry and more independent of political ties, since many California judgeships are elected posts.

In 2008, citizens got the ballot initiative they sought, and passed Proposition 11, the Voters First Act. It created the California Citizens Redistricting Commission, a 14-member panel tasked with re-drawing the lines of state legislative districts. The commission's composition would be: five Democrats, five Republicans, and four citizens unaffiliated with either major party.

In 2010, the passage of Proposition 20 added the re-drawing of California's congressional districts to the commission's tasks. On the same 2010 ballot, an initiative largely funded by special interests and incumbent legislators sought to repeal the commission itself and give redistricting back to the legislature. Citizens voted it down, with 60 percent choosing to keep its new independent citizens panel.

How were the commission's members chosen?

The state auditor's office initiated the process. It established the application procedure and set up a website with an application form for citizens wishing to serve on the commission. About 30,000 people applied. Of that total, 5,000 were disqualified for not meeting basic eligibility requirements set forth in the Voters First Act. The remaining 25,000 were then invited to complete a supplemental application, but only 5,000 of that total actually did so. These 5,000 applications were then sent to the Applicant Review Panel, composed of three independent auditors from California's Bureau of State Audits. The review panel narrowed the field to 120 of the most qualified applicants, dividing them into three pools—40 Republicans, 40 Democrats, and 40 unaffiliated applicants. Each pool was then whittled down to 20 each, for a total of 60 applicants.[19]

Next, in accordance with the Voters First Act guidelines, the majority *and* minority leaders in each house of the legislature were allowed to reject up to two applicants in each of the three pools of 20. So, each of the four leaders could strike two from each of the three pools, for a total of six strikes apiece—or a total of 24 rejections from the 60 remaining applicants. The three pools were now down to 12 applicants apiece—36 total.[20]

The next step was a lottery—random selections from the 36 applicants to fill the first eight seats of the 14-member commission. Weeks later, the new commissioners worked together to choose the final six members from the remaining applicants.[21]

The commission got to work right away designing the new redistricting maps. Its outreach for the process included holding 34 public hearings throughout the state, listening to about 2,700 people who spoke at the hearings, and reading more than 20,000 written statements submitted by citizens.[22]

California Republican Tony Quinn, a redistricting expert and a fervent commission critic, was pleased after looking over the panel's first redistricting drafts. "There is no partisan advantage in these first maps," he wrote in his political blog. "Both parties have reason to be pleased and displeased. The maps do not have weird gerrymanders of ethnic neighborhoods for partisan purposes, as was encouraged upon the commission by some interest groups." He added, "For those Republicans who don't learn how to respond to ethnic voter concerns, it will soon be bye-bye." [23]

The state's Republican leaders, nevertheless, seeking to protect their incumbents, launched two legal challenges against the commission—one contesting the panel's state senate map and the other contesting the panel's congressional map.

In January 2012, the seven-member California Supreme Court dismissed the lawsuit challenging the state senate map. Six of the Court's seven justices were appointed by Republican governors. [24] Peter Yao, a Republican and the commission's acting chairman, called the Court's decision "a great victory for the people of California." He also noted, "It is regrettable that these challenges, based on partisan self-interest, have cost precious taxpayer dollars to defend the work of the people's commission." [25]

The second lawsuit went down in flames as well.

The new redistricting maps stood.

So how well did the independent, nonpartisan citizens panel perform?

Quite well, by most accounts.

Of the total 53 U.S. House seats in California up for election in 2012, 14 newcomers won. [26] Seven incumbents had decided against re-election after seeing their newly-drawn districts. In some cases, two incumbents of the same party found themselves competing for the same seat. Others found their artificial power bases stripped away, broken up, or attached to neighboring districts, making a number of the races highly competitive for the first time in decades. Seven more incumbents lost their seats in the general election. The result: a 26 percent turnover rate for the California House delegation. In comparison, the previous elections of 2008 and 2010 produced only two freshmen per election cycle, for a 4 percent turnover rate.

It was a similar story for California legislative elections. There were 39 freshmen elected—about one third of the entire 120-member state legislature. It was the highest number of new faces since 1966.[27] Most of the change came in the Assembly, the legislature's lower house. Almost half of the chamber's 80 members were incoming freshmen, one fewer than the high of 39 new members in 1934.[28] The map also created the state's first Asian-American majority state assembly seat—the 49th District near Los Angeles.

In May 2013, a comprehensive study by the League of Women Voters (LWV) hailed the California Citizens Redistricting Commission's performance an overall success. The LWV had sponsored Proposition 11, with support from the California Taxpayers' Association; Small Business Action Committee; California Republican Assembly; California Democratic Council; California Small Business Association; California Black Chamber of Commerce; Central California Hispanic Chamber of Commerce; AARP (formerly the American Association of Retired Persons); and the California Police Chiefs Association.

The LWV study, *"When the People Draw the Lines,"* reached the following conclusions:

- Overall, the California redistricting process was a success.
- Four independent studies, including two studies incorporated into the "When the People Draw the Lines" study also generally found the commission's performance a success.
- Incumbent elected officials had little influence over the selection of commissioners.
- The designers of the redistricting process maximized deliberation, transparency, and independence.
- A wide outreach effort to the state's diverse and geographic communities was conducted to encourage applicants to serve on the panel.
- The selection process, operating in public view, did indeed

yield a diverse group of commissioners.

- The final maps earned approval from all three groups serving on the commission: Democrats, Republicans, and unaffiliated.
- The commission sought and obtained a massive amount of public input used to craft the maps.
- The commission completed its work on time.
- Opinion polls showed the majority of voters responded positively to the commission's work.[29]

The study also cited a number of flaws and made recommendations to improve the process.

In 2013, the commission tightened its membership rules to prohibit the following people from serving: federal and state elected officials; candidates for federal and state office; appointees to federal or state office; paid staff of federal and state elected officials; elected or appointed members of a political party's central committee; federal or state lobbyists; paid consultants to federal and state elected officials; anyone who donates $2,000 or more to any congressional, state, or local candidate in any year; and family members of federal and state elected officials.

As long as incumbents and political partisans are prevented from infecting the process, the California Citizens Redistricting Commission will continue serving the public in an outstanding capacity for decades to come. It stands as an excellent template for other independent, nonpartisan citizens panels.

PROTECTING PANELS' INDEPENDENCE

TO ENSURE THAT INDEPENDENT CITIZENS PANELS are impartial and will make decisions that truly reflect the will and consensus of the public, it is essential to protect the panels' funding from elected officials, partisan party leaders, and special interests.

In politics, as in the private sector, those who control the purse strings, control the power. And giving politicians the power to jerk a panel's funding away to influence its decisions would completely undercut the panel's independence.

The campaign spending limits amendment proposed in this book requires that federal, state, and local citizens panels must be granted the authority to determine their own base funding, in conjunction with the appropriating legislative body and an impartial arbiter. The base will then be adjusted annually for inflation. And Congress, state, and local legislative bodies will be subsequently banned from unilaterally increasing or decreasing a panel's funding without the panel's approval.

In 2000, Arizona voters passed a law to strip the state legislature's authority to draw redistricting maps, granting that authority to an independent commission. Unfortunately, the law that created the commission did not sufficiently protect it from partisan politics. When a group of Republicans got wind that the new maps would endanger their state house careers, they teamed up with Republican Governor Jan Brewer to oust the independent commission's chairwoman. The law allowed elected officials to remove commissioners exhibiting "gross misconduct." The chairwoman, Colleen Mathis, a registered independent voter, was ousted because the Republicans were alarmed by the commission's decision to hire a mapping consultant with Democratic ties. Gov. Brewer and her party members also attempted to fire the commission's two Democrats, but failed.[30]

Citizens panels should also be insulated from special interests who can afford to use litigation to undermine them. Limits set by a citizens panel in any election should not be subject to court suspension, for example, but should remain in full effect until after the election. Otherwise, candidates or spending interests could routinely mount legal challenges, claiming the limits are too low for candidates to sufficiently get their messages out. Such lawsuits could hobble the entire system.

A citizens panel will need the power, freedom, and flexibility to operate freely and adjust the correct mix of spending and donation limits, allowing candidates to raise enough money, get their messages out to voters, and reasonably compete.

These panels are a critical component for a sound democracy.

ENSHRINING CITIZENS PANELS

POLITICAL PARTISAN WISEGUYS don't like to lose.

They think they own government. After all, it's the *business* they've chosen. They're the hardened pols, and worse, the faceless powerbrokers and advisers behind the pols.

These wiseguys forget who they work for.

They forget who they exist for.

So when Arizona voters spoke out and kicked the legislature to the redistricting curb, did these wiseguys obey the consent of the governed?

Of course, not!

They sued.

Fearing the loss of political power and their perpetual incumbency, Arizona's Republican-led legislature claimed the state's voters had violated the U.S. Constitution by stripping away its power to draw district lines. The Republicans staked their case, *Arizona State Legislature v. Arizona Independent Redistricting Commission,* on Article 1, Section 4 of the U.S. Constitution, which reads:

> The times, places and manner of holding elections for senators and representatives shall be prescribed in each state in the legislature ...

The U.S. Supreme Court decided the case in June 2015.

The wiseguys lost—barely.

In a 5-4 decision, Justice Ruth Bader Ginsburg, writing for the majority, asserted:

> The animating principle of our Constitution is that the people themselves are the originating source of all the powers of government.[31]

This was a truly scary moment in American political history that garnered little attention from the media and the public. The right of American citizens to control our own government and instill a semblance of integrity was nearly crushed.

A campaign spending limits constitutional amendment must enshrine the right of Americans to appoint independent citizens panels and forever protect our democracy from partisan wiseguy hacks seeking self-aggrandizing power and naïve judges clueless about American realpolitik.

16

PUBLIC FINANCING, TERM LIMITS, & OTHER ALTERNATIVES

EMILIE BOYLES SEEMED LIKE the perfect candidate to answer the call of Portland's new public financing system.

Portland, Oregon's largest city, was to hold its first "voter-owned elections" in May 2006. There were high hopes public funding would attract a larger and more diverse field of candidates.

Boyles worked for a number of nonprofit organizations, most specializing in helping people with mental health issues or developmental disabilities. She served on public boards and took an interest in the plight of the city's growing population of Russian and Ukrainian immigrants. She earned a modest income and lived in a mobile home with her 16-year-old daughter.

Boyles's popularity around the city encouraged her to challenge incumbent Erik Sten for his Portland City Council seat. As a candidate, Boyles portrayed herself as a working class, no-nonsense plain-talker, unbeholden to special interests. She collected the required 1,000 donations of at least $5 each, qualifying her to receive $145,000 in taxpayer funding. She now had more than $150,000 to spend on her campaign.

After losing the race, Boyles skipped town when city officials questioned some of her campaign expenditures. Turns out her "no-nonsense" style didn't extend to her use of public election funds. Among the abuses uncovered were: $12,000 Boyles paid her daughter for undocumented campaign work and a $3,000 payment made by her daughter shortly thereafter toward the overdue mortgage on the family's mobile home.[1]

The city ordered Boyles to return the $145,000 given to her and pay a $14,000 fine for misuse of public funds. Boyles briefly resurfaced and returned only the $68,565 she had not spent as of August 2006, then fled for parts unknown. She left the city on the hook for about $92,000 (balance, plus fine and interest).[2] To make matters worse, it was later revealed that a number of her qualifying signatures had been forged. *The Oregonian*, Portland's major newspaper, dubbed Boyles the city's new "voter-owned deadbeat." It lambasted the new public financing measure as "flawed and unnecessary," and said the city should learn from its $92,000 mistake.[3]

It could be argued that the sad story of Emilie Boyles is not endemic to public financing systems in the United States—that she was just an anomaly. But it sure shows some of the system's flaws.

Public financing, of course, is not a new idea in American politics. It has deep roots in America's past, and it has shown some promise.

BENEFITS AND FLAWS

IN 1907, PRESIDENT THEODORE ROOSEVELT proposed public financing for federal elections, but the idea died in Congress.

In 1966, Congress passed a presidential public financing bill, but suspended the measure a year later. Congress then passed several laws in 1971, setting the foundation for presidential public financing. It was not until the Federal Election Campaign Act (FECA) Amendments of 1974 passed that the system was put into effect.

Although the Supreme Court never gave campaign spending limits a chance to work, presidential public financing has been in effect since the 1976 election, receiving mostly positive reviews. Even candidates who weren't fans of public financing, like Ronald Reagan, didn't seem to mind using taxpayer dollars to win the White House.

Campaign reform critics predictably contend that the presidential public financing system has failed to stem political corruption. They're not interested in evidence that shows it has been somewhat effective.

In 1986, a bipartisan commission headed by Melvin Laird, former Nixon administration defense secretary, and Robert Strauss, former Democratic National Committee chairman, studied public financing's effect on the presidential elections of 1976, 1980, and 1984. The commission concluded: "Public financing of presidential elections has clearly proved its worth in opening up the process, reducing the influence of individuals and groups, and virtually ending corruption in presidential election finance."[4] Keep in mind the commission was referring to candidates' capped spending, not the millions of special interest dollars flowing through independent expenditure groups and soft money laundered through the major parties. Still, there was a positive effect.

Congress in recent years has refused to adjust the amounts given to presidential candidates to reflect the hyperinflation of campaign costs.

Although then-Senator Barack Obama (D-IL) supported public financing, he decided against opting in for the 2008 election so he could collect more money than the spending cap allowed. His challenger, Senator John McCain (R-AZ), remained in the system and received about $84 million in public funds. In the 2012 presidential election, Obama and former Massachusetts Governor Mitt Romney (R) both turned down public funds, as did Donald Trump (R) and Hillary Clinton (D) in 2016.

On January 28, 2011, the U.S. House voted 239-160 to scrap the presidential public financing system altogether. Senate Minority Leader Mitch McConnell (R-KY) quickly filed a companion bill in the Senate. Obama refused to sign it, and the bill died.

Despite Republican plans to kill the system, it still exists, although on life support.

Public financing on the state and local level, however, is still alive and functioning. A study by the Center for Governmental Studies, a nonprofit, nonpartisan think tank, echoed all the known benefits of public financing systems that have been in place in a handful of cities and states. The benefits cited:

- freeing politicians from special interests;
- allowing more average-income Americans from diverse backgrounds and occupations to reasonably compete in elections;
- increasing the opportunities for average voters to engage in the political process.

The study concluded: "No political reform is perfect or without flaws, but public financing is perhaps the best solution to solving campaign finance problems in a given jurisdiction."[5]

Public financing is certainly far better than America's current system of unlimited campaign spending. It has the ability to somewhat curb the money incentive in American politics—but only if wealthy candidates decide to participate in the system.

While public financing is the next best option to campaign spending limits, it would be beneficial at this point to clarify the similarities and differences between the two systems.

A campaign spending limits law would set *mandatory* spending and donation caps for all candidates. And all candidates would be funded by *private* donations—as they are today. Public financing sets *voluntary* spending and donation limits. Only those opting into the system must obey spending and donation caps as a condition of receiving public funds to run their campaigns. Candidates who refuse to obey the limits or decide against opting into the system are not entitled to public money.

Now, let's compare further.

Both campaign spending limits and public financing seek to accomplish the following:

- cutting candidates' dependence on special interest money to fund campaigns;
- leveling the playing field by requiring all candidates to abide by spending caps;
- attracting more candidates with broader and more diverse viewpoints;
- attracting more voters by offering more choices;
- allowing candidates more time to meet voters and debate issues;
- instilling more faith and integrity in the political system.

But public financing has the following drawbacks:

- allowing wealthy candidates to sidestep the system and virtually eliminate the chances of publicly-funded candidates to win by vastly outspending them;
- raiding state and local budgets for taxpayer dollars to pay for elections;
- finding scapegoats (usually corporations) rather than taxpayers to provide the public funds for elections;
- funding "one-issue" or frivolous candidates;
- forcing citizens to use their tax dollars to fund candidates they find frivolous or abhorrent;
- inviting court meddling and legal challenges;
- allowing wealthy individuals and independent expenditure groups, like Super PACs and political nonprofits, to pour money into elections, distorting voter information and influencing outcomes;
- allowing wealthy individuals and independent groups to pour money into out-of-state elections, including ballot initiatives, distorting voter information and influencing outcomes.

Campaign spending limits, on the other hand, would address all these flaws.

Let's explore some of these points in more depth.

Perhaps public financing's biggest weakness is that wealthy candidates or those who can raise great sums almost always bypass the voluntary system. There is simply no incentive for them to limit their campaign spending, an essential idea of public financing. They have far more personal resources to put toward their campaigns than a public financing system could offer. The mere mention that a millionaire may enter a race and use their personal fortune for campaign funds makes them the instant frontrunner. The power of their money scares away potential candidates and gives them a huge advantage over those who stay in the race.

And if you think these wealthy candidates aren't buying public office, then why would they refuse to take hundreds of thousands of "free" taxpayer dollars and compete just with their ideas instead of their bank accounts?

Even most contrarians agree that there are more wealthy candidates today vying for public office than ever before. And this trend under our unlimited spending system will only continue with ever wealthier people winning public office.

So how does public financing deal with the "wealthy-candidate syndrome?"

It throws good money after bad.

If a wealthy candidate enters a race and refuses public money to maintain his or her money advantage, most public financing schemes set the spending caps higher, which throws even more taxpayer dollars to less-wealthy candidates who have opted into the system. So in an attempt to achieve spending parity and a level playing field, public financing pumps up the remaining candidates as if they *were* millionaires. The result is that more taxpayer dollars are spent while the wealthy candidate just pitches in more personal resources to regain their money advantage.

Sound familiar?

It's really just another version of the arms race for unlimited spending that the current system promotes, except that it's fueled by taxpayer dollars that would be better spent elsewhere.

The U.S. Supreme Court frowned on another public financing

scheme to boost the campaign coffers of modestly wealthy candidates.

On June 27, 2011, the Court ruled 5-4 in *Arizona Free Enterprise Club's Freedom Club PAC, et al. v. Bennett, Secretary of State of Arizona* to strike down Arizona's public financing provision that gave escalating matching funds *during* the campaign cycle to less-wealthy, publicly-financed candidates competing against wealthy self-financed candidates. The Court's decision left intact Arizona's right to implement public financing and the right to increase taxpayer dollars to candidates, but only at the *beginning* of a race. So, a major tool used by public financing advocates to blunt the skewing of elections by wealthy candidates is gone.

Public financing's other major flaw is that it siphons off millions of taxpayer dollars from federal, state, and local budgets already straining to provide basic services. It drains public dollars away from chronically under-funded programs for vulnerable citizens, who usually bear the brunt of budget cuts. When revenue is tight, governments often trim health and human services programs for seniors, the disabled, the mentally ill, and children. Also on the chopping block are public school programs for general education, early education, special education, nutrition, sports, arts, music, the gifted and talented, and more.

Although well-intentioned, public financing of elections creates a permanent budget hole—often unpredictable in size—since any candidate who gathers enough signatures is entitled to public funds.

Citizens, of course, could vote themselves a tax increase to fund the system. But why spend such large sums on campaigns when we don't have to?

Some states and municipalities have sought to placate taxpayers' distaste of public financing's high cost by targeting outside sources to fund their schemes.

In California, public-financing advocates placed an initiative on the 2006 ballot that tapped the business sector to foot the bill. Proposition 89 sought to fund publicly-financed campaigns by hiking corporate taxes by $200 million every year.[6] But not all corporations are huge, multi-national conglomerates that pollute the political system. Many are moderate to small in size and are arguably good corporate citizens, fueling the economy and providing many well-paying jobs. Good businesses should not be lumped in and punished with bad ones. And they should not be forced to pay for elections, particularly when many are scrambling to compete globally with rising economies in Asia and government-subsidized industries in Europe. Californians saw Proposition 89 for what it was—a discriminatory slap at business. Voters quashed the initiative by a 3-1 margin.

Next, let's look at qualifying campaign contributions in public financing systems. Candidates seeking public money must solicit voters for qualifying donations, usually in low amounts like $5, $10, or $20. If they gather a certain number of donations, they receive a lump sum or several large payments of taxpayer funds with which to run their campaigns. The problem is the dollars a citizen pays in taxes, that are then used to fund candidates, may be used to fund candidates the taxpayer loathes. Most Americans don't mind paying taxes if we know exactly where our dollars are going and are being used wisely. It's when taxes are wasted, stolen, or lost in a black hole of spending that makes us furious. Most people feel the same way about donating to candidates. We don't want to throw our dollars into a big, bottomless pit to be doled out by some faceless government bureaucrat.

The thing is, Americans are thoroughly consumer-oriented. We like to sample the candidates and donate to those we like. By donating directly to a candidate who inspires us, for example, we feel like we're part of the campaign or movement. Campaign spending limits would preserve this traditional element of the culture.

To further illustrate public financing's benefits and flaws, let's examine the Massachusetts "Clean Elections" measure voters passed by ballot initiative in 1998 (but never implemented) and New York City's public funding law.

MASSACHUSETTS CLEAN ELECTIONS LAW

IN 1998, MASSACHUSETTS VOTERS overwhelmingly approved a public financing ballot initiative dubbed "Clean Elections" by a 2-1 margin.

Advocates sold Clean Elections to citizens as the best way to "clean up" the Bay State's "dirty" political system. On Election Day, voters were focused on the benefits of the system, not the flaws.

The legislature, however, focused on the costs and refused to fund the new law. It cited the large bite it would take out of state funding for vulnerable citizens who depended on public programs. In truth, a strong sense of self-preservation and self-interest ran through the incumbents who resisted funding the measure. They didn't want to appropriate funds that would have resulted in more and better-funded challengers. The legislature stood its ground, insisting the lengthy 1998 ballot question was too confusing to voters. Clean Elections supporters seethed at that accusation. A common refrain heard around the state was: "How dare lawmakers insinuate that voters were too dumb to understand what they were voting on!"

But the Clean Elections law *was* complicated, and its overall costs unclear. Some estimates put the tab at $100 million per election cycle.

As fate would have it, poor timing hurt the Clean Elections law. The funding was due to come on line just when the national economy was tanking and the state was battling budget deficits of several billion dollars per year.

In an attempt to silence the outcry of Clean Elections supporters, the legislature decided on an unusual maneuver. It voted to put its own question on the 2002 ballot asking voters if they were in favor of "taxpayer-funded elections."

The result?

A loud "no" from voters.

Four years earlier, voters supported Clean Elections by a 2-1 margin. Four years later, voters opposed it by a 2-1 margin. So, even in "liberal" Massachusetts, while it was clear voters wanted "clean elections," they didn't want to pay for them. They didn't want their taxes raised, and they didn't want to cannibalize the state budget either.

Further, if Massachusetts' Clean Elections law *had* been in effect in 2002, it wouldn't have mattered in the gubernatorial race. Multi-millionaire Mitt Romney won the contest, shattering state election records by spending $9.3 million on his campaign.[7] The total included $6 million of his own money. Romney would have surely rejected the Clean Elections system to maintain his all-important money advantage.

So while public financing is less effective in higher profile races, there is evidence it's more effective in smaller, less costly campaigns.

New York City's public financing law is a good example.

NEW YORK CITY: A PARTIAL SUCCESS

NEW YORK CITY'S 2001 ELECTION illustrates the mixed results of a voluntary system. The city's 1998 public financing law was overwhelmingly successful in drawing more grassroots candidates, who won city council seats.

But the mayor's race was a different story.

Billionaire Michael Bloomberg snubbed public financing and spent a total of $74 million on his campaign, including $50 million from his own pocket. He narrowly beat Mark Green, who spent a paltry $16.2 million in comparison, including $4.5 million in public funds. Indeed, it was impossible and impractical for the city to try and match Bloomberg's spending by subsidizing Green with another $58 million in taxpayer dollars to close the gap. There is simply no remedy other than a campaign spending limits law that would have created a level playing field in such a race. Bloomberg outspent Green by nearly 5 to 1. The billionaire would have likely lost, and lost big, had he been forced to compete relying on his ideas rather than his wallet.

What happened in that 2001 race was an outright purchase.

In 2013, Bloomberg's exit from the mayor's office exposed another large flaw with the city's public financing system. During his tenure, the wealthy mayor rarely saw a real estate development project he didn't like. His exit unnerved wealthy builders, fearing a more liberal mayor and city council would tighten the reins on new, lucrative projects. To ensure their gravy train would continue, the Real Estate Board of New York, which includes some of the city's biggest developers and landlords, set up a political action committee (PAC) called Jobs For New York. The group virtually soaked some of the council races with outside money, winning 16 of 20 races they helped fund.[8]

As for the mayoral race, a coalition of liberal unions and wealthy activists created an independent expenditure group called "NYC Is Not For Sale" to kill the bid of Christine Quinn, the city council speaker. The group viewed Quinn as Bloomberg's pawn in fast-tracking numerous construction deals in the city and launched a vicious, negative ad blitz against her. And although the wealthy Quinn had money to fight back, the relentless attack ads crippled her candidacy. All told, independent expenditure groups dropped $15.9 million to influence the election.[9] There's nothing the city can do to stop this outside spending. These special interests will continue to up the ante, tipping the outcomes even more as candidates accepting public funds are limited to spending $168,000.

FREE RIDERS

HANDING OUT PUBLIC DOLLARS to anyone who can collect a batch of signatures and small donations will definitely attract more candidates, but what kind or quality?

One of the unintended consequences of public financing is that "free" public money, in addition to creating a larger candidate pool, attracts enterprising "free riders," including those who may be a tad askew in the noggin. These free riders are prone to launch narrow one-issue campaigns that have little chance of winning while wasting public dollars. Some states like Connecticut have tried to devise public financing laws to weed out the free riders. But that just opens up another can of worms with cries of "discrimination!"—with lawsuits sure to follow.

In 2012, a fellow calling himself Vermin Supreme ran for president and sought public financing from the Federal Election Commission. Vermin's a scraggly, weathered, old guy with a long, scraggly, weathered, gray beard. As if he didn't already stand out from the field, he wore a black, two-foot tall boot on his head while campaigning. His main promise was to give every American a pony so we can transition to a "pony-based economy," thus lowering our dependence on fossil fuels and generating new jobs.[10] Vermin also proposed a plan to trick zombies into physically turning our energy-generating turbines by dangling human brains in front of them. It will use the latest in "giant hamster wheel technology," he assured voters.[11]

In 2016, Vermin ran again. This time, he received 256 votes in the New Hampshire Democratic primary. Former Governor Martin O'Malley (D-MD), who participated in nationally-televised debates with Hillary Clinton and Bernie Sanders, received 619 votes. Supreme actually received more primary votes than former Governor Jim Gilmore (R-VA), who received 131 votes in the state's Republican primary.[12]

While Vermin didn't receive federal funding, it's quite plausible he could have gathered a batch of signatures and small donations in a state or local publicly-financed race to access a large sum of taxpayer dollars. Whether he was serious or ran as a joke, he aptly demonstrates how public financing is susceptible to the wasting of taxpayer dollars and mocking of elections.

In comparison, spending limits would not attract such freeloaders. Campaigns are like job interviews. Even a terrible job applicant can fool prospective employers during a one-hour interview. But if the applicant must pass several interviews before selection, there is more time for the real person to emerge and for bad candidates to be weeded out. Political campaigns are the same way. With spending limits, a candidate—even in an abbreviated campaign of six to eight weeks—would need to meet and convince voters to donate right up to Election Day. But a public financing candidate only needs to convince citizens to give qualifying donations in the beginning of the race to access public funds. Then, once those public funds are disbursed, there is no impetus for the candidate to continue meeting voters to acquire more donations. Candidates could conceivably spend all that public money on a few expensive TV ads in the campaign's final weeks, or they could take the money and head for the hills like Emilie Boyles.

In the final analysis, campaign spending limits would achieve all the benefits of public financing without the negatives. It would allow candidates to get their messages out and average citizens to show their support. There would be broader participation on both ends.

And let's not overlook those citizens who wish to exercise their right to *not* participate in elections, which is a political statement in itself. Yes, we all benefit when more citizens vote, but there are times when voters just don't like any of the candidates in a particular race. Campaign spending and donation limits would not force them to fund any of these candidates through their tax dollars as would a public financing system.

TERM LIMITS

"THROW THE BUMS OUT!"

It's a common refrain from American voters fed up with political corruption.

But hold on.

How do we know who the bums *are*?

The idea behind term limits is that the political system is so corrupt, the only way to fix it is to limit how long a public official may serve. The supposed trick is to end a lawmaker's tenure before they get co-opted into the system.

Good luck.

Wealthy power brokers and special interests get their hooks into most politicians well before they're elected, supplying them with much-needed cash to outspend their opponents. It's likely a freshly-anointed public servant has already been co-opted before his or her fanny hits the chair on their first day in office.

Instead of attacking corruption at its root, term limits attacks the outgrowth of that corruption. That is to say, it penalizes people who are forced to function within the corrupt system. It discards good as well as bad lawmakers. It also penalizes voters by eliminating a candidate who may be the best choice for the job.

With term limits, the people who remain the constants in government are lobbyists, bureaucrats, and legislative staffers. Their power increases simply because they're the ones left with the deepest institutional knowledge of how things run. With term limits, greenhorn lawmakers are left to lean on these groups and are often led by the nose through the governmental process.

On the plus side, term limits costs nothing—and it's equally applied to politicians regardless of party affiliation or income level.

While many Americans scream for term limits, few know that Congress is exempt from this policy. The Supreme Court ruled in 1995 in *U.S. Term Limits, Inc. v. Thornton* that term limits for members of Congress is unconstitutional. However, term limits may be applied to state and local government elected offices.

It's easy to understand why term limits is popular. Ever since the American Revolution threw off the chains of monarchy, Americans have been wary of any one political figure lingering around, amassing too much power. George Washington, following the example of the great Roman leader Cincinnatus, set the tone for American presidents by stepping down at the height of his popularity and power. Instead of remaining in politics, he returned to Mount Vernon after two terms in office to tend his estate. Franklin Delano Roosevelt broke the tradition and won an unprecedented third consecutive term in 1940 and then a fourth in 1944, largely because Americans balked at changing leadership during World War II. After the war, Americans amended the Constitution to limit presidents to two terms.

But the Twenty-second Amendment made no provisions to limit the service of appointed officials.

There have been episodes in American government when enormous power has been concentrated in the hands of crafty bureaucrats. Federal Bureau of Investigation (FBI) Director J. Edgar Hoover is a prime example. Hoover slyly exploited the political system for 48 years from his perch to amass an inordinate amount of power, developing a fiefdom that intimidated members of Congress and even presidents. Several years after his death, Congress in 1976 voted to limit the FBI director post to one 10-year term.

The unsavory Hoover episode illustrates the one great benefit of term limits: they are best used to limit the power of high-ranking politicians and government employees who are not elected by citizens, but are either appointed to a post or elected from within a body. The danger of these high-level positions is they can be abused by dominating personalities like Hoover, not accountable to voters.

It has often been noted that term limits for elected officials embodies the curious American belief that politics is the only profession where experience is a negative. People tend to choose doctors, for example, who have the most experience. A patient needing heart surgery generally avoids hiring a doctor with the least experience to perform the operation. Yet voters find inexperience a highly favorable quality in political candidates.

Why?

Because voters prefer a clean slate—a candidate unsullied by the vulgarities of American politics. But trying to fix the political system by advocating term limits is like a car mechanic trying fix the engine by installing a new radio.

There is a huge disconnect.

The origin of the problem is not the people. It's the system.

"Throw the bums out" is not a solution. It's a temporary feel-good reaction that does virtually nothing to address the root cause of corruption in American politics.

TOP-TWO PRIMARY

IN 2010, CALIFORNIA VOTERS passed a ballot initiative that changed primary elections in an effort to promote more competitive races in general elections.

In California's "top-two primary" system, the two candidates who receive the most votes, regardless of party affiliation, advance to the general election. Since California is heavily Democratic, the real election was usually the primary, since whoever won would likely win the general election. And the general elections were too often between a Democrat and a long-shot Republican.

Further, primary candidates often play to the base—the passionate, fringe wings of the respective parties—while candidates in the general election tend to adopt more moderate policies to appeal to voters of all stripes. In California, since the winner of the primary was almost always the de facto winner of the general, more polarizing candidates were getting elected. It didn't sit well with the majority centrist voters.

The results of the new primary system have been mixed.

A 2015 study by University of California at Berkeley researchers found the top-two primary system encouraged more citizens to run for office, but generally failed to keep its promises of creating more competitive races and electing more moderate candidates. Researchers said many voters lacked the knowledge needed to distinguish between moderate and more extreme candidates. The study concluded: " . . . voters held fuzzy beliefs about candidate ideology that came nowhere close to the knowledge necessary for identifying the moderate candidates reformers presumed would be favored."[13]

RANKED-CHOICE VOTING

IN 2016, MAINE BECAME THE FIRST STATE to adopt a new election system in which voters rank the entire field of candidates—from first to last—instead of choosing just one candidate.

"Ranked-choice" voting (RCV), used in Australia for more than a century, is designed to increase voter turnout, discourage negative campaigning, and reduce outside groups from funding single-issue, partisan political ads.

Here's how it works: Voters rank the candidates from one down to however big the field is. If one candidate wins a majority of all votes cast, they win the election. If no candidate wins a majority, the candidate in last place is eliminated and the votes they received are distributed according to how their voters ranked the rest of the field. This process is repeated until one candidate receives a majority of votes.

Proponents of RCV say it increases voter turnout because it ensures the candidate elected best represents the consensus of the people. To illustrate, Republican Paul LePage won the governor's race by a plurality in 2010 and 2014, when he was re-elected. So, while he was the top vote-getter, he did not win a majority of the votes. Many Maine residents believed several candidates to the left of LePage were closer to the voters' consensus, but these candidates split the Independent-Democratic vote. If RCV voting had been in effect, they asserted, LePage would have lost.

RCV also discourages negative campaigning, proponents say, because candidates know they need to win not just first-place votes but likely second- and third-place votes as well. Candidates understand that showing respect and kindness to their competitors may likely result in higher rankings among voters who do not rank them first. And by cultivating a more genial election, supporters say RCV discourages single-issue, negative ads funded by outside, divisive partisans. Of course, this element of RCV is open to gaming the system, with candidates determining which competitors to befriend, based on the political leanings of their voter bases.

RCV opponents, mostly Maine Republicans, claim the system is too confusing and unworkable. They have launched court and legislative battles to stop it. In 2017, the Maine Supreme Judicial Court ruled RCV violated the state constitution. In 2018, the law was only in effect for congressional races, and RCV decided one of them. The highest vote-getter, incumbent U.S. Rep. Bruce Poliquin (R), won 46.3 percent of the vote, while challenger Jared Golden (D) won the second highest tally at 45.6 percent. The votes of the two remaining candidates, unaffiliated with the major parties, were then redistributed. Golden won the majority and the election.

It will take a while, if the law stands, before sufficient data can determine whether ranked-choice voting will achieve its heralded benefits.

SECRET DONATION BOOTH

TWO YALE UNIVERSITY PROFESSORS have been championing a concept they call "voting dollars" to help clean up America's political system.

In their 2002 book, "*Voting With Dollars: A New Paradigm for Campaign Finance*," professors Bruce Ackerman and Ian Ayres trumpet that they've swept aside the "old paradigm" of campaign finance thinking, such as spending limits, public financing, and disclosure of donors' identities.

First, to offset the influence of large private contributions given to candidates, Ackerman and Ayres propose taking $5 billion in taxpayer money and giving every American voter a "Patriot card" tied to an account that is seeded with $50. During the campaign, a voter can donate money from their "Patriot account" to the federal candidates they like. The professors reason that the $5 billion spent this way would neutralize the $3 billion spent by private donors during an election.

Second, to prevent the *quid pro quo* of big donors seeking favors from successful candidates, Ackerman and Ayres propose the "secret donation booth." In this scheme, all political contributions are deposited into a booth or box, which functions as a "blind trust." Then, a "secrecy algorithm" is applied to the accounts, mixing up the donations into varying amounts before being deposited into candidates' coffers. That way, candidates won't know who contributed the money, and the donors won't have proof they've given big donations to any particular candidate.

Evidently, Ackerman and Ayres have found the cosmic seam that leads to a new campaign finance galaxy. Unfortunately, their "new paradigm" looks a lot like the old paradigm they both criticize.

Patriot dollars?

Try taxpayer dollars.

Their secret donation booth and concepts like the "secrecy algorithm," however, are quite inventive and worthy of consideration. These ideas could be used to complement a campaign spending limits law. The funds could be seeded to challengers, lessening the amounts needed to reach the spending cap.

That said, most Americans would still prefer to donate directly to the candidates they like, which is completely consonant with campaign spending limits, but not public financing or the secret donation booth.

LIST OF REFORMS

THERE ARE MANY GROUPS IN AMERICA proposing their own remedy for curbing corruption in America's political system.

RepresentUs is a nonprofit that bills itself as the "nation's largest grassroots anti-corruption campaign."

The group aims to clean up corruption by passing anti-corruption laws on all levels of government. Their bill template is a collection of actions, including many discussed in this book:

- ban lobbyist donations to politicians
- ban lobbyist bundling
- close the revolving door of politicians leaving office and working as lobbyists
- ban politicians from fundraising during working hours
- institute full and immediate disclosure of campaign donations
- end dark money donations
- prohibit politicians from gerrymandering political districts
- establish the top-two primary system
- adopt ranked-choice voting
- register voters automatically at any government agency
- increase mail-in ballot option for voters
- encourage states to award their Electoral College votes for president to the candidate who wins the most votes nationwide
- establish the secret donation booth (Yale professors Ackerman and Ayres serve on the RepresentUs advisory council)
- enforce strict rules for PACs
- eliminate lobbyist loopholes
- overhaul the Federal Election Commission to restore its power to regulate elections

These are all worthy measures to enact.

But they need campaign spending limits as the bedrock to support them and function in a cohesive, collaborative manner and as the bulwark needed to protect them from wily partisans who will surely seek to undermine, manipulate, and kill them, if possible.

17

THE CONSTITUTION
Living, Breathing or Dying, Wheezing Document?

THOMAS JEFFERSON PLUCKED a quill pen from his desk at Monticello on July 12, 1816, and fired off a remarkable response to Samuel Kercheval, who sought the former president's advice on constitutional and democratic reform.

Kercheval, a Virginia innkeeper and political activist, was agitating for a state constitutional convention for Virginia. He sought equal rights and representation for citizens in the western part of the state. The area was far less populated than the eastern portion, which Kercheval believed ran roughshod over all Virginians.

Jefferson, drawing on his experience drafting the Declaration of Independence and other important documents, offered Kercheval insights that were pragmatic and insightful. Jefferson did not see constitutions as religious-like documents. To him, they framed a time and a culture. And that frame should be adapted or rebuilt by each successive generation for the country to grow and thrive.

Jefferson nor the Constitution's Framers could have imagined the future: Electricity. Radio. The automobile. Television. The camera. Automatic weapons. The atom bomb. World War II. The combustion engine. The airplane. The telephone. Rock 'n Roll. Civil rights. Stem cells. The phonograph. Smart phones. Vietnam. Movies. Medicare. Satellites. The Internet. Gay marriage. Texting. Space exploration. And much more.

All these things profoundly changed America and its culture.

Jefferson could not see *what* changes were coming. But he knew change *was* coming. And he knew the law of the land must adapt. In this respect, he maintained a sober view of the U.S. Constitution and other democratic mission statements, which he communicated in his reply to Kercheval:

> Some men look at constitutions with sanctimonious reverence, and deem them like the ark of the covenant, too sacred to be touched. They ascribe to the men of the preceding age a wisdom more than human, and suppose what they did to be beyond amendment. I knew that age well; I belonged to it, and labored with it. . . . I am certainly not an advocate for frequent and untried changes in laws and constitutions. . . . But I know also, that laws and institutions must go hand in hand with the progress of the human mind. As that becomes more developed, more enlightened, as new discoveries are made, new truths disclosed, and manners and opinions change with the change of circumstances, institutions must advance also, and keep pace with the times. We might as well require a man to wear still the coat which fitted him when a boy as civilized society to remain ever under the regimen of their barbarous ancestors.[1]

Benjamin Franklin, in a speech to the Constitutional Convention in Philadelphia, shared a similar mindset:

> I confess that there are several parts of this Constitution which I do not at present approve, but I am not sure I shall never approve them. For having lived long, I have experienced many instances of being obliged by better information, or fuller consideration to change opinions even on important subjects, which I once thought right, but found to be otherwise.[2]

In his earlier years, Jefferson held a more extreme view of constitutions and laws. He believed that each successive generation should junk their constitution and all laws of the land, re-writing them from scratch to be relevant to the "living generation." He believed that those living in their prime years should not be bound by the actions of previous generations.

In a 1789 letter to James Madison, Jefferson proclaimed 19 years as the natural span of this "living generation." He calculated the number using the mortality tables of French naturalist and mathematician Georges-Louis Leclerc, Comte de Buffon.

In the letter, Jefferson wrote:

> On similar ground it may be proved that no society can make a perpetual constitution, or even a perpetual law. The earth belongs always to the living generation. . . . . Every constitution then, and every law, naturally expires at the end of 19 years. If it be enforced longer, it is an act of force, and not of right.[3]

Jefferson wrote the letter six years after the Revolutionary War. The country stood on young, tender roots while shouldering an onerous $54 million owed to creditors like France, which helped finance the war effort. Soon, the U.S., at the urging of U.S. Treasury Secretary Alexander Hamilton, would also assume the states' $25 million war debt. Jefferson, an ideological adversary of Hamilton, worried the debt would hinder America's growth and survival. Jefferson believed that any debts of previous "living generations" should remain unpaid and extinguished:

> No nation can make a declaration against the validity of long-contracted debts so disinterestedly as we, since we do not owe a shilling which may not be paid with ease, principal, and interest within the time of our own lives.[4]

So when Jefferson derived his living generation theory of 19 years, his judgment was likely colored by the expediency of erasing debt rather than scrapping the constitution and all established law. But as Jefferson and the rest of the country settled into life under the new Constitution, it became apparent that the document exhibited much wisdom and durability. The Framers, Americans realized, gave the country a solid foundation with which to build. And the idea of repealing and re-writing the Constitution every 19 years never took hold.

This sense of constitutional consistency continues today, providing us with a direct link to our Founding Fathers. It gives us a sense of grounding and security. Swapping out a new constitution every 19 years would surely propagate a sense of national instability to the citizens and the world.

We have, however, passed amendments throughout our history to adapt to changing times and situations.

No.	Description	Ratified	Years between amendments
CONSTITUTIONAL AMENDMENTS			
1-10	Bill of Rights	1791	-
11	Lawsuits against states	1795	4
12	Separate P/VP Ballots	1804	9
13	Abolition of slavery	1865	61
14	Negro citizenship	1868	3
15	Negro suffrage	1870	2
16	Income tax	1913	43
17	Popular election of senators	1913	0
18	Prohibition	1919	6
19	Women's suffrage	1920	1
20	Lame duck Congress	1933	13
21	Prohibition repealed	1933	0
22	President's term limited	1951	18
23	Washington, D.C. electors	1961	10
24	Abolition of poll tax	1964	3
25	President - transfer of power	1967	3
26	Vote at age 18	1971	4
27	Congressional pay raises	1992	21

Note that the largest gap between amendments is 61 years, from 1804 in the post-Revolutionary War era (Twelfth Amendment) to 1865 in the Civil War era (Thirteenth Amendment).

The Twenty-seventh Amendment is the last to be added to the Constitution. While states ratified it 27 years ago in 1992, Congress proposed it in 1789 as one of the original 12 measures under consideration of what became known as the Bill of Rights. Only 10 at the time were ratified.

The Twenty-sixth Amendment, passed in 1971, set the voting age at 18. It was the last amendment Americans passed *and* ratified in the same era that addressed an issue of their times. That was 48 years ago. If an amendment were ratified today, it would be the second longest gap between amendments passed and ratified in the same generation.

Much has changed since 1971. The Watergate scandal exploded, heralding a period of hyper-binging on political money. It bore some of the most corrupt, dirty politics this nation has ever witnessed. It forced a president to resign in disgrace. It shook this country enough to pass the most comprehensive law possible to get money out of politics—the Federal Election Campaign Act Amendments of 1974. But the Supreme Court thwarted the people's will.

In hindsight, a better strategy would have been to amend the Constitution in 1974 rather than pass a law curbing unlimited campaign spending. Perhaps it was left for this generation to accomplish. There is no issue more vital in America today than getting money out of politics.

Do you believe, as Jefferson, that allowing an ancient pox of our "barbarous ancestors" such as unlimited campaign spending, to continue corrupting our political system is akin to requiring a man to "wear still the coat which fitted him when a boy?"

If you do, then you need to think hard about amending the Constitution and adapting it to modern times.

Some have proposed a constitutional convention to pass a slew of amendments dealing with such issues as: balancing the federal budget, banning American flag burning, eliminating the Electoral College, among others.

Should there be wholesale change of the Constitution?

No.

As noted throughout this book, campaign spending limits is the *only* amendment that would have the capacity to positively affect every law and action in the halls of American government.

It stands alone.

It deserves our *full* attention.

There is no other amendment proposal in its class.

A political system inoculated against rigging by wealthy elites will reach consensus directly, efficiently, and fairly on all other issues.

Proposing a slate of amendments, however, would divide the public's attention.

This would be folly.

The public is already skittish about amending the Constitution. Besides the Bill of Rights, there is no precedent in American history for ratifying a long list of amendments. Our custom has been to ratify one at a time, except for 1913 and 1933 when two amendments in each of those years were ratified.

We've gotten out of the change habit. But amending the Constitution is in our DNA, as past generations have shown. We must do this together—with focus, clarity, and purpose.

LIVING, BREATHING OR DYING, WHEEZING?

AT 230 YEARS OLD, the United States Constitution is the longest surviving single document constitution still in effect in the world. (Some nations are governed by two or more charter documents.)

In its first 200 years, the Constitution served as a template for other nations seeking freedom and democracy. When many new countries formed, they wrote their constitutions based in large part on America's mission statement.

In 1987, *Time* magazine published a special issue celebrating the Constitution's bicentennial and its global influence. The magazine cited 170 nations that had liberally used ideas and language from the document to write their own constitutions and charters.

Since then, however, the U.S. Constitution has suffered a precipitous decline in influence. Countries today seeking constitutional inspiration turn to the Canadian Charter of Rights and Freedoms and other documents that embody a "global constitutionalism" that include more enumerated human rights, according to a 2012 study by David S. Law of Washington University in St. Louis and Mila Versteeg of the University of Virginia.

The study, *The Declining Influence of the United State Constitution*, examined 729 working constitutions from 1946 to 2006 adopted by 188 countries. The authors analyzed and coded 237 different variables extracted from these documents, whittling them down to a rights index of 60 variables.[5] The authors then compared which constitutions were the most copied around the world. The U.S. Constitution did not fare well.

Law and Versteeg cited the following reasons for the U.S. Constitution's waning influence:

1. brevity of the Constitution;
2. extreme difficulty amending the document;
3. omission of some basic human rights used in new constitutions;
4. inclusion of outdated rights.

First, because of the Constitution's age and brevity, different schools of thought have cropped up—similarly to different Christian denominations interpreting scripture—claiming to decipher the true meaning of each passage of the "ancient, hallowed" document. These schools of thought include: fundamentalism, sometimes called originalism; perfectionism, majoritarianism, and minimalism.

Fundamentalists, like Supreme Court Justices Clarence Thomas and the late Antonin Scalia, interpret the Constitution's rights, principles, and ideas as they believe the Framers intended—"through their eyes," so to speak. Other schools of thought approach the Constitution as a "living, breathing" document that contains enough elasticity in its sinews to apply to issues of the day.

The Constitution's brevity invites broad interpretation because of its sparse language contained in highly important passages. The Second Amendment, for example, is one sentence long, yet it has been shaped by hundreds of federal and state court cases and laws. Does it mean that the right to bear arms only includes those weapons of the Revolutionary Era, such as muskets? Or is it elastic enough to include semi- and fully-automatic rifles?

Second, amending the Constitution has become as rare as a major comet sighting. The vast majority of Americans have no memory of the last amendment that was both passed and ratified. According to Law and Versteeg, the nearly impossible task of amending the document "raises the possibility that (the U.S. Constitution) is simply becoming obsolete." The authors state the average working constitution today has a "38 percent chance of being revised in any given year and is replaced every 19 years." As discussed earlier, amending the Constitution at this frequency is far out of our comfort zone and would likely lead to instability. California's state constitution is a cautionary tale of easy and frequent amending. It is changed nearly every election by ballot initiatives. It is a mess. The document is riddled with contradictory passages—often including spending authorizations—passed by partisan factions or wealthy interests that blew a huge hole in the state budget for years.

Third, the study's top 25 most popular constitutional provisions used by other nations comprise a "shared or generic" core, wholly influenced by the U.S. Constitution, that is used in about 70 percent of all constitutions:

- freedom of religion
- freedom of the press

- right to private property
- right to privacy
- right of assembly

But after analyzing newer constitutions, the authors found the following provisions gaining wide popularity:

- rights for the family
- rights for women
- rights for children
- rights for the disabled
- right to a healthy environment

The study quantified this shift toward more enumerated rights, beginning around 1987 and continuing today:

> . . . the U.S. Constitution is increasingly atypical in the purely quantitative sense that it offers relatively few enumerated rights. While the catalog of rights found in other constitutions has steadily grown, the laconic U.S Constitution has not added any rights at all over the last century. As a result, it contains only 21 of the 60 provisions in (the study's) rights index, whereas the average constitution currently contains 34.[6]

The U.S. Constitution, for example, does not include any enumerated rights for women aside from suffrage, yet women's rights provisions are included in over 90 percent of the world's constitutions in effect today.[7] In the U.S., the Equal Rights Amendment was introduced in 1923, but was not passed by Congress until 1972. After Congress extended the original seven-year ratification deadline to 1982, only 35 states had ratified—three short of the required 38.

The U.S. Constitution, according to the study, also fails to include "physical needs rights," such as the right to retirement payments, health care, and food. These rights are found today in about 80 percent of the world's constitutions.[8]

In 1944, President Franklin Delano Roosevelt proposed a "Second Bill of Rights" that included many of the rights now espoused by more modern constitutions. The following is an excerpt from the president's 1944 State of the Union Address in which he proposed these rights to the American people:

> This Republic had its beginning, and grew to its present strength, under the protection of certain inalienable political rights—among them the right of free speech, free press, free worship, trial by jury, freedom from unreasonable searches and seizures. They were our rights to life and liberty. As our Nation has grown in size and stature, however—as our industrial economy expanded—these political rights proved inadequate to assure us equality in the pursuit of happiness. We have come to a clear realization of the fact that true individual freedom cannot exist without economic security and independence. Necessitous men are not free men. People who are hungry and out of a job are the stuff of which dictatorships are made. In our day, these economic truths have become accepted as self-evident. We have accepted, so to speak, a second Bill of Rights under which a new basis of security and prosperity can be established for all regardless of station, race, or creed.
>
> Among these are:
>
> - the right to a useful and remunerative job in the industries or shops or farms or mines of the nation;
> - the right to earn enough to provide adequate food and clothing and recreation;
> - the right of every farmer to raise and sell his products at a return which will give him and his family a decent living;
> - the right of every businessman, large and small, to trade in an atmosphere of freedom from unfair competition and domination by monopolies at home or abroad;
> - the right of every family to a decent home;
> - the right to adequate medical care and the opportunity to achieve and enjoy good health;

- the right to adequate protection from the economic fears of old age, sickness, accident, and unemployment; and
- the right to a good education.

All of these rights spell security. And after this war is won we must be prepared to move forward, in the implementation of these rights, to new goals of human happiness and well-being. America's own rightful place in the world depends in large part upon how fully these and similar rights have been carried into practice for our citizens. For unless there is security here at home there cannot be lasting peace in the world.

The president's initiative failed.

Conservatives and Southern Democrats in Congress turned their noses up at a truly American idea, just like they had done with the League of Nations. But the world took notice, and the United Nations was born, as were so many enumerated rights written into constitutions around the globe. The reason for the U.S. Constitution's stinginess on human rights, Law and Versteeg note, is that "the U.S. Constitution is . . . rooted in a libertarian tradition that is inherently antithetical to the notion of (social and cultural) rights."[9]

Fourth, the study states the U.S. Constitution's declining influence may also be caused by the inclusion of outdated provisions, such as the Second Amendment's right to bear arms. The only other nations in the world that enshrine gun rights in their constitutions are Mexico and Guatemala. Argentina's constitution includes a right to bear arms, but only to *protect* the "fatherland." America's Second Amendment zealots, in contrast, defend their gun rights to protect themselves *against* the "fatherland."

It must be noted that although some European countries have laws allowing campaign spending caps, there is no nation that includes such a provision in its constitution. Perhaps the U.S. could recapture some of its international luster by passing such an amendment. After all, there is no shortage of political scandals involving the lust for money in any country.

While we may no longer rank first in the world for democratic inspiration, we must temper the popularity of global constitutions in comparison with the U.S. Constitution. Just because a country has a constitution does not mean those rights are granted expeditiously, if ever. After all, the Nazis had a constitution (Weimar Constitution), as do Cuba and Libya. Supreme Court Justice Antonin Scalia once weighed in on this issue while testifying before the Senate Judiciary Committee:

> Every banana republic in the world has a bill of rights. The bill of rights of the former evil empire, the Union of Soviet Socialist Republics, was much better than ours. We guarantee freedom of speech and of the press. Big deal. They guarantee freedom of speech, of the press, of street demonstrations and protests, and anyone who is caught trying to suppress criticism of the government will be called to account. Whoa, that is wonderful stuff! Of course, it's just words on paper, what our framers would have called a 'parchment guarantee.'[10]

Noted U.S. judge Learned Hand put it best concerning the real power and importance of constitutions, laws, and courts. In a famous 1944 speech in New York City's Central Park during a patriotic rally for "I Am An American Day," he mused:

> I often wonder whether we do not rest our hopes too much upon constitutions, upon laws, and upon courts. These are false hopes, believe me, these are false hopes. Liberty lies in the hearts of men and women; when it dies there, no constitution, no law, no court can save it; no constitution, no law, no court can even do much to help it.[11]

There are many other countries that enjoy freedom and democracy. But it's *embedded* in America's DNA like no other. There is no doubt we draw incredible strength from our direct link to the Founding Fathers and the Framers through the Constitution. Their spirit is very much alive today in our hearts. Many Americans are fearful of opening up the Constitution for amendment. To them, it's like opening up a Pandora's Box—afraid our freedom will somehow fly away if we tinker with the contents.

Yet we must change.

Those who are too fearful to imagine amending the document should remember the Eighteenth Amendment, which prohibited alcoholic beverages in America. Turns out it was not the right move.

Did the country implode?

No.

Did freedom die?

No.

America simply passed the Twenty-first Amendment to revert back to prior law.

The Constitution needs to breathe. And it hasn't taken a breath in 48 years.

THE AMENDMENT PROCESS

THE CONSTITUTION'S ARTICLE V permits only two ways to propose and approve an amendment and only two ways to ratify it.

Proposing and approving an amendment:

1. *Legislation*: A bill must be introduced in Congress and passed by a two-thirds majority vote in each house.
2. *Constitutional convention*: Two-thirds (34) of the nation's state legislatures must call for a national constitutional convention where the amendment will be proposed. (This method has never been used.)

Ratifying an amendment:

1. *State legislatures*: Three-fourths (38) of the nation's state legislatures must pass the amendment.
2. *State conventions*: Three-fourths of the nation's states must each call a convention and pass the amendment.

Twenty-six of the Constitution's 27 amendments have been passed by proposing a bill in Congress and ratifying the proposal by three-fourths of the state legislatures.

Only the Twenty-first Amendment, which repealed Prohibition (Eighteenth Amendment), was passed by proposing a bill in Congress and then ratifying the proposal in conventions in three-fourths of the states.

The Framers saw no role for the president in the amendment process, other than the office's bully pulpit. An amendment does not require the president's signature for ratification. There have been occasions, however, when a president has held a signing ceremony for a ratified amendment to raise awareness of its significance.

IS AN AMENDMENT ACHIEVABLE?

THE MERE THOUGHT OF AMENDING the Constitution to enshrine campaign spending limits may sound farfetched to average Americans. Amending the Constitution is difficult, of course, but not impossible.

It is instructive to know that since the Bill of Rights passed into law in 1791, nine of the 17, or 53 percent, of constitutional amendments ratified since then have amended the nation's election system. The last three were passed in 1961, 1964, and 1971 (granting Electoral College representation to Washington, D.C.; eliminating poll taxes, and establishing the voting age at 18, respectively).

It is also instructive to know that Americans have amended the Constitution to overrule the Supreme Court. The Twenty-sixth Amendment, lowering the voting age to 18, passed because the Democrat-controlled Congress and Republican president, Richard M. Nixon, understood the public demanded common sense change. The government passed the Voting Rights Act Amendments of 1970 to grant suffrage to citizens reaching age 18. After all, Americans reasoned, if these citizens were mature enough to fight and die in Vietnam, they should have the right to vote. But the Supreme Court partially nullified the law after Texas and Oregon successfully challenged its constitutionality in the case of *Oregon v. Mitchell* (1970). The Court ruled that Congress had the authority to lower the voting age to 18 for federal elections, but not state elections.

The public, however, would not be denied. The citizens called on Congress to overrule the Court with a constitutional amendment requiring Congress *and* the states to allow citizens as young as 18 to vote. Just three months after the Supreme Court decision, Congress swiftly proposed and passed an amendment bill by the requisite two-thirds vote in each house. Three months and eight days later, the required three quarters of the state legislatures ratified the amendment. On July 1, 1971, North Carolina became the 38th state to ratify, thus adding the Twenty-sixth Amendment to the Constitution.

The Twenty-sixth Amendment is one of seven amendments that fully or partially overruled a Supreme Court decision. The Nineteenth Amendment in 1920, one of the more well-known amendments, granted suffrage to all women by overruling *Minor v. Happersett* (1875).

So is it realistic to believe Americans could support a campaign spending limits amendment?

Yes.

But not in the current hyper-partisan political climate.

Of course, that can change. And there's been quite a bit of change in American politics since 2016.

Keep in mind that this country did not grant women the right to vote after a short public discussion. The process took 100 years to complete. There were pioneers who began the cause, like writer Fanny Wright in the 1820s, and those who sustained it and nurtured it over many years, like Elizabeth Cady Stanton, Lucretia Mott, and Susan B. Anthony. And there were those lucky enough to be at the finish line on August 26, 1920, when America added the Nineteenth Amendment—women's suffrage—to the Constitution. The suffragettes knew their cause was just, and they knew it was vital for the nation's future, and they persevered.

Today's campaign finance reformers are not pioneers in this process, but are at a key moment in the arc of this issue. Watergate provided the biggest flashpoint by propelling Congress to pass campaign spending limits. Although extremist ideologues and wealthy special interests quickly snuffed it out, mainstream America's hunger for spending caps has never subsided.

Polls conducted since the 1960s consistently show average Americans of both parties heavily favor campaign finance reform, including spending limits, to curb political corruption.

Rodney A. Smith, a longtime, noted Republican fundraiser and anti-reform advocate admitted in his 2006 book, *Money, Power & Elections: How Campaign Finance Reform Subverts American Democracy*, that Republicans as well as Democrats favor campaign finance reforms to cut the corrupting link between politicians and money. Smith noted that 68 percent of Americans in 1968 favored campaign spending limits, rising to 78 percent in 1970—several years before the spiking of citizen outrage in reaction to the Watergate scandal.[12]

In January 2006, the nonpartisan National Voting Rights Institute released a poll stating 87 percent of voters "overwhelmingly support a law to limit campaign spending."[13] The poll showed that this support was strong regardless of gender, age, income, geography, or party affiliation, finding that 90 percent of women and 84 percent of men favored spending limits. The Northeast registered the strongest support for spending limits at 91 percent, followed by the West at 90 percent, the Midwest at 85 percent, and the South at 84 percent. As for political affiliation, Democrats led with a 90-percent support rate; Independents at 89 percent; and Republicans at 84 percent.[14]

In January 2012, a *CBS News* poll found that 67 percent of Americans favored campaign spending limits.[15] In June 2015, a *New York Times/CBS News* poll showed 78 percent of respondents favoring spending limits on independent expenditure groups.[16] A Pew Research Center poll in November 2015 showed that 84 percent of Democrats and 72 percent of Republicans favored campaign spending caps.[17] Those polled cited the influence of special interest money as the biggest problem plaguing the U.S. political system and that it corrupted the "integrity and honesty" of their elected officials. Also, 64 percent said the "high cost of campaigns discourages good candidates."[18]

According to these and other sources, there seems to be strong bipartisan support across America for instituting campaign spending limits to curb political corruption. But the issue hasn't reached critical mass since the 1970s because a sound proposal has not been articulated in a way that makes sense to average Americans.

In today's political climate of Invisible Empire dominance, rabid partisanship, so-called fake news, empty sound bites, and ugly character assassinations, such a proposal must be strong enough to rise above the din of naysayers who profit from the status quo.

It will also likely take another major political scandal like Watergate to spur Americans to take action. Perhaps, Senator Evan Bayh (D-IN) said it best in 2010 when asked if there were any hope that America would throw off the chains of its corrupted political system. Bayh replied, "There'll be a major scandal at some point that'll shock the public. It'll be worse than what happened with (super lobbyist Jack) Abramoff. And at that point, the system will be changed."[19]

There is no doubt that the issue of our times is getting money out of politics. Every poll shows Democrats, Republicans, and unaffiliated voters are in agreement.

America is at a crossroads.

Do we take back our democracy or lay down like lambs?

Will future generations revere us for our courage and wisdom in restoring our democratic foundation and setting the nation on a renewed course of freedom?

Or will we pass into oblivion, too timid to act; shirking our responsibility to future Americans?

An interviewer recently asked Pulitzer Prize-winning historian David McCullough, a prolific writer on early American history, what the Founding Fathers would think if they could observe
the current state of our democracy. McCullough replied:

> I think that their stomachs might turn a little at the role of money in
> our politics now, and the degree to which politics has been turned
> into merchandising, and marketing, and advertising, and ballyhoo.

The same could be said for the vast majority of Americans—
that we are sickened at the role of money in politics and how the
Invisible Empire, moneyed politicians, political wiseguys, and
other reform foes have cynically used our freedom and democracy
against us to steal our political power.

We have the opportunity *now* to amend the Constitution for
our benefit and the benefit of so many generations to come.

The Founding Fathers would be proud of us.

18

AMENDMENT DRAFT

A CONSTITUTIONAL AMENDMENT granting Congress, the states, and local governments the right to enact campaign spending limits is gravely serious, and it is unique.

It is gravely serious because it will mend the lingering hole in our Constitution that has torn at the fabric of our equality-based democratic institutions.

It will repair the American political system's one major flaw that is sapping the strength and integrity of our democracy. It will overthrow the Invisible Empire that has been set up by wealthy special interests above the forms of democracy. And it will restore citizens as the sovereign power in the United States.

Under the Constitution, citizens are the masters, not the slaves. To remain the masters, the power and value of our individual votes must forever remain sacrosanct and equal to all others.

A campaign spending limits amendment is unique because it has the capacity to change the dynamic of the entire political system, strengthening the integrity of every decision and vote on virtually every issue lawmakers face in the halls of government. It is not a narrow amendment addressing a single issue, like flag burning, the federal budget deficit, or the Electoral College. It is an all-encompassing amendment that will allow these and all other issues to be addressed impartially by lawmakers with decisions and votes that truly reflect citizens' consensus and will. There is no other amendment that will have a more positive and profound effect on our democracy and who we are as a people.

A campaign spending limits amendment is no slippery slope. It is not an assault on our First Amendment rights. It's not the germ of a police state. It won't lead to jailing or executing citizens wishing to speak their minds in public. It will simply provide the democratic bulwark needed to contain the baser elements of capitalism that have been weakening the bonds between citizens and government.

A constitutional spending limits amendment will restore citizens' freedom and right to manage our elections by limiting spending that political extremists and the U.S. Supreme Court killed before it could be implemented.

This amendment will not force Congress, states, and municipalities to adopt spending limits. It will not force anybody to do anything. It will simply *reserve a right* for citizens to adopt such laws if they choose.

Our collective vision of America is that of a beacon for other nations to follow—a successful example of self-governance based on openness, honesty, equality, impartiality, and integrity. We strive to inspire others by striving ourselves to form a "more perfect union." That means participating in our democracy, individually and through our government representatives, to better our laws, culture, and the lives of all citizens.

But how can we be an effective beacon to others when our own house is not in order? How can we advocate adopting democracy when our own system is corrupt to its core?

America must stop deceiving itself that the problem can be solved with a few Band-Aids—like weak disclosure requirements and porous lobbying and ethics laws.

It is not working.

We all know it.

And the nation's children know it. They see it every day on television, radio, newspapers, and the Internet. It serves no purpose to hide our nation's dirty laundry behind statues of Washington, Jefferson, and Lincoln.

In years past, America led the world because of its willingness to embrace change and innovation. If we refuse to acknowledge the structural design flaw in our political system and neglect to repair it, it will continue to fester. It will undermine and degrade our moral and economic standing in the world.

A constitutional amendment granting citizens the power to enact campaign spending limits will help create the stronger and truer America we all envision. And the stronger, truer democracy that will emerge will help set all Americans free, as well as our fellow citizens around the world.

AMENDMENT ESSENTIALS

LET'S REVIEW THE MAJOR TENETS a campaign spending limits amendment must include.

The amendment is needed to curb political corruption—as well as the *appearance* or *perception* of political corruption—in our political system. The amendment will reserve the right for citizens to enact campaign spending and donation limits on all levels of government and amend or repeal such laws at our discretion.

As a general rule, "one citizen, one vote" must be the guiding principle when setting spending and donation limits, ensuring that wealthy partisans cannot abuse the system by giving large contributions (donation votes) that expand their political power at the expense of average Americans' ballot votes.

Campaign spending limits must be designed in tandem with donation caps that reflect average American income levels for the right balance, allowing candidates to raise sufficient funds to get their messages out to voters.

Spending limits must apply to all individuals, businesses, and groups who fund, produce, and run television, radio, Internet, or other mass media political advertisements or conduct mass marketing activities designed to influence election outcomes. The rules will apply to all political advertising activities, including all independent expenditure groups and wealthy individuals regardless of whether or not their ads clearly identify a candidate. Proper spending caps will eliminate the practice of Super PACs and other independent groups conducting campaign activities that the candidate's campaign traditionally performs, such as phone banking, administrative work, and get-out-the-vote drives, etc. The amendment will not apply to policy research, news and commentary, and other activities that do not involve paid political advertisements.

The amendment must enshrine citizens' right to create independent, nonpartisan citizens panels to oversee government activities, including redistricting. These panels will set, regulate, and administer campaign spending and donation limits. Congress or any other partisan-elected body or individual must never be given this power, since they cannot be trusted to regulate themselves.

The amendment must apply to ballot initiatives, referendums, and other issue-related elections, as well as political spending to influence issues pending in Congress and other legislative bodies.

The amendment must grant control to states and local jurisdictions to limit or ban out-of-state or out-of-jurisdiction contributions to candidates and ballot initiative campaigns. Citizens deserve the right to choose their own representatives and decide ballot initiatives that will directly affect them without outside interference.

Finally, the amendment must ensure flexibility by granting sufficient enforcement powers to the citizens panels to quickly address and block any violations or attempts to exploit loopholes that would impact a current election cycle. Panels will have the power to ban all schemes used to circumvent spending and donation limits.

So how should this amendment be written? Although the Constitution's First Amendment, for example, is short and uncluttered, its brevity and broadness have invited voluminous legal challenges and interpretations. Knowing the tendencies of special interests to exploit any weakness in a law's language, a spending limits amendment must therefore have more on its bones, yet still retain some broadness and freedom bound by basic structure.

The following is a draft constitutional amendment bill that embodies the ideas expounded on in this book.

JOINT RESOLUTION

Proposing an amendment to the Constitution of the United States relating to contributions and expenditures intended to affect elections.

Resolved by the Senate and House of Representatives of the United States of America in Congress assembled (two-thirds of each House concurring therein), that the following article is proposed as an amendment to the Constitution of the United States, to be valid only if ratified by the legislatures of three-fourths of the several states after the date of final passage of this joint resolution:

ARTICLE

SECTION 1.

Money is not speech. Money expended by individuals or groups to fund, produce, and run mass media political advertisements or conduct activities, other than policy research or journalistic news and commentary, designed to influence the outcome of lawmaking or elections, including ballot initiative elections, is not a protected right under the First Amendment of this Constitution. All political expenditures and contributions may be fully regulated by the People.

SECTION 2.

Congress, states, and local jurisdictions shall have the power to enact legislation allowing campaign expenditure and contribution limits for all elections. Once passed, such laws may be repealed by a three-fourths majority vote. States and local jurisdictions may enact such laws by ballot initiative, if available. The law may only be repealed by a three-fourths majority vote using the same method by which the measure was adopted.

SECTION 3.

Citizens shall have the power to create independent, nonpartisan panels to oversee government activities, including redistricting.

Congress, the states, and local jurisdictions may enact campaign expenditure and contribution limits, provided that the power of setting the limits and administering the law with appropriate enforcement powers be granted to independent, nonpartisan citizens panels.

The law must grant authority to a nonpartisan government agency or nonpartisan nonprofit organization to oversee the selection of citizens panel members. The composition of such panels shall reflect the demographics of the citizens these panels will represent.

Such citizens panels shall have the power to enact reasonable expenditure and contribution limits on all individuals and groups seeking to influence elections and lawmaking.

Such federal, state, and local citizens panels shall have the power to restrict or ban practices or constructs that circumvent the law and expand an individual's or group's voting power at the expense of the voting power of each individual citizen.

Such panels shall have the power to limit or ban out-of-state or out-of-jurisdiction contributions and political advertisements funded by individuals or groups that do not have voting rights in the elections they seek to influence.

Such panels shall have the authority to determine whether any political expression is deemed a political advertisement.

Such panels shall have the power to immediately block

expenditures or contributions made to circumvent the law and expand an individual's or group's voting power at the expense of the voting power of each individual citizen. Violations by any individual or group that willfully violates a panel's expenditure or donation limits may result in fines or imprisonment, as set forth in the enacting law.

Such federal, state, and local panels shall conduct research to assess the effects of prior elections' limits and adjust the limits accordingly for subsequent elections to ensure candidates may accept and spend amounts sufficient to communicate their messages to voters.

Federal, state, and local citizens panels, in conjunction with the appropriating legislative body and an impartial arbiter, will determine and establish their base funding needed to administer their duties. The funding shall increase or decrease at the annual rate of inflation. Congress, state and local legislative bodies, and elected or appointed officials shall be banned from subsequently increasing or decreasing a panel's funding without the panel's approval.

Panels shall have the sole authority by a two-thirds majority vote to remove a fellow panel member for misconduct or party partisanship intended to undermine the panel's independence and nonpartisanship. Partisan elected bodies and partisan elected or appointed officials shall be banned from removing or appointing panel members. Federal, state, local jurisdictions, or ballot initiatives shall determine the manner and length of terms.

SECTION 4.

Residual powers of a campaign expenditure and contribution limits law shall be vested in the independent, nonpartisan citizens panels, which shall have the power to administer the law through rules and guidelines in consonance with the federal, state, or local enacting legislation or ballot initiative. The guiding principle governing the panels' decisions shall be the democratic precept of "one citizen, one vote" to protect the equal voting power of every

American citizen.

SECTION 5.
There is no time limit to ratify this amendment.

FINAL THOUGHTS

I HOPE THIS BOOK ILLUMINATED the structural problems that hobble our democracy, steal our individual and collective rights, and degrade our quality of life.

I believe that if you evaluate all possible questions and seek all possible explanations for why our government is broken, you will come to the same conclusion: that unlimited political spending—that is a near guarantee of political power in elections and passing laws—is the root cause of political corruption in our country. It is robbing us of our political power as guaranteed by the Constitution, fleecing average Americans of their hard-earned income every day, and undermining the trust that binds all Americans together. Unless we do something about it, we will never have a legitimate, responsive government imbued with impartiality and integrity that we can trust. And we will surely and completely become the slaves of our own democracy, rather than its masters.

The solution can only be achieved if we believe together, act together, and persevere together through the din of vested interests, naysayers, and cynics who will seek to divide us. The odds will be difficult to overcome—American indifference being the most feared opponent. Famed historian Will Durant once said, "The political machine triumphs because it is a united minority acting against a divided majority."

And divided we are.

Our attention is divided by relationships, marriages, families, children, work, entertainment—and everything else that is important to us or holds our daily interest.

But we are also angry, particularly when government corruption is splashed over the news, such as when we learn our tax dollars have been wasted or misused. Or when our government lets moneyed special interests gouge us for services such as electricity, cable television, banking, credit cards, cell phones, etc., and sends us bills written in unintelligible, tiny legalese that are hard to read without a magnifying glass and impossible to understand without a law degree. And you wonder how things got so out of control.

The next time you get angry about government corruption, think of this book.

Think of campaign spending limits.

And think of amending the Constitution.

Absent our willingness to act—even in simple ways—nothing will change. And you and your children will continue to be robbed by the Invisible Empire—the people who have corrupted the system and exert immense control over it for their benefit. They've mastered the government, and in a very real sense, they've become our masters. And they will continue to act every single day to enrich themselves at our expense until we stop them.

We must no longer be duped by special interests, partisans, and extremists wanting us to believe that corruption is part of the deal of a democracy—like a dog resigned to fleas. Why should we settle for less and tolerate these parasites? They continue to rule over us only because we aren't organized enough, outraged enough, and determined enough.

It is our country.

It is our democracy.

It belongs to all of us.

The Constitution declares that "We the People" are the masters, not the slaves.

Let us clean up our house once and for all.

And let us fulfill our promise and destiny as the shining beacon to all nations.

APPENDIX

IT'S BROKEN

Presidential Quotations & More

WHO WOULD REALLY KNOW if America's political system is corrupt and rotten to the core?

Who would know if the system's money incentive, coupled with special interests' greed for power, control, and profits is a lingering hole in our Constitution that's killing the integrity of our democracy?

And who would have more intimate, first-hand, behind-the-scenes, insider knowledge of what's *really* going on in the system?

It would logically be those who've run the big-money gauntlet seeking high office.

Earlier in this book, congressional politicians spoke of the debilitating effect unlimited campaign spending has on their ability to effectively perform their duties for the people. We've even heard from lobbyists who corroborated the politicians' stories.

We will now hear from our presidents, governors, and other elected officials and candidates on the overall effect that unlimited spending has on the entire political system.

PRESIDENTS

Theodore Roosevelt (R): In a fiery campaign speech on August 31, 1910, in Osawatomie, Kansas, Roosevelt declared that his "square deal" for all Americans meant that all hardworking citizens deserved an equal chance at prosperity, and that corporations and moneyed special interests must be thwarted from accumulating outsized power and influence with which to corrupt the government:

> It is necessary that laws should be passed to prohibit the use of corporate funds directly or indirectly for political purposes; it is still more necessary that such laws should be thoroughly enforced. Corporate expenditures for political purposes, and especially such expenditures by public service corporations have supplied one of the principal sources of corruption in our political affairs. . . . Exactly as the special interests of cotton and slavery threatened our political integrity before the Civil War, so now the great special business interests too often control and corrupt the men and methods of government for their own profit. We must drive the special interests out of politics. . . . For every special interest is entitled to justice, but not one is entitled to a vote in Congress, to a voice on the bench, or to representation in any public office... [1]

Calvin Coolidge (R): In a June 21, 1926, speech in Washington, D.C., "Silent Cal" chillingly foretold the consequences of an out-of-control political system allowing influence peddlers to manipulate the nation's lawmakers and the federal budget:

> It shows how hard it is in these times to reduce the costs, taxes, and debts of governments. But it can be done if the people will cooperate. Unless they do, however, special interests will continue to overwhelm the legislative bodies for more expenses and more taxes. The limit is close at hand when further expansion in the costs of government will bring the danger of stagnation and financial depression. [2]

Three years later the stock market crashed and America sank into the Great Depression.

Herbert Hoover (R): In a May 6, 1932, news conference, Hoover decried the influence of special interests, who he believed were preventing the passage of a balanced budget by stuffing it with pork-barrel projects:

> It is an issue of the people against delays and destructive legislation, which impair the credit of the United States. It is also an issue between the people and the locust swarm of lobbyists that haunt the halls of Congress seeking selfish privilege for special groups and sections of the country, and misleading (congressional) members on the real views of the people by showers of propaganda.[3]

Franklin Delano Roosevelt (D): In his annual message to Congress in 1936, Roosevelt, struggling to shake the nation from the Great Depression's grip, warned against the moneyed interests meddling in government affairs and threatening to roll back the progress and momentum created by his New Deal initiatives:

> We, you in the Congress and I as the executive, had to build upon a broad base. Now, after 34 months of work, we contemplate a fairly rounded whole. We have returned the control of the federal government to the city of Washington. To be sure, in so doing, we have invited battle. We have earned the hatred of entrenched greed. The very nature of the problem that we faced made it necessary to drive some people from power and strictly to regulate others. I made that plain when I took the oath of office in March 1933. I spoke of the practices of the unscrupulous money-changers who stood indicted in the court of public opinion. I spoke of the rulers of the exchanges of mankind's goods, who failed through their own stubbornness and their own incompetence. I said that they had admitted their failure and had abdicated.
>
> Abdicated? Yes, in 1933, but now with the passing of danger they forget their damaging admissions and withdraw their abdication. They seek the restoration of their selfish power. They offer to lead us back 'round the same old corner into the same old dreary street. Yes, there are still determined groups that are intent upon that very thing. Rigorously held up to popular examination, their true character presents itself. They steal the livery of great

national constitutional ideals to serve discredited special interests. As guardians and trustees for great groups of individual stockholders, they wrongfully seek to carry the property and the interests entrusted to them into the arena of partisan politics. They seek, this minority in business and industry, to control and often do control and use for their own purposes legitimate and highly honored business associations; they engage in vast propaganda to spread fear and discord among the people—they would 'gang up' against the people's liberties. The principle that they would instill into government if they succeed in seizing power is well shown by the principles which many of them have instilled into their own affairs: autocracy toward labor, toward stockholders, toward consumers, toward public sentiment. Autocrats in smaller things, they seek autocracy in bigger things. 'By their fruits ye shall know them.'[4]

Harry S. Truman (D): During his relentless barnstorming across America to overcome New York Governor Thomas E. Dewey's lead in the presidential polls, Truman stopped at Rock Island, Illinois, on September 18, 1948, at 5:45 in the morning and gave a blistering speech, standing on the rear platform of his campaign train. Although he owed his political career to a party boss in his home state, Truman scorned the poison of corruption:

> You must, if you want this country to go forward, you must always be sure that you have people in control of the government whose interest is yours and not the special interests who want special privilege in everything that takes place. . . . There is one thing I want to bring home to you. I am on a crusade for the welfare of the everyday man in the United States. I am not working for special privilege. I am not working for the speculators' lobby. I am not working for the real estate lobby. I am not working for any special interests in the United States but the interests of the everyday man whose interest is my interest—and that interest is your interest.
>
> You know, Lincoln said that the Lord certainly loved the common people or He wouldn't have made so many of them. I think that is just as true as it can be.[5]

Dwight D. Eisenhower (R): In a May 4, 1956, news conference, a reporter asked Eisenhower if he favored federal campaign
spending laws to curb corruption in states' congressional primary
elections. The president replied:

> Well, for me it is a very difficult (question) because, as I read the
> Constitution, the determination of their voting laws and so on is
> left to the states. I think if we could have comparable laws in these
> cases in all of the states and properly enforced, it would be a good
> thing. Everybody of good will in America wants to take any pos-
> sibility of corruption, graft, and everything else out of politics.
> We should try to do it; but it is not easy . . .[6]

John F. Kennedy (D): In a May 29, 1962, letter to congressional leaders, Kennedy summed up the recommendations of the
Commission on Campaign Costs, which he appointed in 1961:

> In these days when the public interest demands basic decisions so
> essential to our security and survival, public policy should enable
> presidential candidates to free themselves of dependence on large
> contributions of those with special interests.[7]

Lyndon B. Johnson (D): The president, who just one month
earlier had decided to withdraw from politics and not seek re-
election, made the following remarks on April 24, 1968, at a
Democratic Party dinner in Chicago, Illinois:

> From the first days of the republic to our times, the leaders who
> have loved America have warned continuously against the divisive
> spirit of faction and special interests. Every generation of Ameri-
> cans has had to heed that warning. . . . In this time, and at this
> place here in this great city of Chicago with the presence of these
> devoted leaders, it is fitting to recall the words of one of our great
> American leaders, Abraham Lincoln, when he spoke 110 years ago
> in a small Illinois town. He was then referring to the authors of
> our Declaration of Independence. Abraham Lincoln had this to
> say:
> 'Wise statesmen as they were, they knew the tendency of

prosperity to breed tyrants, and so they established these great self-evident truths, that when in the distant future some man, some faction, some interest, should set up the doctrine that none but rich men or none but white men, were entitled to life, liberty and the pursuit of happiness, their posterity might look up again to the Declaration of Independence and take courage to renew the battle which the fathers began . . . '[8]

Gerald R. Ford (R): On October 15, 1974, the president made the following remarks at the White House signing ceremony for the Federal Election Campaign Act (FECA) Amendments of 1974 that instituted campaign spending limits for federal candidates:

It is really a great privilege for me to have a part in what I think is historic legislation. As all of my good friends from the Congress know, a tremendous amount of work, a lot of extra labor, went into the putting together of this legislation. Quite frankly, I had some strong reservations about one version or one provision or another of the legislation, and I suspect some of the people here on both sides of the aisle have the same. But we got together in a spirit of cooperation, a willingness to work together, to give a little and take a little, and the net result is legislation that I think the American people want. It is legislation for the times. . . . I can assure you from what I have heard, from the American people in writing and other communications, they want this legislation. So, it will soon be law. I think we do recognize that this legislation seeks to eliminate to a maximum degree some of the influences that have created some of the problems in recent years. And if that is the end result, certainly it is worth all the labor and all the compromises that were necessary in the process.[9]

Jimmy Carter (D): In 2015, the former president reflected on the fallout of the Supreme Court's 2010 *Citizens United* ruling:

Now (America is) just an oligarchy, with unlimited political bribery being the essence of getting the nomination for president or to elect the president. And the same thing applies to governors and U.S. senators and Congress members. So now, we've just seen a complete subversion of our political system as a payoff to major contributors who want and expect and sometimes get favors for themselves after the election's over.[10]

Ronald Reagan (R): In his March 9, 1981, budget message to Congress, the new president warned the public that influence peddlers would be fighting to protect longtime "sacred cow" spending items that he planned to cut:

> We must see to it that the voice of the average American, not that of special interests or full-time lobbyists, is the dominant one.[11]

George H. W. Bush (R): On June 29, 1989, Bush proposed campaign finance reform legislation that would "free our electoral system from the grip of special interests." Although Bush opposed spending limits, he favored a number of other key reforms, which he outlined in his speech:

> Parties are the indispensable organizers of democracy. And yet times have changed, and today's special interest political action committees (PACs) and their $160 million war chests overshadow the great parties of Thomas Jefferson and Abraham Lincoln. . . .
> By necessity, members of Congress engage in time-consuming and often degrading appeals for money outside the party structure. As vigorous competition between candidates and between ideas wanes, the clear winner in the race for PAC dollars is incumbency.
> More than 90 percent of all PAC contributions come from PACs sponsored by corporations, unions, and trade associations. So the cornerstone of this reform . . . is the elimination of those political action committees. . . . I propose to end a practice that's known as bundling, where business and unions encourage or coerce contributions from employees or members and then give these contributions as one single donation. . . . Today, incumbents stay in office for decades, amassing huge war chests to scare off strong challenges in election after election. This is not democracy in the spirit of Madison and Jefferson. This is not the spirit of democracy at all. And so, I propose to end the rollover of campaign war chests, requiring any excess campaign funds to be donated to

the parties, to a fund to retire the national debt, or to be given back to the contributors.[12]

Bill Clinton (D): In his weekly radio address on July 22, 1995, Clinton bemoaned the steep rise and power of lobbyists and their wealthy clients:

> It's clearer than ever that we need political reform. The American people believe their political system is too influenced by narrow interests, that our government serves the powerful but not hard-working families. Even before the '94 elections, the special interests prevented passage of both campaign finance reform and lobby reform legislation that I had strongly asked the Congress to pass. When a minority in the Senate killed lobbying reform in 1994, lobbyists were standing right outside the Senate chamber cheering. Since the new Congress came in, I'm sad to say, it's gotten worse, for even more power has been given to the lobbyists. Now this new majority lets lobbyists for polluters write legislation rolling back environmental and public health protections. They've brought them in to explain the legislation. They even gave them a room off the House floor to write the amendments and the statements the members would have to give explaining the bills that the lobbyists had written for them.[13]

George W. Bush (R): In 2002, the president signed the McCain-Feingold bill into law, although he had reservations about the measure. Bush believed the best way to improve the political system was full disclosure of donors and recipients. In his signing statement for the bill, Bush wrote:

> These provisions of the bill will go a long way toward fixing some of the most pressing problems in campaign finance today. They will result in an election finance system that encourages greater individual participation and provides the public more accurate and timely information than does the present system. All of the American electorate will benefit from these measures to strengthen our democracy.[14]

Barack Obama (D): Obama issued the following response to the U.S. Supreme Court's 2010 *Citizens United* decision:

> With its ruling today, the Supreme Court has given a green light to a new stampede of special interest money in our politics. It is a major victory for Big Oil, Wall Street banks, health insurance companies, and the other powerful interests that marshal their power every day in Washington to drown out the voices of everyday Americans. [15]

The next day, Obama commented on the special interest tactics to scuttle his health care reform bill:

> I mean, it's just an ugly process. You're running headlong into special interests, and armies of lobbyists, and partisan politics that's aimed at exploiting fears instead of getting things done. And then you've got ads that are scaring the bejesus out of everybody. And the longer it takes, the uglier it looks. [16]

GOVERNORS

Mitt Romney (R-MA): Romney supported campaign spending limits in 1994 when he couldn't outspend his incumbent opponent, Senator Ted Kennedy (D-MA). He railed against big money and insinuated Kennedy had changed his positions on issues because of campaign donations:

> And to get that kind of money, you've got to cozy up as an incumbent to all of the special interest groups who can go out and raise money for you from their members. And that kind of relationship has an influence on the way you're going to vote. . . . I saw that the American Trial Lawyers Association and lawyers in general have contributed, I think, well over $1 million to Ted Kennedy's campaign. Well, does that have anything to do with the fact that he was unwilling to cut off a filibuster for product liability reform? Who knows? But these kinds of associations between money and politics in my view are wrong. And for that reason, I would like to have campaign spending limits—and to say we're not going to spend more than this in certain campaigns, in a campaign for

senator or U.S. representative and so forth, because otherwise I think you have money playing far too important a role. I also would abolish PACs. . . . The kinds of demands that are being placed on the economics of running a campaign suggest an increasing power on the part of moneyed interests, and I think it's wrong, and we've got to change it.[17]

After losing to Kennedy, Romney flip-flopped on campaign spending limits. With the $250 million fortune he made running Bain Capital, a private equity firm, he could now outspend virtually all competitors for public office and had no use for capping political spending.

Jim McGreevey (D-NJ): After resigning as governor in 2004 over a sex scandal, McGreevey wrote in his memoir:

> You can't take large sums of money from people without making them specific and personal promises in return. People weren't shy about saying what they expected for their 'investments'—board appointments to the Sports Authority or the New Jersey Economic Development Authority, for example, which were coveted not just for their prestige, but because they offered control over tremendously potent economic engines with discretionary budgets in the tens of millions. The plum was the Port Authority of New York and New Jersey; directors there controlled a multi-billion-dollar budget. I tried to stay as naïve about this horse-trading as much as possible. But I allowed my staff to intimate things to donors.[18]

Arnold Schwarzenegger (R-CA): The actor and former body builder raked in millions of special interest, corporate donation dollars for his two successful gubernatorial campaigns. He also worked his Hollywood connections for all their worth. In a candid moment at a San Francisco campaign stop during his 2006 re-election effort, he lamented:

> The practice of money in and favors out . . . is the most horrible thing in politics.[19]

George Pataki (R-NY): In a June 16, 1999, press release, the governor, who ran for president in 2016, outlined his plan for campaign finance reform, which included lowering contribution limits from $30,700 to $5,000 for statewide races:

> This comprehensive proposal will provide much needed reform to improve the campaign finance laws and provide a level playing field for all candidates regardless of their political party. . . . At the same time we are putting an end to so-called advocacy ads, which have been exposed as nothing more than vehicles for big-money special interests to bypass campaign finance laws.

U.S. SENATORS

Mitch McConnell (R-KY): The Senate majority leader, much like Mitt Romney, ardently supported campaign spending limits as he sought to break into politics. And, like Romney, ardently opposed spending limits soon after his bank account swelled into the millions of dollars.

McConnell, in fact, became one of the nation's most passionate reform foes—and richest members of Congress. While Romney made his money in the private sector, McConnell's current $30 million net worth curiously accumulated mostly while holding public office. As a party leader for many years, millions of special interest dollars naturally flowed through his office. But back in 1973, as a budding Kentucky lawyer and Jefferson County Republican Party chair, McConnell wrote a scathing column in the *Louisville Courier-Journal* blasting a proposed local campaign finance ordinance as too weak. While calling political money a "cancer" on democracy, he wrote:

> With regard to a spending limitation, past events have shown how close we are to a 'bought' nation, state, and city. . . . The lack of an overall limit on spending is an open invitation for special interests to circumvent this ordinance and lavishly finance future candidates . . .

John McCain (R-AZ): During the 1997 Senate campaign finance reform debate, McCain tried in vain to convince colleagues to support his bill:

> We do not want corporations, unions, or wealthy individuals to buy and sell elections. This is not a country where a royal class controls the government. No one here wants corporations to give directly to campaigns. The fact is that at certain times and certain places, there is a role for some regulation and restraint in order to protect the greater public good.[20]

Lindsey Graham (R-SC): Graham, Senator McCain's close friend, who ran for president in 2016, was one of only several Republicans who believed campaign spending cap laws do not violate the Constitution's First Amendment. He made the following statement after the 2003 *McConnell v. FEC* Supreme Court ruling that upheld the McCain-Feingold campaign finance bill:

> The ruling reaffirms my belief that money is property, not speech.[21]

Susan Collins (R-ME): During the 1997 Senate campaign finance reform debate, Collins responded to colleagues who asked why special interest six-figure campaign donations are a problem, since the U.S. Supreme Court equates them with free speech:

> Why should this matter, we are asked by those, by those all too eager to equate freedom of speech with freedom to spend? It should matter because political equality is the essence of democracy, and an electoral system driven by big money is one lacking in political equality.
>
> It strikes me that the Maine attitude may be shaped by the fact that many communities in my state still hold town meetings. I am not talking about the staged, televised town meeting, which has become so fashionable of late. I am talking about a rough-and-tumble meeting held in the town office or the high school gym or the grange hall. Attend one of these sessions and you will observe an element of true democracy; people with more money do not

get to speak longer and louder than people with less money. What is true at Maine town meetings is unfortunately not true in Washington.[22]

Joseph Lieberman (I-CT): Lieberman, a Democrat at the time, penned a *New York Times* column during the Senate hearings investigating the 1996 Clinton-Gore fundraising irregularities:

> Our campaign finance system is without controls and therefore corrupting. Everyone knows this. And most agree on what we should do about it . . . limit spending on campaigns and force independent groups that get into political campaigns to at least disclose who they are and where their money comes from.
>
> If a demoralized public can't summon the anger to force these reforms and we in Congress can't find the courage to enact them, that will be the biggest act of chutzpah of all.

He added that the nation's election system is riddled with loopholes that "invite abuse and send the message that for the right price, influence *can* be bought."[23]

Barry Goldwater (R-AZ): Goldwater was no fan of circumvention schemes. When Congress debated a cap on the amount political action committees (PACs) could donate to candidates, Goldwater railed against the myopic view of special interests:

> (PACs are) destroying the election process . . . with their selfish and narrow view about what is good for this country." [24]

Dale Bumpers (D-AR): The longtime Arkansas governor and senator penned a *New York Times* opinion piece in 1999 in which he wrote:

> Democracy is threatened when the candidates we elect and laws we enact hinge on how much money is spent. To claim that campaign spending is a legitimate exercise of free speech is to deny the constitutional principle that each one of us counts. A donor who gives $100,000 gets a lot more free speech than the assembly line

worker, who cares just as deeply about the issues but doesn't give because he can't afford to and doesn't vote because he doesn't think his views matter, unless his interests happen to coincide with those of the big donors, and they seldom do.[25]

Gary Hart (D-CO): Hart ran for president in 1988, but dropped out after being caught in a sex scandal that captured national headlines for months. Hart was one of several senators during the Senate's 1997 campaign finance debate who called for restrictions on rampant PAC activity. In a speech decrying the growing power of PACs, he asserted:

PAC money is the toxic waste of American politics.[26]

John Glenn (D-OH): Glenn, the famous American astronaut and 1984 presidential candidate, stated in a PBS interview on campaign finance reform in September 23, 1997:

. . . when an individual donor can give vast amounts of money to a campaign, the potential for corruption is enormous.[27]

Bob Dole (R-KS): Dole, known for bluntness, spoke candidly about political corruption. During the October 6, 1996, presidential debate, moderator Jim Lehrer asked Dole: "How do you avoid being influenced by people who contribute money and services to your campaign?" Dole replied:

I think it's very difficult. Let's be honest about it. That's why we need campaign finance reform. . . . We're never going to fix it by the parties because Democrats want a better advantage to themselves, we want a better advantage as Republicans, and that's not how it's going to work . . . we're going to get it when we have a bipartisan commission. Take it out of politics; get people who don't have any interest in politics but understand the issue, and let them make a recommendation to Congress.

President Clinton responded, "I agree."

Bill Bradley (D NJ): In his book that accompanied his 2000 run for the presidency, the former basketball great wrote:

> Money is to politics what acid is to cloth—it eats away at the fabric of democracy. Democracy doesn't have to be a commodity that is bought and sold. Most politicians enter politics to do good, not to ask for donations. There's no reason we can't have a political process in which everyone's voice can be heard, in which dissent is respected, and in which candidates run on the strength of their ideas, not the weight of their wallets.

Fred Thompson (R-TN): In a March 11, 2007, TV interview, the actor, 2008 presidential candidate, and former lobbyist explained why he voted for the McCain-Feingold bill that passed into law in 2002:

> I came from the outside to Congress. And it always seemed strange to me. We've got a situation where people could give politicians huge sums of money, which is the soft money situation at that time, and then come before those same politicians and ask them to pass legislation for them. I mean, you get thrown in jail for stuff like that in the real world. And so I always thought that there was some reasonable limitation that ought to be put on that, and you know, looking back on history, Barry Goldwater in his heyday felt the same thing.[28]

U.S. REPRESENTATIVES

House Speaker Newt Gingrich (R-GA): Known as a rabid foe of campaign finance reform, Gingrich, in the wake of the Abramoff scandal, had this to say in 2006 about our corrupt, dysfunctional government:

> There is $2.6 trillion spent (U.S. budget) in Washington, with the authority to regulate everything in your life. Guess what? People will spend unheard-of amounts of money to influence that. The underlying problems are big government and big money.[29]

Timothy Penny (D-MN): Penny left the House after 12 years, disgusted with the level of corruption, incompetence, and waste in Congress. Looking back in 1993, he noted:

> I was enough of a true believer that I ran for office. I wanted to show people that government can work and that partisanship doesn't have to be the dominant force in politics, that interest groups don't have to be a deciding factor on every vote. And with all that enthusiasm and idealism, I've been kind of worn down. . . . And maybe what bothers me the most is having been within the system, kind of an outsider on the inside, I've grown more cynical.[30]

OTHER VOICES

Justice John Paul Stevens, *United States Supreme Court*: In his 2006 *Randall v. Sorrell* dissenting opinion, Stevens wrote:

> When campaign costs are so high that only the rich have the reach to throw their hats into the ring, we fail to 'protect the political process from undue influence of large aggregations of capital and to promote individual responsibility for democratic government.' . . . I am firmly persuaded that the Framers would have been appalled by the impact of modern fundraising practices on the ability of elected officials to perform their public responsibilities.[31]

Pat Buchanan (R): In a March 16, 2000, speech at Harvard University, the political commentator, 2000 presidential candidate, and former aide to President Nixon, spoke of the grip campaign money has on the nation's capital:

> Friends, neither Beltway party is going to drain this swamp, because to them it is not a swamp at all, but a protected wetland and their natural habitat. They swim in it, feed in it, spawn in it. Washington is a city where corporate PACs bid against union PACs to contribute to congressional PACs. Each month, Washington lobbyists spend $100 million to influence Congress. . . . What does that kind of cash buy? Your laws and your government.

Cheryl Rivers (D), Vermont state senator: Vermont, as noted in this book, passed a campaign spending limits law in 1997 that was subsequently killed by the Supreme Court in its 2006 *Randall v. Sorrell* ruling. Rivers testified in court how corporate campaign donations influenced voting in the Vermont legislature. When the Vermont Senate president was asked to sign off on a bill to label food products that contained genetically-engineered food, he refused. Rivers quoted him as saying:

> We've already lost the drug money, and I don't need to lose the food manufacturer money, too.[32]

Elizabeth Ready (D), Vermont state senator: During trial testimony in support of Vermont's 1997 campaign spending limits law, Ready made several revealing comments about how unlimited campaign spending corrupted her state's government:

> Some Vermont citizens have reported that they do not vote because 'all the big money controls everybody in Montpelier, anyways.' They think it's all wrapped up and that the special interests control it and, quite frankly, they aren't that wrong. . . . There is an agenda out there that is pretty much set by folks that are not elected. . . . The need to raise unlimited funds precludes normal people, even people that have a lot of political experience, from getting into the running for lieutenant governor or governor, because who wants to go out and raise . . . a hundred thousand, two hundred thousand, a half million dollars?. . . And quite frankly, who can amongst normal members of the public? [33]

Dale Schultz (R), former Wisconsin state senator: After his 32-year career in the state house ended in 2015, Schultz reflected on his ouster by wealthy special interests who did not appreciate his independent streak:

> Legislation is coming to the legislature entirely pre-packaged. And anybody who wants to work on it, who wants to think about it, or wants to change it gets in trouble. . . . When some think tank comes up with the legislation and tells you not to fool with it, why

are you even a legislator anymore? You just sit there and take votes and you're kind of a feudal serf for folks with a lot of money.[34]

IN CLOSING

IT IS STUNNING to realize how many of our elected leaders through the years have acknowledged our political system's fatal flaw of unlimited spending and its debilitating effect on our democracy, yet never managed to solve the problem.

Their failure has been abetted by average Americans who cannot agree on the best approach to address the issue.

I hope this book put to rest any doubts you may have had about which is the best approach.

Campaign spending limits is the only reform that *literally means* getting money out of politics.

It stands alone.

No other reform comes close.

Endnotes

Pre-Introduction Quotation

1. Ian Christopher McCaleb, "Bradley, McCain Converge in New Hampshire to Swear Off Soft Money," *CNN.com-The Associated Press*, December 16, 1999.

Introduction

1. Peter Nicholas, "Donald Trump Walks Back His Past Praise of Hillary Clinton," *The Wall Street Journal*, July 29, 2015.
2. Charlotte Alter, "The View: At the NRA's TV Network, Guns Are A Weapon in the Culture Wars," *Time*, November 27-December 14, 2017.
3. Caitlin Yilek, "GOP Mega-donor Sheldon Adelson 'Furious' Over Rex Tillerson Comments: Report," Washington Examiner, May 14, 2017.
4. Staff Writer, "Jane Mayer on Robert Mercer & the Dark Money Behind Trump and Bannon," *Democracy Now!*, March 23, 2017.
5. Thomas Jefferson, Letter to Francis A. van der Kemp, March 22,1812.

Chapter 1
Why Should You Care About Campaign Spending Limits?

1. Staff Report, "Nixon & Detroit: Inside the Oval Office," *PBS Frontline*, February 21, 2002.
2. Ibid.
3. Ibid.
4. Carl Bernstein and Bob Woodward, "Woodward and Bernstein: 40 Years After Watergate, Nixon Was Worse Than We Thought," *The Washington Post*, June 8, 2012.
5. Barry Sussman, A Watergate Lesson: Secret Money Means Payoffs, Bribes, and Extortion, *Nieman Watchdog-Nieman Foundation for Journalism at Harvard University*, October 19, 2010.
6. Chris Isidore, "ExxonMobil Profit Is Just Short of Record," *CNNMoney*, February 1, 2013.
7. PharmacyChecker.com, November 2018.
8. Joe Nocera, "Big Money Wins Again in a Romp," *The New York Times*, November 7, 2014.
9. Robert G. Kaiser, "Big Money Created a New Capital City," *The Washington Post*, April 8, 2007.

CHAPTER 2
Assumption of Impartiality

1. Brendan Sasso, "Hollywood or Silicon Valley?—Obama Faces a Difficult Choice on SOPA," *The Hill*, January 12, 2012.
2. Ibid.
3. Peter Schweizer, "Politicians' Extortion Racket," *The New York Times*, October 21, 2013.
4. Ibid.
5. Macon Phillips, Victoria Espinel, Aneesh Chopra, and Howard Schmidt, "Combating Online Piracy While Protecting an Open and Innovative Internet," *The White House Blog*, January 14, 2012.
6. Nick Allen, "Hollywood Threatens to Withdraw Funding for Barack Obama Over SOPA," *The Telegraph*, January 20, 2012.
7. Jim Drinkard, "Industry Money Rings Up Votes," *The Associated Press-Cape Cod Times*, March 18, 1996.
8. Ibid.
9. Pew Research Center Poll, "Public Trust in Government," December 14, 2017.
10. Staff, "75% in U.S. See Widespread Government Corruption, *Gallup*, September 19, 2015.
11. Frank Newport, "Americans' Confidence in Institutions Edges Up," *Gallup*, June 26, 2017.
12. Staff, "Judicial Selection: Significant Figures," *Brennan Center for Justice*, May 8, 2015.
13. Adam Liptak and Janet Roberts, "Campaign Cash Mirrors a High Court's Rulings," *The New York Times*, October 1, 2006.
14. Ibid.
15. Sandra Day O'Connor, "How to Save Our Courts," *Parade Magazine*, February 24, 2008.
16. Ibid.
17. Ibid.
18. Adam Liptak, "U.S. Voting for Judges Perplexes Other Nations," *The New York Times*, May 25, 2008.
19. Ibid.
20. Staff, "Is Congress for Sale?" *Rasmussen Reports*, July 9, 2015.
21. Pew Research Center Poll, conducted January 4-8, 2006.
22. Staff, "Gallup Historical Trends: Party Affiliation," *Gallup*, June 1-13, 2018.
23. Editorial Staff, "The Worst Voter Turnout in 72 Years," *The New York Times*, November 12, 2014.
24. General Election Turnout: 1945-2015, UK Political Info, 2002.

25. Voter Turnout in Presidential Elections: 1828-2012, The American Presidency Project, University of California at Santa Barbara.
26. Rafael Lopez Pintor, Maria Gratschew, et.al., "*A Global Report: Voter Turnout Since 1945*, International Institute for Democracy and Electoral Assistance, 2002.
27. Harry S. Truman, "Rear Platform Remarks in Missouri, Illinois, Indiana, and Ohio," The American Presidency Project, University of California at Santa Barbara, June 17, 1948.
28. Clare Feikert, "*Campaign Finance: United Kingdom*," Library of Congress-Law Library of Congress, April 2009.
29. Ibid.
30. Stephen Castle, "An Affinity for American-Style Politics Meets Tight Spending Rules in Britain," *The New York Times*, May 5, 2015.
31. Nicholas Kulish, "And on Your Left, Behind Those Walls, Lobbyists Are at Work," *The New York Times*, November 23, 2012.
32. Randal C. Archibold, "Arizona Ballot Could Become Lottery Ticket," *The New York Times*, July 17, 2006.
33. Ilya Somin, "President Obama Endorses Mandatory Voting," *The Washington Post*, March 19, 2015.
34. Filip Palda, *How Much Is Your Vote Worth – The Unfairness of Campaign Spending Limits*, Institute for Contemporary Studies Press, San Francisco, California, 1994, p. 113.

CHAPTER 3

"Representative" Democracy

1. Thomas Jefferson, Letter to John Adams, October 28, 1813.
2. Edmund S. Morgan, *The Birth of the Republic*, The University of Chicago Press, Third Edition, 1992, p. 149.
3. The Founding Fathers: Massachusetts, U.S. National Archives & Records Administration.
4. Ibid.
5. Kathleen Maher, "*By The Numbers: The Jobs of the First Congress vs. the Jobs of the 112th Congress*," National Constitution Center, February 16, 2012.
6. Russ Choma, "Millionaire's Club: For First Time, Most Lawmakers Are Worth $1 Million-Plus," *Center for Responsive Politics*, January 9, 2014.
7. David Hawkings, "Wealth of Congress: Richer Than Ever, But Mostly at the Very Top," *Roll Call*, February 27, 2018.
8. Staff, "Millionaire Freshmen Make Congress Even Wealthier," *Center for Responsive Politics*, January 16, 2013.

9. Russ Choma, "One Member of Congress = 18 American Households: Lawmakers' Personal Finances Far From Average," *Center for Responsive Politics*, January 12, 2015.

10. Nicholas Carnes, *White-Collar Government: The Hidden Role of Class in Economic Policy Making*," The University of Chicago Press, 2013, p. 20.

11. Carnes, p. 19.

12. Carnes, pp. 15-16.

13. Jonathan Martin, "Tales of Working-Class Roots Are Political Perennials," *The New York Times*, March 10, 2015.

14. Andrew Rosenthal, "Bush Encounters the Supermarket, Amazed," *The New York Times*, February 5, 1992.

15. Lydia Saad, "Snapshot: Congress Approval Still Low Heading Into Midterms," *Gallup*, October 15, 2018.

16. Dale Bumpers, "How the Sunshine Harmed Congress," *The New York Times,* January 3, 1999.

17. Staff, "Supreme Court History: Expanding Civil Rights, Landmark Cases," *Reynolds v. Sims* (1964), Public Broadcasting Service.

18. *Gray v. Sanders*, U.S. Supreme Court, No. 112, (1963)

19. Ibid.

20. *Reynolds v. Sims,* U.S. Supreme Court, 377 U.S. 533, (1964).

21. Ibid.

22. Thomas Jefferson, Letter to Samuel Kercheval, July 12, 1816.

23. Charles Riley, "Tom Perkins Big Idea: The Rich Should Get More Votes," *CNNMoney*, February 14, 2014.

24. Ajay Kapur, *Global Equity Strategy*, Citigroup, September 29, 2006.

25. Ibid.

26. Ajay Kapur, *Equity Strategy, Revisiting Plutonomy: The Rich Getting Richer*, Citigroup, March 5, 2006.

27. *Shelby County v. Holder*, No. 12-96 (2013).

28. Ibid.

29. Ibid.

30. Ibid.

31. Ibid.

32. *North Carolina State Conference of the NAACP, et al. v. Patrick L. McCrory*, et. al, No. 16-1468 (2016).

33. Ibid.

34. Ari Berman, "Is the Voting Rights Act History?," *The New York Times*, August 6, 2015.

35. E.J. Dionne, Arizona's Voting Outrage is a Warning to the Nation, *The Washington Post*, March 27, 2016.

36. Staff, "Judge Slams Kansas Voter ID Law's 'Magnitude of Harm,'" *CBS News-Associated Press*, May 18, 2016.

37. Keesha Gaskins and Sundeep Iyer, "The Challenge of Obtaining Voter Identification," *Brennan Center for Justice*, July 18, 2012.
38. Staff, "Judge Slams Kansas Voter ID Law's 'Magnitude of Harm,'" *CBS News-Associated Press*, May 18, 2016.
39. Ibid.
40. Stephen Koranda, "Rule Creating Two-Tiered Kansas Voting System Approved With Little Notice," *KMUW Radio Wichita*, July 12, 2016.
41. Josh Gerstein, "Judge Slams Kobach for Flouting Court Rules," *Politico*, June 18, 2018.
42. Eli Rosenberg, "The Most Bizarre Thing I've Ever Been A Part Of: Trump Panel Found No Voter Fraud, Ex-member Says," *The Washington Post*, August 3, 2018.
43. Ibid.
44. Eli Rosenberg, "Experts Say Kris Kobach Used Flawed Research to Defend Trump's Voter Fraud Panel," *The Washington Post*, August 7, 2018.
45. Ibid.
46. Ibid.
47. Donie O'Sullivan and Drew Griffin, "Cambridge Analytica Ran Voter Suppression Campaigns, Whistleblower Claims," *CNN.com*, May 16, 2018.
48. Ibid.
49. Editorial Staff, Blocking the Vote, *The New York Times*, October 25, 2012.
50. Stephanie Saul, "GOP Operative Long Trailed by Allegations of Voter Fraud," *The New York Times*, October 4, 2012.
51. Staff, "Senator Strom Thurmond Dead at 100," *The Association Press-The New York Times*, June 26, 2003.

CHAPTER 4
Capitalism & Democracy: An Uneasy Balance

1. Steve Coll, *Private Empire: ExxonMobil and American Power*, Penguin Books, 2012, p.71.
2. Staff, "What's Gone Wrong With Democracy," *The Economist*, March 1, 2014.
3. Michael Forsythe, "Another Chinese Mogul Is Reported to Be Missing," *The New York Times*, December 11, 2015.
4. Staff, "Founder Securities Ex-Chairman Said to Have Assisted a Probe," *BloombergBusiness*, November 25, 2015.
5. Lianna Brinded, "Another Chinese Billionaire Is Missing, *Business Insider*, January 8, 2016.

6. Paul Mozur and Michael Forsythe "China Extends Crackdown to Billionaire's Employees," *The New York Times,* February 14, 2017.

7. Staff, "Chinese Government Accused of Burning Crosses in Christian Crackdown," *CBS News*, March 10, 2016.

8. Javier C. Hernandez, "Young Activists Go Missing in China," *The New York Times*, November 12, 2018.

9. Sui-Lee Wee, "After One-Child Policy, Outrage at China's Offer to Remove IUDs," *The New York Times,* January 7, 2017.

10. Chris Buckley and Vanessa Piao, "Rural Water, Not City Smog, May Be China's Pollution Nightmare," *The New York Times,* April 12, 2016.

11. Barbara Finamore, "What China's Second Red Alert Means for the Future Of Clean Energy," *Fortune*, January 6, 2016.

12. Ibid.

13. Anneta Konstantinides and Khaleda Rahman, "Pharmaceutical Entrepreneur Who Jacked Up AIDS Pill Prices by 5,000 Percent Says He Should Have Charged Even More," *Daily Mail*, December 5, 2015.

14. Paul Piff, *"Wealth and the Inflated Self: Class, Entitlement, and Narcissism,"* Personality and Social Psychology Bulletin, January 2014.

15. Nathan Bomey, "Martin Shkreli Pleads the Fifth, Then Tweets About 'Imbeciles' in Congress," *USA Today*, February 4, 2016.

16. Aaron Smith, "Martin Shkreli Sentenced to Seven Years in Prison for Fraud," *CNN.com*, March 9, 2018.

17. Documentary, *Money For Nothing: Inside the Federal Reserve*, 2013.

18. Brian Knowlton and Michael M. Grynbaum, "Greenspan 'Shocked' that Free Markets are Flawed," *The New York Times*, October 23, 2008.

19. Howard Berkes, "Massey CEO's Pay Soared as Mine Concerns Grew," *National Public Radio*, April 17, 2010.

20. Barry Meier, "A New Round in a Long Coal Battle," *The New York Times*, November 9, 2010.

21. *Caperton v. A.T. Massey Coal,* U.S. Supreme Court, No. 08-22, (2009).

22. Ibid.

23. Ibid.

24. Ibid.

25. Kelly Holleran, "Capterton Files Motion with U.S. Supreme Court," *The West Virginia Record*, December 31, 2008.

26. Barry Meier, "A New Round in a Long Coal Battle," *The New York Times,* November 9, 2010.

27. *Caperton v. A.T. Massey Coal,* (2009).

28. Lydia DePillis, "Coal Baron Convicted of Misdemeanor After Mine Disaster that Killed 29," *The Washington Post*, December 3, 2015.

29. Thomas Jefferson, Letter to Francis A. van der Kemp, March 22,1812.

CHAPTER 5
Money As Speech

1. Audio recording, Koch brothers Donor Summit, Dana Point, California, June 15, 2014.
2. Nicholas Confessore and Jonathan Martin, "GOP Race Starts in Lavish Haunts of Rich Donors," *The New York Times*, March 1, 2015.
3. Woodrow Wilson, The New Freedom, Doubleday, Page & Co., 1913, P.35.
4. Nicholas Confessore, Sarah Cohen, and Karen Yourish, "From Only 158 Families, Half the Cash for '16 Race," *The New York Times*, October 11, 2015.
5. Matea Gold, "Big Money in Politics Emerges as a Rising Issue in 2016 Campaign, *The Washington Post*, April 19, 2015.
6. Kenneth P. Vogel, "Blue Billionaires on Top: Politico's List of Top 100 Donors of Disclosed Money Tilts Leftward," *Politico*, January 11, 2015.
7. Interview transcript, "'500 People Will Control American Democracy' If Supreme Court Overturns Campaign Finance Law," *DemocracyNow.org*, October 11, 2013.
8. Staff, "McCutcheon v. FEC," *Center for Responsive Politics*, 2014.
9. Bob Biersack, "McCutcheon's Multiplying Effect: Why an Overall Limit Matters," *Center for Responsive Politics*," September 17, 2013.
10. Ben Jacobs, "McCutcheon v. FEC: Big Money Fights Back at the Supreme Court," *The Daily Beast*, October 9, 2013.
11. *Shaun McCutcheon v. Federal Election Commission*, No. 12-537, 527 U.S. (2014).
12. Andy Kroll, "Follow the Dark Money," *Mother Jones*, July/August 2012.
13. Nicholas Confessore, Sarah Cohen, and Karen Yourish, "A Wealthy Few Lead in Giving to Campaigns," *The New York Times*, August 2, 2015.
14. Staff, David Koch profile, www.forbes.com, December 27, 2018.
15. Koch Global Presence, www.kochind.com, 2018.
16. Staff, David Koch profile; Charles Koch profile, www.forbes.com, December 27, 2018.
17. Lisa Graves, "The Koch Cartel: Their Reach, Their Reactionary Agenda, and Their Record," *The Progressive*, July/August 2014.
18. Kenneth P. Vogel, "The Koch Intelligence Agency," *Politico*, November 18, 2015.
19. Staff, David Koch profile; Charles Koch profile, www.forbes.com, December 27, 2018.
20. Staff, Thomas Steyer profile, www.forbes.com, December 28, 2018.
21. Nicholas Confessore, "'16 Koch Budget is $889 Million," *The New York Times*, January 27, 2015.

22. Jane Mayer, "Covert Operations: The Billionaire Brothers Who are Waging a War Against Obama," *The New Yorker*, August 30, 2010.

23. Jacob Fenton and Peter Olsen-Phillips, "Outside Groups' Return on Investment: Rove Leads 2014 Conservative Rebound," *Sunlight Foundation*, November 5, 2014.

24. Lisa Graves, "The Koch Cartel: Their Reach, Their Reactionary Agenda, and Their Record," *The Progressive*, July/August 2014.

25. Peter Roff, "Charles G. Koch: Addicted to the Cause of Economic Freedom," *U.S. News & World Report*, November 7, 2011.

26. Staff, "Post Election 2018 State & Legislative Partisan Composition," *National Conference of State Legislatures*, November 21, 2018.

27. Drew DeSilver, "Ahead of Redistricting, Democrats Seek to Reverse Statehouse Declines," *Pew Research Center*, March 2, 2015.

28. Staff, 2012 REDMAP Summary Report, January 4, 2013.

29. Staff, "The Multimillionaire Helping Republicans Win N.C.," *NPR*, October 6, 2011.

30. Mary Bottari, "Hi-Tech Hyper-Partisan Gerrymandering on Trial in Wisconsin," *PR Watch*, May 24, 2016.

31. Ibid.

32. Ibid.

33. Ibid.

34. Richard Kreitner, "Conventional Wisdom," *The Nation*, November 20-27, 2017.

35. *Coleman v. Miller,* 307 U.S. 433 (1939).

36. Michael Wines, "Push to Alter Constitution Via the States," *The New York Times*, August 23, 2016.

37. Ibid.

38. Staff, "Conventional Follies," *The Economist*, September 30, 2017.

39. Gregory Krieg, "Texas Governor Joins Marco Rubio in Call for New Constitutional Convention," *CNN.com*, January 8, 2016.

40. Jim Tankersley, "Inside Charles Koch's $200 Million Quest for a 'Republic of Science,'" *The Washington Post*, June 3, 2016.

41. Tom Hamburger, "The Koch Brothers' Impact On the American Political System," *The Washington Post*, January 15, 2016.

42. Tankersley, "Inside Charles Koch's . . .," *The Washington Post*, June 3, 2016.

43. Jo Ann Taube, "I Lost My Seat to the Koch Brothers," *The Progressive*, July/August 2014.

44. John Eligon, "To Koch Group, No Election is Too Small," *The New York Times*, November 3, 2013.

45. Ibid.

46. Matea Gold, "Charles Koch's Focus on 'Injustices' is Fueled By an Unlikely

Partnership," *The Washington Post,* August 3, 2015.

47. Patty Wooten, "Study Says Crossett Residents Sickened by GP Chemicals," *Southeast Arkansas News,* March 20, 2013.

48. Lucia Graves and Jordan Howard, "Koch-Owned Georgia-Pacific Plant Linked to High Cancer Rates, Film Alleges," *Huffington Post,* October 12, 2011.

49. Corporate Toxics Information Project, Political Economy Research Institute, University of Massachusetts.

50. Tim Dickinson, "Inside the Koch Brothers' Toxic Empire," *Rolling Stone,* September 24, 2014.

51. Ibid.

52. Ibid.

CHAPTER 6

Lobbying: The Fourth Branch of Government

1. Peter Grier, "BP Oil Spill: Harrowing Escapes of Deepwater Horizon Survivors," *The Christian Science Monitor,* May 27, 2010.

2. Suzanne Goldenberg, "Deepwater Horizon Survivor Describes Horrors of Blast and Escape From Rig," *The Guardian,* May 20, 2010.

3. Laura Strickler, "BP Lobbying Team's Revolving Door," *CBSNews.com,* June 1, 2010.

4. National Commission on the BP Deepwater Horizon Oil Spill and Offshore Drilling, Deep Water, *The Gulf Oil Disaster and the Future of Offshore Drilling,* (January 2011).

5. Ibid.

6. Press Release, "BP Exploration and Production Inc. Pleads Guilty, Is Sentenced to Pay Record $4 Billion for Crimes Surrounding Deepwater Horizon Incident," U.S. Department of Justice, January 29, 2013.

7. Robert W. Wood, "In BP's Final $20 Billion Gulf Settlement, U.S. Taxpayers Subsidize $15.3 Billion," *Forbes,* April 6, 2016.

8. Matt Smith, "Massive Tar Mat Dug Up Off Louisiana Coast, 3 Years After Gulf Spill, *CNN.com,* June 26, 2013.

9. Nicholas St. Fleur, "Study Links Dolphin Deaths to BP Oil Spill," *The New York Times,* May 21, 2015.

10. Brody Mullins, "Growing Role for Lobbyists: Raising Funds for Lawmakers, *The Wall Street Journal,* January 27, 2006.

11. Congressional Budget Office, Historical Budget Data.

12. Steven Brill, "On Sale: Your Government. Why Lobbying is Washington's Best Bargain," *Time Magazine,* July 12, 2010.

13. Ibid.

14. Michael J. Cooper, Huseyin Gulen and Alexei V. Ovtchinnikov, *Corporate Political Contributions and Stock Returns*, October 24, 2006.
15. Ibid.
16. Stephen Ansolabehere, John M.P. DeFigueiredo and James M. Snyder Jr., *Are Campaign Contributions Investment in the Political Marketplace or Individual Consumption? Or 'Why is There So Little Money In Politics?,'* MIT Sloan Working Paper No. 4272-02.
17. Ken Silverstein, *Washington On $10 Million A Day: How Lobbyists Plunder the Nation*, Common Courage Press, Monroe, Maine, 1998, p. 225.
18. Jeffrey H. Birnbaum, "Washington's Once and Future Lobby," *The Washington Post*, September 9, 2006.
19. Raquel Meyer Alexander, Stephen W. Mazza, and Susan Scholz, *Measuring Rates of Return for Lobbying Expenditures: An Empirical Case Study of Tax Breaks for Multinational Corporations*, Journal of Law and Politics, Vol. 25, April 8, 2009.
20. Staff, "Investment and Lobbying: Money and Politics," *The Economist*, October 1, 2011.
21. Dan Weil, "Companies That Spend Most on Lobbying Outperform S&P 500," *Newsmax*, February 27, 2014.
22. Staff, Forbes 400 List: 2018 Ranking, *Forbes*.
23. Warren E. Buffet, "The Billionaire's Buyout Plan," *The New York Times*, September 10, 2000.
24. Kevin Bogardus, "Lobbyist Spending Jumps 5 Percent Last Year Despite Nation's Recession Woes," *The Hill*, February 10, 2012.
25. Greg Jaffe and Jim Tankersley, "Capital Gains: Spending on Contracts and Lobbying Propels A Wave of New Wealth in D.C.," *The Washington Post*, November 17, 2013.
26. U.S. Bureau of Labor Statistics, Expenditures on Housing By Area, 2014.
27. Greg Jaffe and Jim Tankersley, "Capital Gains: Spending on Contracts and Lobbying Propels A Wave of New Wealth in D.C.," *The Washington Post*, November 17, 2013.
28. Steven Brill, "On Sale: Your Government. Why Lobbying is Washington's Best Bargain," *Time Magazine*, July 12, 2010.
29. Ibid.
30. Michael Isikoff, Holly Bailey and Evan Thomas, "A Washington Tidal Wave," *Newsweek*, January 16, 2006.
31. Terry Frieden, "DeLay Ex-Aide Pleads Guilty in Abramoff Case," *CNN Washington Bureau*, November 21, 2005.
32. Susan Schmidt, "Lobbyist Cited US Help in Blocking Rival Casino," *The Washington Post*, August 29, 2005.
33. Staff Report, "Ex-Interior Official Gets 10 Months in Abramoff Scandal," *The Associated Press-CBSNews.com*, June 26, 2007.

34. Press Release, "Former Public Relations Specialist Michael Scanlon Pleads Guilty to Corruption and Fraud Conspiracy," United States Department of Justice, November 21, 2005.
35. Michael Kranish, "Abramoff Ties to Russians Probed," *The Boston Globe,* February 23, 2006.
36. Ibid.
37. Ibid.
38. Michael Isikoff, "More Trouble Ahead?" *Newsweek,* August 22, 2005.
39. Ibid.
40. Pete Yost, "White House Secretly Removed Visitor Records from Public Eye," *The Associated Press-San Francisco Chronicle,* January 6, 2007.
41. Ibid.
42. Periscope, "Sports Tickets and Springsteen: The Email Trail," *Newsweek,* October 9, 2006.
43. Ibid.
44. Ibid.
45. Curt Anderson, "U.S. Suggests Cutting Abramoff Sentence," *The Associated Press-The Washington Post,* March 22, 2007.
46. Matt Apuzzo and David Dishneau, "Abramoff, Ruing 'Nightmare,' Begins Six-Year Prison Term," *The Associated Press-The Boston Globe,* November 16, 2006.
47. Eric Lichtblau, "Abramoff Speaks, With Limits," *The New York Times,* February 7, 2012.
48. Carrie Levine, "Jack Abramoff is Back – As A Registered Lobbyist," *Center for Public Integrity,* June 22, 2017.

CHAPTER 7
The Revolving Door: Mr. Smith Goes to K Street

1. Eric Lipton, "Breathtaking Waste and Fraud in Hurricane Aid," *The New York Times,* June 27, 2006.
2. Editorial, "Heckuva Idea, Brownie," *St. Louis Post-Dispatch,* November 29, 2005.
3. Eric Lipton, "Ex-Head of FEMA Returns to Disaster Work," *The New York Times,* April 26, 2006.
4. Revolving Door: Former Members, Center for Responsive Politics, 201
5. Staff Report, "Penn. GOP Congressman Indicted in Influence Peddli Case," *Associated Press-The Boston Globe,* May 6, 1992.
6. Sean Connolly, "McDade, Acquitted of Wrongdoing, Feted,"
   (Harrisburg, Penn.), August 14, 1996.
7. Dave Janoski, "Witness Describes McDade's Behavior,"

(Wilkes-Barre, Penn), February 16, 2007.

8. Jeffrey Birnbaum, "The Road to Riches Is Called K Street," *The Washington Post*, June 22, 2005.

9. Elliot Gerson, "To Make America Great Again, We Need to Leave the Country," *The Atlantic*, July 10, 2012.

10. Lewis F. Powell Jr., Attack on American Free Enterprise System, August 23, 1971.

11. Ibid.

12. Ibid.

13. Ibid.

14. Ibid.

15. Ibid.

16. Josh Hicks, "Rick Santorum and the K Street Project (Fact Checker Biography)," *The Washington Post*, January 9, 2012.

17. Ibid.

18. Eric Lipton, "Former Anti-Terror Officials Find Industry Pays Better," *The New York Times*, June 18, 2006.

19. Ibid.

20. Ibid.

21. Ibid.

22. Laura Strickler, "BP Lobbying Team's Revolving Door," *CBS News*, June 1, 2010.

23. Chuck Raasch, "After Switching Positions, Gephardt and His Lobbying Firm Have Taken $8 million from Turkish Government," *St. Louis Post-Dispatch*, June 7, 2015.

24. Ibid.

25. Ibid.

26. Emily Heil, "Sheriff, Congressman, Liquor Store Owner . . . Now Lobbyist," *The Hill*, November 29, 2006.

27. Matt Kelley, "Iraqis Deploying More Lobbyists," *USA Today*, June 27, 2007.

28. Anna Palmer, "Iraq to Hire D. C. Lobbyist," *Politico*, February 13, 2013.
Washington Lobbying Machine to Fund
k Times, May 6, 2016.
e to Influence Congress," *The Hill*,

up Gets a Washington Lobbyist," *The Hill*,

t Bind," *Time*, February 26, 1996.

the Highway Bill," *The Washington Post*,

35. Charles R. Babcock, "Life After Congress," *The Washington Post*, July 29, 2001.
36. Anna Palmer, Jake Sherman, and John Bresnahan, "Shuster Lounges Poolside with Airline Lobbyists as He Pursues FAA Bill," *Politico*, February 23, 2016.
37. John Bresnahan, Anna Palmer, and Jake Sherman, "Shuster Admits Relationship With Airline Lobbyist," *Politico*, April 16, 2015.
38. Editorial Staff, "All in the Family," *St. Petersburg Times*, July 9, 2003.
39. Ibid.
40. Eleanor Clift, "Blunt Makes a Big-Time Blunder," *Newsweek*, June 23, 2003.
41. David S. Fallis and Dan Keating, "In Congress, Relatives Lobby on Bills Before Family Members," *The Washington Post*, December 29, 2012.
42. Editorial Staff, "All in the Family," *St. Petersburg Times*, July 9, 2003.

CHAPTER 8

The Cost of Unlimited Spending

1. Gerald F. Seib, "Capital Journal: One Good Guy Says Goodbye to Money Hunt," *The Wall Street Journal*, February 19, 1997.
2. Ibid.
3. Steve Israel, "Confessions of a Congressman," *The New York Times*, January 9, 2016.
4. Ibid.
5. Ibid.
6. Ibid.
7. Eric Lipton, "For Freshmen in the House, Seats of Plenty," *The New York Times*, August 10, 2013.
8. Ibid.
9. Ibid.
10. Ibid.
11. Ezra Klein, "For Lawmakers Like Evan Bayh, the Price of Fundraising is Too Steep," *The Washington Post*, October 31, 2010.
12. Alan Simpson, "Limit Campaign Fundraising," *The Boston Globe*, March 10, 2006.
13. Helen Dewar, "Sen. Ford Announces He Will Retire," *The Washington Post*, March 11, 1997.
14. Congressional Record—Senate, January 19, 1999, p. S712.
15. Staff, "Michele Bachmann: Washington is 'Corrupt Paradigm,' and I'll Change It," *Newsmax*, June 26, 2011.
16. Francis X. Clines, "Senators Bemoan Unshakable Habit," *The New York*

Times, March 20, 1997.
17. United States Senate website, www.senate.gov.
18. Citizens Against Government Waste, www.cagw.org.
19. Newt Gingrich website, Gingrich Outlines Campaign Finance Reform, www.newt.org.
20. John Berlau, "Spending Limits a Good Idea Whose Time May Not Come," *Insight On The News*, March 10, 1997.
21. Staff Report, Transcript, *Meet The Press,* December 17, 2006.
22. Brian McGrory, "Hard to Pull for Kerry," *The Boston Globe*, September 16, 2003.
23. Ibid.
24. Money Games, *PBS*, November 28, 1996.

CHAPTER 9

Buckley v. Valeo, Part I: Need for a Constitutional Amendment

1. President Gerald Ford, Remarks on Signing the Federal Election Campaign Act Amendments of 1974, October 15, 1974.
2. 1911 Amendments to the Publicity Act, 37 Statute 25, August 19, 1911.
3. Anthony Corrado, Thomas E. Mann, Daniel R. Ortiz, and Trevor Potter, "*The New Campaign Finance Sourcebook*," Brookings Institution Press, 2005, p. 14.
4. Corrado, Mann, Ortiz, and Potter, p. 20.
5. Federal Election Campaign Act of 1971, Public Law 92-225, (1971).
6. Staff Report, "Campaign Finance: The States Push for Reform," *Congressional Quarterly Political Report*, 2360-2365, August 31, 1974.
7. Federal Election Campaign Act Amendments of 1974, Public Law 93-443, (1974).
8. Staff Report, "Campaign Finance: The States Push for Reform," *Congressional Quarterly Political Report*, 2360-2365, August 31, 1974.
9. Ibid.
10. Ibid.
11. Ibid.
12. *Buckley v. Valeo*, 171 U.S. Court of Appeals for the District of Columbia Circuit, 172 (1975).
13. Ibid.
14. Ibid.
15. *Buckley v. Valeo,* 424 U.S. 1 (1976).
16. Ibid.
17. Ibid.
18. Ibid.

CHAPTER 10
Buckley v. Valeo, Part II: Name Recognition & Free Speech

1. Maurice Carroll, "Moynihan Defeats Buckley for New York Senate Seat," *The New York Times*, November 3, 1976.
2. James Taranto, "Nine Decades at the Barricades," *The Wall Street Journal*, August 1, 2014.
3. Andrew T. Karron, "Lord Buckley Meets Professor Moynihan," *The Harvard Crimson*, November 2, 1976.
4. Ibid.
5. James Lane Buckley, Lecture at Quinnipiac University School of Law, November 10, 2010.
6. *Buckley v. Valeo,* 424 U.S. 1 (1976).
7. Telephone interview with Gary Jacobson, July 23, 2007.
8. Election Overview, Center for Responsive Politics, 2016.
9. *New York Times v. Sullivan*, U.S. Supreme Court, 376 U.S. 254, (1964).
10. *Buckley v. Valeo,* 424 U.S. 1 (1976).
11. *Randall v. Sorrell*, U.S. Supreme Court, No. 04-1528, (2006).
12. Ibid.
13. Ibid.
14. *Buckley v. Valeo,* 424 U.S. 1 (1976).
15. Alex Lundry, "Microtargeting: Knowing the Voter Intimately, Winning Campaigns," Volume 4, No. 1: http://www.winningcampaigns.org.
16. Ibid.
17. Ibid.
18. Ibid.
19. Derek Willis, "Campaigns Use Facebook Tool to Deliver Targeted Political Ads," *The New York Times*, September 11, 2014.
20. Ibid.
21. Michael Scherer, "Elections Will Never Be the Same," *Time*, August 27, 2012.
22. Kevin Randall, "Looking the Voter In the Eye and Trying to Track Emotions," *The New York Times*, November 4, 2015.

CHAPTER 11
The Art of Circumvention: What Hath Buckley Wrought?

1. Staff, Top Lobbying Firms, Center for Responsive Politics, 2005.
2. Larry Margasak, "House Eases Some Lobbying Rules," *The Associated Press-Columbian*, January 8, 2003.
3. Jake Stump, "Mollohan Named 'Porker of the Year,'" *Charleston Daily Mail*,

March 1 2007.

4. Jeffrey H. Birnbaum, "West Virginia Democrat Is Scrutinized," *The Washington Post*, May 15, 2006.

5. Ibid.

6. Editorial Staff, "Mollohan: His Pork-Barrel Award Is a Reminder of a Failed Plan," *The Charleston Gazette*, March 3, 2007.

7. Alex Isenstadt, "Rep. Mollohan loses in West Virginia," *Politico*, May 12, 2010.

8. Jennifer Martinez and Tom Hamburger, "Target Feels Backlash From Shareholders," *Los Angeles Times*, August 19, 2010.

9. Eric Lichtblau, "I.R.S. Expected to Stand Aside as Nonprofits Increase Role in 2016 Race," *The New York Times*, July 6, 2015.

10. *Buckley v. Valeo*, Footnote 52, 424 U.S. 1 (1976).

11. Staff Report, *"Straight Talk on Campaign Finance: Separating Fact From Fiction – Paper No. 5,"* Brennan Center for Justice at New York University School of Law.

12. Anthony Corrado, Thomas E. Mann, Daniel R. Ortiz, and Trevor Potter, *"The New Campaign Finance Sourcebook,"* Brookings Institution Press, 2005, p. 18.

13. Ibid.

14. Staff, Leadership PACs, Center for Responsive Politics, 2014.

15. Brody Mullins, "Loose Change: Lawmakers Tap PAC Money to Pay Wide Array of Bills," *The Wall Street Journal,* November 2, 2006.

16. Taryn Luna, "Legislation Bills Lawmakers Who Resign Early," *The Sacramento Bee*, April 10, 2016.

17. Ibid.

18. Jim Drinkard and Laurence McQuillan, "Bundling Contributions Pays for Bush Campaign," *USA Today*, October 16, 2003.

19. Ibid.

20. Johannes W. Fedderke and Dennis C. Jett, *What Price the Court of St. James?: Political Influences on Ambassadorial Postings of the United States of America,* Economic Research Southern Africa, September 2012.

21. Staff Report, "We've Got Some Dancing to Do, Bush Says," *CNN.com,* January 20, 2001.

22. Ron Edmonds, "Bush Inaugural Fundraising Hits $18M," *The Associated Press-USA Today*, January 7, 2005.

23. Ibid.

24. Scott Mayerowitz and Nick Tucker, "What Recession? The $170 Million Inauguration," *ABC News Business Unit*, January 19, 2009.

CHAPTER 12
Citizens United & Super PACs

1. Barry Goldwater, The Conscience of A Conservative, Victor Publishing Company, Inc., 1960, P.54.
2. *Citizens United v. Federal Election Commission*, No. 08-205, (2010).
3. *Shaun McCutcheon v. Federal Election Commission*, No. 12-537, (2014).
4. Jack Abramoff, "I Know the Congressional Culture of Corruption," *The Atlantic*, July 24, 2012.
5. *Citizens United v. Federal Election Commission*, No. 08-205, (2010).
6. Theodore Roosevelt, New Nationalism Speech, August 31, 1910.
7. Carl Hulse, "Is the Supreme Court Clueless About Corruption? Ask Jack Abramoff," *The New York Times*, July 5, 2016.
8. Eric Lichtblau, "Advocacy Group Says Justices may Have Conflict in Campaign Finance Cases," *The New York Times*, January 19, 2011.
9. *First National Bank v. Bellotti*, No. 76-1172, (1978).
10. *Buckley v. Valeo*, 424 U.S. 1, (1976).
11. Nicholas Confessore, "Lines Blur Between Candidates and PACs With Unlimited Cash," *The New York Times*, August 27, 2011.
12. Kevin Liptak, "Florida Primary 'the Most Negative Campaign Ever' Says Media Group," *CNN.com*, January 31, 2012.
13. Seth Cline, "Sheldon Adelson Spent $150 Million on Election," *U.S. News & World Report*, December 3, 2012.
14. 2012 Presidential Race, Center for Responsive Politics.
15. Staff, "Briefing," *Time*, July 2, 2012.
16. Bill Moyers and Michael Winship, "Netanyahu Speaks, Money Talks," bill.moyers.com, March 4, 2015.
17. Ravi Somaiya, Ian Lovett, and Barry Meier, "Purchase of Las Vegas Newspaper Is Seen as a Mogul's Power Play," *The New York Times*, January 3, 2016.

CHAPTER 13
The Do-Nothing Republicans: Free Speechers or Free Loaders

1. Staff, "Senate Divided on Campaign Finance Bill," *All Politics CNN*, February 24, 1998.
2. Staff, "Top Spenders on Lobbying," Center for Responsive Politics, 2016.
3. Bradley A. Smith, Testimony to House Judiciary Subcommittee on the Constitution, February 27, 1997.
4. Staff, "The Great Debate: A Look at the Provisions of McCain-Feingold," *PBS*, September 29, 1997.

5. Michael W. Lynch, "Federal Election Commission Member Bradley A. Smith Takes on Campaign Finance Laws," *Reason*, July 2001.

6. Hans A. Von Spakovsky, "Will This Election Be Stolen?" *The Wall Street Journal*, November 1, 2008.

7. Thomas Fleming, "The Long, Stormy Marriage of Money and Politics," *American Heritage Magazine*, November 1998.

8. Ibid.

9. *Biographical Directory of the United States Congress*.

10. Thomas Fleming, "The Long, Stormy Marriage of Money and Politics," *American Heritage Magazine*, November 1998.

11. Jeff Brindle, "The Next Campaign Finance Challenge: Are Contribution Limits the Next to Go?," *Campaigns & Elections*, August 19, 2014.

12. Adam Liptak, "Justices Strike Down Law That Aids Campaign Rivals of Rich Candidates," *The New York Times*, June 27, 2008.

13. *American Tradition Partnership, Inc., FKA Western Tradition Partnership, Inc., et. al., v. Steve Bullock, Attorney General of Montana*, No. 11-1179, (2012).

14. Michael Scherer and Pratheek Rebala, "Campaign Inflation: The Cost of Campaigns Has Been Growing at a Staggering Rate," *Time*, November 3, 2014.

15. George Will, "Corrupt Campaign 'Reform,'" *The Washington Post*, June 29, 2006.

16. George Will, "Academy's Dress Code Falls Just Short of Uniform Acceptance," *Newsweek*, January 29, 1996.

17. Ibid.

18. Ibid.

19. Elizabeth Mendes, "Americans Down on Congress, OK With Own Representative," *Gallup*, May 9, 2013.

CHAPTER 14
The Benefits of Campaign Spending Limits

1. Seema Mehta, "Poizner, Trailing in Polls, Slams Whitman's 'Obscene' Spending," *Los Angeles Times*, May 31, 2010.

2. Seema Mehta and Maeve Reston, "Jerry Brown Nearly Matched Meg Whitman's Spending On TV in Final Weeks of Race," *Los Angeles Times*, February 1, 2011.

3. Ibid.

4. Will Rogers, Daily Telegram #1538, June 28, 1931.

5. Curtis Kalin, "Top 20 Worst Ways the Government Wastes Your Tax Dollars," *CBSNews.com*, October 23, 2014.

6. Liz Essley Whyte, "Big Business Gave Heavily to Thwart Ballot Measures in 2014," *Center for Public Integrity*, February 5, 2015.
7. *Randall v. Sorrell*, U.S. Supreme Court, No. 04-1528, (2006).

CHAPTER 15

The FEC & Independent, Nonpartisan Citizens Panels

1. Sheryl Gay Stolberg, "Senate Approves Lobbying Limits by Wide Margin," *The New York Times*, March 30, 2006.
2. Staff, "Congress Exempt from Several Federal Laws," *Fox News / Associated Press*, February 3, 2012.
3. Dan Keating, David S. Fallis, Kimberly Kindy, and Scott Higham, "Members of Congress Trade in Companies While Making Laws that Affect Those Same Firms," *The Washington Post*, June 23, 2012.
4. Ibid.
5. Tamara Keith, "How Congress Quietly Overhauled its Insider-Trading Law," *NPR*, April 16, 2013.
6. Ibid.
7. Tal Kopan, "Poll: Lobbyists Rank Last On Ethics," *Politico*, December 16, 2013.
8. Federal Election Campaign Act of 1976, Public Law 94-283, (1976).
9. Nicholas Confessore, "Election Panel Enacts Policies by Not Acting," *The New York Times*, August 25, 2015.
10. Anthony Herman, "The FEC: Where A Tie Can Be (Almost) a 'Win,'" Inside Political Law-Covington & Burling LLP, March 20, 2014.
11. Eric Lichtblau, "Paralyzed FEC Can't Do Its Job, Chairwoman Says," *The New York Times*, May 3, 2015.
12. Christopher Rowland, "Deadlock by Design Hobbles Election Agency," *The Boston Globe*, July 7, 2013.
13. Federal Election Campaign Act Amendments of 1974, Public Law 93-443, (1974).
14. The Gerrymander, American Treasures of the Library of Congress, Library of Congress, 2016.
15. Kyle Hughes, "New York State Redistricting Amendment Comes Under Fire," *Daily Freeman*, June 23, 2014.
16. Gabrielle Levy, "Redistricting Reform Gains Steam," *U.S. News & World Report*, December 1, 2015.
17. Ibid.
18. Editorial, "Channeling Money Westward," *The New York Times*, August 24, 2005.

19. We Draw the Lines, Application and Selection Process.
20. Ibid.
21. Ibid.
22. Ibid.
23. Dan Walters, "New California Legislative Maps Make Good on Promise of Reform," *The Sacramento Bee*, June 7, 2011.
24. Judy Lin and Juliet Williams, "California Supreme Court Upholds State Senate Maps," *The Associated Press-Press Democrat (Santa Rosa, California)*, January 27, 2012.
25. Ibid.
26. Staff Report, "California House Delegation Includes 14 Newcomers," *The Sacramento Bee*, November 19, 2012.
27. Jim Sanders, "California Legislature Welcomes Largest Freshman Class Since 1966," *The Sacramento Bee*, December 3, 2012.
28. Ibid.
29. Raphael J. Sonenshein, *When the People Draw the Lines: An Examination of the California Citizens Redistricting Commission*, League of Women Voters of California, May 2013.
30. Editorial Staff, "Gov. Brewer's Power Grab," *The New York Times*, November 5, 2011.
31. *Arizona State Legislature v. Arizona Independent Redistricting Commission*, No. 13-1314 (2015).

CHAPTER 16
Public Financing, Term Limits, & Other Alternatives

1. Phil Yost, "Campaign Funding Gets Look," *San Jose Mercury News*, August 15, 2006.
2. Anna Griffin, "Cash Due, But Boyles May Have Left Town," *The Oregonian*, August 2, 2006.
3. Editorial, "The City's Painful $92,000 Lesson," *The Oregonian*, August 3, 2006.
4. David D. Kirkpatrick, "Death Knell May Be Near for Public Election Funds," *The New York Times*, January 23, 2007.
5. Steven M. Levin, "*Keeping it Clean: Public Financing in American Elections*," Center for Governmental Studies, December 2006.
6. Staff, "Initiative Would Finance Campaigns," *San Francisco Chronicle*, June 27, 2006.
7. Press Release, "Gubernatorial Race Paces Statewide Spending to an All-Time High," Commonwealth of Massachusetts Office of Campaign and

Political Finance, December 4, 2002.

8. Mijin Cha, "Outside Money Wins in New York City Elections," *Demos.org*, September 12, 2013.

9. Katrina Shakarian, "Campaign Finance Board, City Council Respond to Unprecedented Outside Spending," *The Gotham Gazzette*, September 16, 2014.

10. Lucy Sweeney, "Vermin Supreme 2016: Alternative U.S. Presidential Candidate Promises Free Ponies for All," *Australian Broadcasting Corporation*, January 25, 2016.

11. Rebecca Kaplan, "Vermin Supreme Finishes Fourth in N.H. Democratic Primaries, *CBS News*, February 10, 2016.

12. Ibid.

13. David Siders, "New Research Offers Four Lessons from California's Top-Two Primary," *The Sacramento Bee*, February 7, 2015.

14. James Pindell, "Maine's Ranked Choice Voting Is Provoking Questions. Here are Some Answers," *The Boston Globe*, November 14, 2018.

CHAPTER 17
The Constitution: Living, Breathing or Dying, Wheezing Document?

1. Adrienne Koch and William Peden, "*The Life and Selected Writings of Thomas Jefferson*," Modern Library Publicans, 1998, pp-615-616.

2. Benjamin Franklin speech to the Federal Convention, September 17, 1787: http://press-pubs.uchicago.edu/founders/documents/a7s3.html.

3. Thomas Jefferson, Letter to James Madison, September 6, 1789.

4. Ibid.

5. David S. Law and Mila Versteeg, *The Declining Influence of the United States Constitution*, May 25, 2012.

6. Ibid.

7. Ibid.

8. Ibid.

9. Ibid.

10. Adam Liptak, "'We the People' Loses Followers," *The New York Times*, February 7, 2012.

11. Judge Learned Hand, Spirit of Liberty Speech, May 21, 1944.

12. Rodney A. Smith, *Money, Power & Elections: How Campaign Finance Reform Subverts American Democracy*, Louisiana State University Press, 2006, p. 17.

13. National Voting Rights Institute Poll, Public Opinion on Election Campaign, January 5, 2006.

14. Ibid.

15. Brian Montopoli, "Most Want Limits on Campaign Spending," *CBS News*, January 18, 2012.
16. Staff, "Americans' Views on Money and Politics," *The New York Times/CBS News*, June 2, 2015.
17. Pew Research Poll, "Beyond Distrust: How Americans View Their Government," *Pew Research Center*, November 23, 2015.
18. Ibid.
19. Ezra Klein, "More Money, More Problems: The Soul-Crushing Life of A Senator," *Newsweek*, November 8, 2010.

APPENDIX
It's Broken: Presidential Quotations & More

1. President Theodore Roosevelt speech, Osawatomie, Kansas, August 31, 1910.
2. President Calvin Coolidge address, Eleventh Regular Meeting of the Business Organization of the Government, June 21, 1926.
3. President Herbert Hoover news conference, May 6, 1932.
4. President Franklin Delano Roosevelt, Annual Message to Congress, January 3, 1936.
5. President Harry S. Truman addresses (from rear train platform) in Illinois, Iowa and Missouri, September 18, 1948.
6. President Dwight D. Eisenhower news conference, May 4, 1956.
7. President John F. Kennedy letter to the President of the Senate and to the Speaker of the House Transmitting Bills To Carry Out Recommendation of the Commission on Campaign Costs, May 29, 1962.
8. President Lyndon B. Johnson address at Democratic Party Dinner in Chicago, April 24, 1968.
9. President Gerald R. Ford remarks at signing ceremony for the Federal Election Campaign Act Amendments of 1974, October 15, 1974.
10. President Jimmy Carter remarks at Democratic National Committee meeting, May 25th, 1979.
11. President Ronald Reagan remarks at signing ceremony for documents transmitting budget revisions to Congress, March 9, 1981.
12. President George H. W. Bush remarks announcing campaign finance reform proposals, June 29, 1989.
13. President Bill Clinton radio address, July 22, 1995.
14. President George W. Bush statement on signing the Bipartisan Campaign Reform Act of 2002, March 27, 2002.
15. President Barack Obama statement on the United States Supreme Court's *Citizen United v. FEC* ruling, January 21, 2010.

16. President Barack Obama remarks at a town hall meeting in Elyria, Ohio, January 22, 2010.
17. Mitt Romney speech to Burlington Business Roundtable, Burlington, Massachusetts, October 17, 1994.
18. Brad Hamilton, Heather Gilmore, and Elizabeth Wolff, "MCG: How I Kept My Skeletons Closeted," New York Post, September 17, 2006.
19. John Wildermuth, "Campaign 2006: Angelides Puts Money on Public Election Finance," The San Francisco Chronicle, August 4, 2006.
20. Staff Report, "Senators' Remarks on Campaign Finance Proposals," The New York Times, September 30, 1997.
21. U.S. Senator Lindsey Graham press release, December 10, 2003.
22. Staff Report, "Senators' Remarks on Campaign Finance Proposals," The New York Times, September 30, 1997.
23. Joseph I. Lieberman, "Chutzpah Hall of Shame," The New York Times, August 21, 1997.
24. Barry Goldwater, "The Conscience of a Conservative," Martino Publishing, 2011, p. 54.
25. U.S. Senator Dale Bumpers, "How the Sunshine Harmed Congress," The New York Times, January 3, 1999.
26. Elmer W. Lammi, "Hart: PAC Money the 'Toxic Waste' of Politics," UPI, November 5, 1985.
27. PBS NewsHour, Transcript, "Senate Standstill," September 23, 1997.
28. Former Senator Fred Thompson, Interview, Fox News Sunday with Chris Wallace, March 11, 2007.
29. Todd S. Purdum, "Go Ahead, Try to Stop K Street," The New York Times, January 8, 2006.
30. Lloyd Grove, "Tim Penny: The Bitter End; Resigning After a Decade, the Frugal Congressman Says the System Plain Stinks," The Washington Post, August 18, 1993.
31. Randall v. Sorrell, U.S. Supreme Court No. 04-1528, (2006).
32. Quotes from the Record and Opinions, National Voting Rights Institute, 2007.
33. Ibid.
34. Jack Craver, "The Last Moderate: Will 'Passionate Pragmatist' Dale Schultz Be Driven Out of the Wisconsin Senate?" The Capital Times, August 7, 2013.

CPSIA information can be obtained
at www.ICGtesting.com
Printed in the USA
LVHW051506250620
658993LV00001B/151

34. Press Release, "Former Public Relations Specialist Michael Scanlon Pleads Guilty to Corruption and Fraud Conspiracy," United States Department of Justice, November 21, 2005.

35. Michael Kranish, "Abramoff Ties to Russians Probed," *The Boston Globe,* February 23, 2006.

36. Ibid.

37. Ibid.

38. Michael Isikoff, "More Trouble Ahead?" *Newsweek*, August 22, 2005.

39. Ibid.

40. Pete Yost, "White House Secretly Removed Visitor Records from Public Eye," *The Associated Press-San Francisco Chronicle*, January 6, 2007.

41. Ibid.

42. Periscope, "Sports Tickets and Springsteen: The Email Trail," *Newsweek,* October 9, 2006.

43. Ibid.

44. Ibid.

45. Curt Anderson, "U.S. Suggests Cutting Abramoff Sentence," *The Associated Press-The Washington Post*, March 22, 2007.

46. Matt Apuzzo and David Dishneau, "Abramoff, Ruing 'Nightmare,' Begins Six-Year Prison Term," *The Associated Press-The Boston Globe*, November 16, 2006.

47. Eric Lichtblau, "Abramoff Speaks, With Limits," *The New York Times*, February 7, 2012.

48. Carrie Levine, "Jack Abramoff is Back – As A Registered Lobbyist," *Center for Public Integrity*," June 22, 2017.

CHAPTER 7
The Revolving Door: Mr. Smith Goes to K Street

1. Eric Lipton, "Breathtaking Waste and Fraud in Hurricane Aid," *The New York Times*, June 27, 2006.

2. Editorial, "Heckuva Idea, Brownie," *St. Louis Post-Dispatch*, November 29, 2005.

3. Eric Lipton, "Ex-Head of FEMA Returns to Disaster Work," *The New York Times*, April 26, 2006.

4. Revolving Door: Former Members, Center for Responsive Politics, 2018.

5. Staff Report, "Penn. GOP Congressman Indicted in Influence Peddling Case," *Associated Press-The Boston Globe*, May 6, 1992.

6. Sean Connolly, "McDade, Acquitted of Wrongdoing, Feted," *The Patriot* (Harrisburg, Penn.), August 14, 1996.

7. Dave Janoski, "Witness Describes McDade's Behavior," *Citizens' Voice*

(Wilkes-Barre, Penn), February 16, 2007.

8. Jeffrey Birnbaum, "The Road to Riches Is Called K Street," *The Washington Post*, June 22, 2005.

9. Elliot Gerson, "To Make America Great Again, We Need to Leave the Country," *The Atlantic*, July 10, 2012.

10. Lewis F. Powell Jr., Attack on American Free Enterprise System, August 23, 1971.

11. Ibid.

12. Ibid.

13. Ibid.

14. Ibid.

15. Ibid.

16. Josh Hicks, "Rick Santorum and the K Street Project (Fact Checker Biography)," *The Washington Post*, January 9, 2012.

17. Ibid.

18. Eric Lipton, "Former Anti-Terror Officials Find Industry Pays Better," *The New York Times*, June 18, 2006.

19. Ibid.

20. Ibid.

21. Ibid.

22. Laura Strickler, "BP Lobbying Team's Revolving Door," *CBS News*, June 1, 2010.

23. Chuck Raasch, "After Switching Positions, Gephardt and His Lobbying Firm Have Taken $8 million from Turkish Government," *St. Louis Post-Dispatch*, June 7, 2015.

24. Ibid.

25. Ibid.

26. Emily Heil, "Sheriff, Congressman, Liquor Store Owner . . . Now Lobbyist," *The Hill*, November 29, 2006.

27. Matt Kelley, "Iraqis Deploying More Lobbyists," *USA Today*, June 27, 2007.

28. Anna Palmer, "Iraq to Hire D.C. Lobbyist," *Politico*, February 13, 2013.

29. Eric Lipton, "Iraqi Kurds Build Washington Lobbying Machine to Fund War Against ISIS," *The New York Times*, May 6, 2016.

30. Kristina Wong, "Iraqi Sunnis See to Influence Congress," *The Hill*, December 22, 2015.

31. Julian Hattem, "Iraqi Militia Group Gets a Washington Lobbyist," *The Hill*, February 23, 2016.

32. Karen Tumulty, "The Ties That Bind," *Time*, February 26, 1996.

33. Ibid.

34. Juliet Eilperin, "Fingerprints on the Highway Bill," *The Washington Post*, April 11, 1998.